TEACH YOURS

GERMAN
VOCABULARY

A COMPLETE LEARNING TOOL

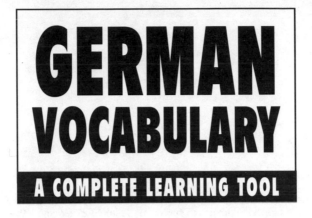

GERMAN VOCABULARY
A COMPLETE LEARNING TOOL

Series Editor: Rosi McNab

Language Editor: Susan Ashworth-Fiedler

TEACH YOURSELF BOOKS

Long-renowned as the authoritative source for self-guided learning – with more than 30 million copies sold worldwide – the Teach Yourself series includes over 200 titles in the fields of languages, crafts, hobbies, sports, and other leisure activities.

British Library Cataloguing in Publication Data
A catalogue record for this title is available from the British Library

Library of Congress Catalog Card Number: 95-71312

First published in UK 1996 by Hodder Headline Plc, 338 Euston Road, London NW1 3BH

First published in US 1996 by NTC Publishing Group, 4255 West Touhy Avenue, Lincolnwood (Chicago), Illinois 60646 – 1975 USA

Typeset by Transet Ltd, Coventry.
Printed in England by Cox & Wyman Ltd, Reading, Berkshire.

Impression number	10	9	8	7	6	5	4	3	2	1
Year			1999	1998	1997	1996				

CONTENTS

INTRODUCTION

An easy-to-use reference book of key language for the language student, business traveller and holidaymaker.

About this book

This book is designed to be EASY to use, both
- as a quick reference to find useful words in a specific area, and
- to increase your word power by building up a stock of new vocabulary

How to use the book

Quick reference
The topics are listed in alphabetical order and the words in each topic are also in alphabetical order for easy reference.Where appropriate, there is an example of how the words in each list might be used in a sentence.

Vocabulary learning
Follow the simple suggestions to help you to increase your vocabulary. There are also games and puzzles to make learning more fun.

How can I learn better?

Most people complain of having a poor memory. They say they are no good at learning a language because they can't remember the words, but few people have difficulty in remembering things which really interest them: the names of members of a football team, the parts of a car, what happened in the last episode of a favourite radio or TV series, the ingredients in a recipe...!

Introduction

How can you make learning a list of words more interesting?

1 First YOU decide which list you are going to learn today.

2 Then YOU decide which words in that list you want to try to learn.
Mark each word. (Put a mark beside each word you have chosen.)
Count them. (How many are you going to try to learn?)
Underline the first letter of each word. (What letters do they begin
with?)

Now you are ready to begin.

3 Say the words ALOUD. If you put your hands over your ears whilst
you read them it will cut out extraneous noise and can also help you
to concentrate by reflecting the sound of your voice and helping you to
hear what you sound like.

4 Next look for ways to remember them. Do you know how YOU
remember words best? Try this quick test to find out:

Look at the grid below for one minute, and then cover it up and try to
remember as many words or pictures as possible.

Then close the book and write down a list of the words you remember.

horse	bottle	knife	bread
scarf	letter	shoe	banana
plane	gate	book	cup

Have you remembered more words or more pictures?

Introduction

Words If you have remembered more of the words than of the pictures, you have a preference for memorising the written word and you may find it helpful to write down the words you are learning.

Pictures If you have remembered more pictures, this shows you have a more visual memory. You will probably find it helpful to 'tie' in the words you learn to a picture.

You didn't remember many at all! Try again:

Pictures
Imagine a composite picture. Imagine a boat, 'put' the elephant, eating an apple, sitting on a chair in the boat . 'Put' the tap on the front of the boat to let the water out. (5 words). Look through the window at a Christmas tree, 'hang' a mini-bicycle, the flower and the clock in the tree like Christmas decorations. Now put the light bulb on the top. What have you got left? The gloves. Put them on to keep your hands warm!

Words
There are four which begin with b: ba_____; boo_____; bo_____; b_____ (you can eat two of them).

There are six others which begin with: c_____; g_____; h_____; k_____; l_____; pl_____ and two which begin with s: sc_____; sh_____ (and you can wear them both)

Now how many can you remember?
Which do you remember better: the words, the pictures or a bit of both? Try again in five minutes . . . and in half an hour . . . and tomorrow.

Now you should know how you prefer to learn!

Below is a list of twelve words. Choose six of them to learn.

bridge	die Brücke
bus stop	die Bushaltestelle
car park	der Parkplatz
corner	die Ecke
crossroads	die Kreuzung
level crossing	die Bahnübergang
one-way street	die Einbahnstraße

pedestrian area	die Fußgängerzone
road	die Straße
station	der Bahnhof
traffic lights	die Ampel
tram	die Straßenbahn

a) **Put a Mark beside the words you would like to learn**
Count them. (Choose six to try.)
Underline the first letter of each word.

b) Read them aloud. (Put your hands over your ears whilst you do it.)

c) Try it again until you are happy with the sound of them.

d) Look at each word carefully for ways to remember it. Find 'pegs' to hang them on.

- Does it sound like the English word? (Parkplatz – *parkplace*)
- Does it sound like a different English word? (Bahn – sounds like *barn*)
- Does part of it look like the English word? (Bushalt{estelle})
- Can you split it up into any bits you recognise? (-gang – *gangway*)
- Can you find any word that might be helpful? (amps – to do with **lighting**)
- Can you see a **picture** of each word, as you say it? Can you picture it as it sounds? (Bahn – a *barn*)
- Can you build all the words into an imaginary composite picture? Say each word as you add it to the picture (Straße, Kreuzung, Ampel, Brücke. . .)

5 Cover up the English and try to remember what your chosen words mean.

6 Write a list of the first letters and put dashes for the missing letters.

Which did you choose? Mark them:

e.g. die A_ _ _ _	*traffic lights* ('amps')
die B_ _ _ _ _ _ _ _ _ _	*level crossing* ('Railway-over-way')
der B_ _ _ _ _ _	*station* ('railway courtyard')
die B_ _ _ _ _	*bridge* (first two letters as in English)
die B_ _ _ _ _ _ _ _ _ _ _ _	*bus stop* ('bus stopping plac'e)
die E_ _ _	*corner*

die E_ _ _ _ _ _ _ _ _ _ _	*one way street*
die F_ _ _ _ _ _ _ _ _ _ _	*pedestrian area* ('foot-goer-zone')
die K_ _ _ _ _ _	*crossing* (K.... = cross; -ung = ing)
der P_ _ _ _ _ _ _	*car park* (park place)
die S_ _ _ _	*street* (first three letters as English)
die S_ _ _ _ _ _ _ _ _	*tram* (street-way)

and try to 'read' the words.

7 Fill in the missing letters and check that you have got them right.

8 Cover up the German and see if you can remember the words you have chosen.

9 Do something else for half an hour.

10 Go back and check that you can still remember the six you chose. (e.g.)

traffic lights	die A _ _ _ _
level crossing	die B _ _ _ _ _ _ _ _ _ _
station	der B _ _ _ _ _ _
bridge	die B _ _ _ _ _
bus stop	die B _ _ _ _ _ _ _ _ _ _ _
corner	die E _ _ _
one way street	die E _ _ _ _ _ _ _ _ _ _
pedestrian area	die F
crossing	die K _ _ _ _ _ _ _
car park	der P _ _ _ _ _ _ _ _
street	die S _ _ _ _ _
tram	die S _ _ _ _ _ _ _ _ _

What do you know already?

Does the word **look** or **sound** like the English or a related word? For example,

- the German word for chair is **Stuhl** – it sounds like *stool*;
- the German word for car is **Wagen** – it looks a bit like *wagon*

English is a particularly rich language with words from many sources. Some of the words we use come from a northern origin, from the ancient Anglo Saxon and Nordic languages and some from a southern origin, from Latin, French and the Celtic languages, as well as many words brought back by the early travellers from all round the globe.

Look for words that are similar to the English ones, for example:

Blumen	*flower* (bloom)	Eisen	*iron*
Bruder	*brother*	Fleisch	*meat* (flesh)

Some words are even the same or almost the same as the English:
Bus Butter Englisch Fisch Gras Haus Hunger Mann Name Supermarkt

Can you guess what the following words are in English? Cover up the English words and try it.

Buch	*book*	Mond	*moon*
Feld	*field*	Polizei	*police*
Fuß	*foot*	Salat	*salad, lettuce*
Gast	*guest*	Salz	*salt*
gut	*good*	Schiff	*ship*
Katze	*cat*	Sturm	*storm*
Land	*country*	Wasser	*water*
Marktplatz	*market place*	Wein	*wine*

Can you find any more examples?

Short cuts. Looking for patterns

Consonant changes

- The English *th* - is often **D** in German:

thanks	Danke	*thirst*	Durst
thin	dünn	*thick*	dick
village	(-thorp) Dorf	*brother*	Bruder

- **t** at the beginnng of a word in English will often become **z**:
  ten – zehn   *to* – zu   *two* – zwei   *twenty* – zwanzig

- *p* often becomes **Pf**:
  pound – Pfund   *pepper* – Pfeffer   *plant* – Pflanze

- *-k-* often becomes **-ch-**:
  to break – brechen   *to make* – machen   *week* – Woche

- *-v-* often becomes **-b-**:
  to give – geben   *to have* – haben   *to live* – leben   *to love* – lieben

- *-t-* often becomes **ss**:
  white – weiß *water* – Wasser *to eat* – essen *better* – besser

Word building
A lot of German words are made up of other words – so you have fewer to learn!

Haus – *house*	+	krank – *ill*	= Krankenhaus – *hospital*
	+	Gast – *guest*	= Gasthaus – *guesthouse*
	+	Hoch – *high*	= Hochhaus – *high-rise flats*

Bahn – *track* + Hof – *yard* or *court* = Bahnhof – *railway station*
or *way*

  + Eisen – *iron* = Eisenbahn – *railway*
  + Kreuz – *cross* = Autobahnkreuz – *motorway junction*
  + Ein – *one* = Einbahnstraße – *one-way street*

The word for *lunch* is: **Mittagessen**: Mit – *mid*; Tag – *day*; essen – *to eat* = *mid-day-eat*. (Remember 'd' in English is often 't' in German.) The word for the evening meal is *evening* + *eat* = **Abendessen**.

Note: the word for breakfast is different. It is Frühstück = früh (*early*) + Stück (*piece*). (A mid-morning snack which someone takes to work or school is still often referred to as 'piece' in some parts of the North and Scotland).

Some tips on spelling and pronunciation
Most English speakers have little difficulty in pronouncing the German sounds because the two languages share some of their linguistic roots and they both belong to the same family of languages. Here are the letters whose sounds differ from English:

  e – an e at the end of a word is always pronounced: **Panne** is pronounced *pan-ne* (*breakdown*)
  j – sounds *y*, for example **jung** (*young*)
  qu – sounds *k + v* (*kv*) , as in **Quiz**
  r – is a more throaty sound in German.
  s – sounds *z* before the vowels a e i o u . **Sonne** is pronounced *zonn-e* (*sun*) BUT
  s – before consonants and at the end of words sounds *s* as in **Haus** (*house*)

s – followed by **p** or **t** sounds *sh* as in *shut*. **Sport** is pronounced *shp-ort*

v – sounds *f*
Remember **Volkswagen** is pronounced *Folksvagen*

w – sounds *v*

And here are some more tips on pronunciation:

1 ¨ is called an Umlaut and is used on an **a**, **o** or **u**. It tells you that the vowel under it has changed its sound. The short form is given first:

ä sounds	*eh*:	Mädchen	*girl*
	ay:	spät	*late*
ö sounds	*uh*:	wöchentlich	*weekly*
	er:	schön	*pretty*
ü sounds	*i*:	fünf	*five*
	u:	Bücher *books*, Tür *door*	

2 **ß** is ss: Straße *street*, Fuß *foot*

3 **ch** is pronounced as in the Scottish word *loch*. i**ch** (*I*); Bu**ch** *book*

4 **au** is pronounced *ow* as in cow: **Frau** *Mrs*, **Auf** Wiedersehen! *goodbye*
äu is pronounced *oy* as in coy: Fr**äu**lein *Miss*

5 At the end of the word:

b is pronounced *p*: hal**b** *half*
d is pronounced *t*: hun**d** *dog*
g is pronounced *k*: Ta**g** *day*
ig is pronounced *ch*: fert**ig** *ready*
s is pronounced *s* (not *z*): Hau**s** *house*

6 **ei** is pronounced *eye*: dr**ei** *three*, W**ei**n *wine*
ie is pronounced *ee*: v**ie**r *four*, B**ie**r *beer*

7 **sch** is pronounced *sh* as in **Sch**uh *shoe*
sp is pronounced **shp**: **sp**ät *late*
st is pronounced **sht**: **St**adt *town*

Introduction

Using your dictionary

infinitive		past participle		
tanzen	*to dance*	**ge**tanzt	*danced*	(regular verb)
schlafen	*to sleep*	**ge**schlafen	*slept*	(irregular verb)

Most past participles begin with **ge**. Take off the **ge** when you want to look up the infinitive or a related word in the dictionary.

Most people make the excuse that they are no good at learning words as they have a poor memory. That's not true! There is nothing wrong with your memory, but it often lacks the guidance and focus it needs. In learning words from a list the learner has not yet decided when he or she is going to use them. There is no immediate goal.

To learn with least effort you need to have a clear goal. Choose your goals:

A I want to use the language to communicate with other speakers of that language:

    (*i*) on a business trip

    (*ii*) on a holiday trip

    (*iii*) on a social visit

    (*iv*) at home, for business reasons

    (*v*) because I know someone I would like to talk to or write to

B I want to be able to understand the language to:

    (i) read something in that language for pleasure, books, magazines, letters, etc

    (ii) read something for business, manuals, letters, faxes, etc

    (iii) listen to the radio

    (iv) watch television programmes

    (v) read signs and instructions on a visit.

C I just enjoy learning languages.

You should choose the words and phrases you are going to learn and focus on them and their meaning. Concentrating on the words and thinking about their meaning and sound, and looking for 'pegs' on which to hang them (looking for related words, imagining them in pictures, remembering the sound of the words, etc.) will help you to put them in your long-term memory.

How many of the picture words can you still remember . . . and how many of the written words?

Introduction

Abbreviations used in this book are listed below:

Akk.	Akkusativ	acc.	accusative
dat.	Dativ	dat.	dative
jdn., jdm.	jemanden, jemandem	sb.	somebody
fam.	familiär	fam.	familiar
förm.	förmlich	form.	formal
Pl.	Plural	pl.	plural
ugs.	umgangssprachlich	coll.	colloquial
sl.	Slang	sl.	slang

When there is a masculine and a feminine form for a noun, the masculine form is given first, for example:

der Chef/in = der Chef / die Chefin *the boss*

Irregular masculine and feminine forms are given in full.

The plural form of nouns is given in brackets after the word.
(¨) means the vowel has an umlaut.
(-e)/ (-en)/ (-s) means the word adds an **e**, **en** or **s** in the plural.
(–) means there is no change in the plural.

CORE
LANGUAGE

Begrüßungen *Greetings*

Guten Morgen!	*Good morning*	Gute Nacht!	*Good night*
Guten Tag!	*Good day,*	Hallo!/Tag!	*Hello*
	Good afternoon	Hi!	*Hi*
Guten Abend!	*Good evening*		

Wie geht es Dir?, Wie geht's? — *How are you? (fam.)*
Wie geht es Ihnen? — *How are you ? (form.)*
Es geht mir gut, danke. — *I'm fine, thanks.*
Und Dir/Und Ihnen? — *And you?*

Auf Wiedersehen!

	Goodbye
Auf Wiederhören!	*Goodbye (on the telephone)*
Adieu!	*Goodbye*
Bis später!	*See you later*
Leb wohl!	*Farewell*
Mach's gut!	*Take care*
Tschüs!	*'Bye*
Wiedersehen!	*'Bye*
Ade, Ada!	*'Bye (Southern German)*
Grüß Gott!	*Good day (South Germany)*
Grützi!	*Good day (Swiss)*
Moin, Moin!	*Good morning, Good day (North Sea coast & Hamburg)*

Remember:
. . . .
In German you have two forms of *you*: **Sie** is formal and **du** is familiar.

Salut!	*Bye / hello (Southwest Germany)*
Servus!	*'Bye (Southern Germany)*
'tschau!	*Ciao!*
Guten Appetit!	*Enjoy your meal*
n'Guten!	*Enjoy your meal (Southern Germany)*
Prost!	*Cheers (with beer)*
zum Wohl!	*Cheers (wines, spirits)*

Herzlich Willkommen! *Welcome!*

Willkommen in Berlin!	*Welcome to Berlin.*
Darf ich mich vorstellen . . . ist mein Name.	*I'd like to introduce myself. I'm . . .*
Darf ich Ihnen Herrn/Frau . . . vorstellen.	*Let me introduce you to Mr / Mrs . . . (form.)*
Darf ich dir . . . vorstellen.	*Let me introduce you to . . . (fam.)*
Sehr angenehm!	*Pleased to meet you.*
Grüßen Sie Ihre Frau/Familie.	*Give my regards to your wife / family. (form.)*

Begrüßungen *Greetings*

Liebe Grüße an	*Give my love to . . . .*
Sag' deiner Frau einen schönen Gruß von mir.	*Remember me to your wife. (fam.)*
Schöne Grüße an deinen Mann.	*Say hello to your husband from me. (fam)*

NOCH MAL!

● *Activity: What would you say? Was würden Sie sagen?*

ANREDEN UND TITEL
FORMS OF ADDRESS AND TITLES

Herr	*Mr*
Frau	*Mrs, Ms*
Fräulein	*Miss*
Doktor	*Doctor* (medical and academic)

Anreden *Forms of address*

meine Dame	*madam*
mein Herr	*sir*
Meine Damen und Herren	*Ladies and gentlemen*
Herr Doktor/ Frau Doktor	*Doctor*

Herr Direktor/Frau Direktorin	*Sir / Madam* (company)
Herr/Frau Professor	*Professor*
Herr Bundeskanzler	*Mr Chancellor*
Herr Minister/Frau Ministerin	*Minister* (politics)
Herr Bürgermeister /Frau Bürgermeisterin	*Mr / Mrs Mayor*
Herr Richter/ Frau Richterin	*my Lord* (a judge)
Herr Wachtmeister	*Officer* (police)
Herr Pastor	*Reverend*
Herr Pfarrer	*Father* (church)

Begrüßungen *Greetings*

Schriftliche Anreden   *Written forms of address*

Lieber Karl/Liebe Moni,	*Dear Karl / Dear Moni,*
Sehr geehrte	
Damen und Herren,	*Dear Sir or Madam,*
Sehr geehrte Frau . . . ,	*Dear Mrs / Ms . . . ,*
Sehr geehrter Herr . . . ,	*Dear Mr . . . ,*
Mit freundlichen Grüßen,	*Yours faithfully, / Yours sincerely,*
Schöne Grüße,	*Best wishes,*
Alles Liebe,	*Love,*

NOCH MAL!

● *Activity 1: How would you address these people?*

● *Activity 2: Letter writing. Complete the opening phrases. How would you close each letter?*

(a) ____ ____ Herr Frank,
(b) ____ Steffi,
(c) ____ ____ Damen und Herren,

Zahlen *Numbers*

Kardinalzahlen
Cardinal numbers

0	null
1	eins (pron. ey-ns)
2	zwei (tsv-eye)
3	drei (dr-eye)
4	vier (fear)
5	fünf
6	sechs (zex)
7	sieben (zee-bn)
8	acht
9	neun(noyn)
10	zehn(ts-ane)
11	elf
12	zwölf (ts-vulf)
13	dreizehn
14	vierzehn
15	fünfzehn
16	sechzehn
17	siebzehn
18	achtzehn
19	neunzehn
20	zwanzig (ts-van-ts-ig)
21	einundzwanzig
22	zweiundzwanzig
23	dreiundzwanzig
24	vierundzwanzig
25	fünfundzwanzig
26	sechsundzwanzig
27	siebenundzwanzig
28	achtundzwanzig
29	neunundzwanzig
30	dreißig
31	einunddreißig
40	vierzig
50	fünfzig
60	sechzig
70	siebzig
80	achtzig
90	neunzig
100	(ein) hundert
1 000	(ein) tausend
1 000 000	eine Million

Remember:
. . . .

zwo is the colloquial form of zwei *(two)*. In two-digit numbers you put the last digit first, for example :**13** = **drei**zehn. For the numbers from 20 upwards, you add **und** between the digits: 24 = vier**und**zwanzig.

Ordinalzahlen
Ordinal numbers

erste	*first*
zweite	*second*
dritte	*third*
vierte	*fourth*
fünfte	*fifth*
zehnte	*tenth*
einmal	*once*
zweimal	*twice*
dreimal	*three times*
viermal	*four times*
x-mal	*umpteen times*

Brüche *Fractions*

ein Drittel	⅓
ein Viertel	¼
ein Halb	½
anderthalb, eineinhalb	*1 ½*
zweieinhalb	*2 ½*
drei Fünftel	⅗

Zahlen *Numbers*

Dezimalbrüche
Decimal fractions

null Komma zwei
  fünf (0,25)   *0.25*
eins Komma sieben
  vier (1,74)   *1.74*

Note: In German decimals are
separated with a comma, not a full stop.

Zeichen *Signs*

plus, und	+
minus, weniger	-
geteilt durch	÷
mal	×
ist, macht, gleich	=
drei hoch zwei	3^2
Wurzel aus 4	$\sqrt{4}$

Telefonnummer(n)
Telephone numbers

die Vorwahl (-en) *code*

Tip
......

Telephone numbers
The code from Britain to Germany is 0049
The code from Germany to Britain is 0044
Read the code as separate digits but the telephone number in pairs, for
example: 0049 30 69 74 13: **null – null – vier – neun – drei – null –
neunundsechzig – vierundsiebzig – dreizehn**

NOCH MAL!

● *Activity 1: Practise reading these telephone numbers and codes:*

(a) Jens in Frankfurt: 0049 69 80 55 07 (b) Rolf in Freiburg: 0049
67 11 23 68 (c) Julia in Wolfsburg: 0049 5361 21 06 44
(d Annette in Hamburg: 0049 40 93 60 79

● *Activity 2: Read these years aloud:*

1966 neunzehnhundertsechsundsechzig
1975 1984 1998 2025
Add important dates in your own life and practise saying them:
I was born in _____ .

● *Activity 3: Calculations. Work out how to answer these in German.*

(a) ⅔ + ⅜ = ?	(f) ½ + ¾ = ?
(b) 1,5 + 2,25 = ?	(g) 2,4 + 3,8 = ?
(c) 7 + 9 = ?	(h) 12 x 5 = ?
(d) 17 + 11 = ?	(i) 30 - 8 = ?
(e) 24 ÷ 4 = ?	(j) 2 x 0.25 = ?

Der Kalender *The calendar*

Der Kalender *The calendar*

das Jahr (-e)	*year*
der Monat (-e)	*month*
das Schaltjahr (-e)	*Leap year*

der Tag (-e)	*day*
die Woche (-n)	*week*

Die Wochentage
The days of the week

Montag	*Monday*
Dienstag	*Tuesday*
Mittwoch	*Wednesday*
Donnerstag	*Thursday*
Freitag	*Friday*
Samstag, Sonnabend	*Saturday*
Sonntag	*Sunday*

am Montag	*on Monday*
der Vormittag (-e)	*morning*
am Vormittag	*in the morning*
der Mittag (-e)	*midday*
der Nachmittag (-e)	*afternoon*
der Abend (-e)	*evening*
die Nacht ("e)	*night*

heute	*today*
heute morgen	*this morning*
heute abend	*this evening*

am nächsten Tag *the next day*

morgen	*tomorrow*
morgen früh	*tomorrow morning*
morgen abend	*tomorrow evening*
übermorgen	*the day after tomorrow*

gestern	*yesterday*
gestern abend, letzte Nacht	*yesterday evening, last night*

vorgestern	*the day before yesterday*
letzte Woche	*last week*

das Wochenende (-n)	*the weekend*
am Wochenende	*at the weekend*

Die Monate *The months*

Januar	*January*
Februar	*February*
März	*March*
April	*April*
Mai	*May*
Juni	*June*
Juli	*July*
August	*August*
September	*September*
Oktober	*October*
November	*November*
Dezember	*December*

Datum *Dates*

Der Wievielte ist heute?	*What's the date today?*
Heute ist Mittwoch, der elfte Januar	*Today is Wednesday, 11th January*
am . . .	*on the . . .*
ersten Januar	*1st January*
zweiten Februar	*2nd February*
dritten März	*3rd March*

18

Der Kalender *The calendar*

zwanzigsten April	*20th April*
vom neunten Juli bis zum elften August	*from 9th July to 11th August*
vom einundzwanzigsten Mai bis zum dreißigsten Juni	*from 21st May to 30th June*

Learning tip

Shortened forms: vom = von dem; zum = zu dem

DIE VIER JAHRESZEITEN, FEIERTAGE UND BESONDERE ANLÄSSE
THE FOUR SEASONS, BANK HOLIDAYS AND SPECIAL OCCASIONS

die Jahreszeit (-en)	*season*
der/im Frühling	*the / in spring*
der Sommer	*summer*
der Herbst	*autumn*
der Winter	*winter*
die Sommerzeit	*summertime*

GESETZLICHER FEIERTAGE
BANK HOLIDAYS

Neujahr *New Year*

Silvester	*New Year's Eve, Hogmanay*
Neujahrstag	*New Year's Day*

Weihnachten *Christmas*

Nikolaus (6. Dez)	*St Nicholas' Day*
Heiligabend	*Christmas Eve*

Erster Weihnachtstag	*Christmas Day*
Zweiter Weihnachtstag	*Boxing Day*
Heilige Drei Könige	*Epiphany*

Ostern *Easter*

Gründonnerstag	*Maundy Thursday*
Karfreitag	*Good Friday*
Ostersonntag	*Easter Sunday*
Ostermontag	*Easter Monday*

Pfingsten *Whitsun*

Pfingstsonntag	*Whit Sunday*
Pfingstmontag	*Whit Monday*
Maifeiertag	*May Day*
Christi Himmelfahrt	*Ascension Day*
Vatertag	*Father's Day*
Fronleichnam	*Feast of Corpus Christi*
Nationaler Gedenktag (3.Okt)	*National Commemoration Day*
Allerheiligen (1. Nov)	*All Saints' Day*

Der Kalender *The calendar*

Buß- und Bettag (Nov)
    Day of prayer and repentance

Valentinstag   **St Valentine's Day**
*Karneval, Fasching (Feb)
    Carnival festival
Rosenmontag   *Monday preceding*
        Ash Wednesday
Rosenmontagszug *Carnival procession*
Fastnacht,
  Faschingsdienstag *Shrove Tuesday*

Aschermittwoch *Ash Wednesday*
Muttertag   *Mother's Day*
Erntedankfest   *Harvest festival*
Volkstrauertag *Remembrance*
        Sunday

*Karneval: This festival is known as Karneval in the north of Germany and as Fasching in the south.

NOCH MAL!

● *Activity 1: When is your birthday?*
Wann haben Sie/hast du Geburtstag?
Mein Geburtstag ist am . . .
Wann hat . . . Geburtstag? (*Your mother, friend, children, etc.*)

● *Activity 2: When are the meetings? Tell your German friend.*

Die Uhr *The clock*

Wie spät ist es?	*What time is it?*
Es ist ...	*It is ...*
ein Uhr	*one o'clock*
fünf nach eins	*five past one*
zehn nach eins	*ten past one*
Viertel nach eins	*quarter past one*
Viertel zwei	*quarter past one*
zwanzig nach eins	*twenty-past one*
zehn vor halb zwei	*twenty past one*
fünf vor halb zwei	*twenty-five past one*
halb zwei	*half past one**
fünfundzwanzig vor zwei	*twenty-five to two*
fünf nach halb zwei	*twenty-five to two*
Viertel vor zwei	*quarter to two*
dreiviertel zwei	*quarter to two*
zehn vor zwei	*ten to two*
zwei Uhr	*two o'clock*

Es ist drei Uhr morgens.	*It's 3 am.*
Es ist sechs Uhr nachmittags/abends.	*It's 6 pm.*

13.07	15.19
Es ist dreizehn Uhr sieben	Es ist fünfzehn Uhr neunzehn

00.15	05.00
Es ist null Uhr fünfzehn	Es ist fünf Uhr

*To say *half past* in German, you say *half before the next hour*, so *half past seven* is **halb acht**, half past eleven is **halb zwölf**, etc.

die Sekunde (-n) *second*	kurz vor/kurz nach	
die Minute (-n) *minute*		*just before / just after*
die Stunde (-n) *hour*	Mittag	*midday*
die Dreiviertelstunde	Mitternacht	*midnight*
three quarters of an hour		

Ich komme in einer Dreiviertelstunde.	*I'll be there in three quarters of an hour.*
Meine Uhr geht vor/nach.	*My watch is fast / slow.*
Tut mir leid. Ich habe mich verspätet.	*I'm sorry, I'm late.*
Meine Uhr geht nicht/ist kaputt.	*My watch doesn't work / is broken.*
aufziehen	*to wind*

Die Uhr *The clock*

NOCH MAL!

● *Activity: When shall we meet?*
Treffen wir uns um . . . (Let's meet at . . .)

Farben *Colours*

die Farbe(-n)	*colour*	violett	*violet*
beige	*beige*	weiß	*white*
schwarz	*black*	gelb	*yellow*
blau	*blue*	lila	*lilac*
braun	*brown*	weinrot	*burgundy*
golden	*gold*	dunkel	*dark*
grün	*green*	dunkelblau	*dark blue*
grau	*grey*	hell	*light / pale*
natur	*natural*	knall	*bright*
marineblau	*navy*	knallrot	*bright red*
orange	*orange*	schreiend	*fluorescent*
rosa	*pink*	grell	*loud*
purpur	*purple*	giftgrün	*bilious green*
rot	*red*	pech(raben) schwarz	
silbern	*silver*		*pitch-black,*
türkis	*turquoise*		*jet-black*

Remember

When two colour adjectives are used together, they are written as one word, for example: ein **blaugrünes** Hemd (*a blue green shirt*).
When an **adjective** comes **after** the verb (known as a **predicative** adjective), it remains unchanged: Das Hemd ist **blau**. (*the shirt is blue*).

When an adjective comes **before** the verb (called an **attributive** adjective) it must be declined; that is, it must **agree with** the noun it describes, for example: Das **blaue** Hemd, (*the blue shirt*). (For more information on adjective agreement see: *Adjectives*, p. 25)

NOCH MAL!

● Activity: What colours are the flags?

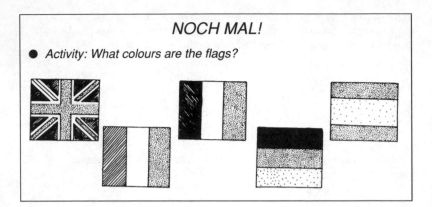

Adjektive *Adjectives*

You can use these words to describe things, people, places or feelings. Look at the end of this list to find examples of these adjectives in sentences. You will also find appropriate adjectives included in the topic areas.

aktiv	*active*		heiß	*hot*
alt	*old*		hell	*light, bright*
bequem	*comfortable*		herzlich	*warm (-hearted)*
berühmt	*famous*		hoch	*high*
beschäftigt	*busy*		höflich	*polite*
besetzt	*engaged (occupied)*		hungrig	*hungry*
billig	*cheap*		in Form, fit	*fit*
bitter	*bitter*		intelligent	*intelligent*
bösartig	*nasty*		interessant	*interesting*
breit	*wide, broad*		jung	*young*
lang	*long*		kalt	*cold*
dick	*fat*		klein	*small*
dumm	*stupid*		klug	*clever*
dunkel	*dark*		kompliziert	*complicated*
dünn	*thin*		kühl	*cool*
einfach	*single* (ticket)		kurz	*short*
einfach, leicht	*simple (easy)*		langsam	*slow*
eng	*narrow*		langweilig	*boring*
erste	*first*		laut	*loud*
fair, gerecht	*fair*		leer	*empty*
falsch	*false, wrong*		leicht	*easy*
faul	*lazy*		leicht	*light* (weight)
flach	*flat*		letzt	*last*
frei	*free (available)*			
kostenlos	*free (no cost)*		lieb	*dear (beloved)*
			links	*left* (side)
frisch	*fresh*		lustig	*funny*
früh	*early*		modern	*modern*
gemein	*unkind*		möglich	*possible*
			müde	*tired*
gemeinsam	*common*		nah	*near*
geschlossen	*closed*		naß	*wet*
gesund	*well*		nett	*nice*
glatt	*smooth*		neu	*new*
glücklich, froh	*happy*		niedrig	*low*
groß	*big*		offen	*open*
gut	*good*		ruhig	*quiet*
hart	*hard*		satt	*full* (food)
hart	*tough*		sauber	*clean*

Adjektive *Adjectives*

schlecht	*bad*	tief	*deep*
schmutzig	*dirty*	tot	*dead*
schnell	*fast*	trocken	*dry, stale* (bread)
schön	*beautiful*	untrainiert	*unfit*
schrecklich	*awful, dreadful, horrible*	voll	*full*
		wahr	*true*
schwach	*weak*	warm	*warm*
schwer	*difficult / heavy*	weich	*soft*
spät	*late*	weit	*far*
stark	*strong*	zäh	*tough* (meat)
süß	*sweet*	zart	*tender*
tapfer	*brave*	zerbrechlich	*fragile*
teuer	*dear (expensive)*		

Er ist mit 80 noch sehr aktiv.	*He's still very active at 80.*
Heute bin ich sehr beschäftigt.	*I'm very busy today.*
Die Toilette ist besetzt.	*The toilet is engaged.*
Einmal einfach nach Köln, bitte.	*A single to Cologne, please.*
Die Broschüre ist kostenlos.	*The brochure is free.*
Das ist wirklich gemein.	*That's really unkind.*
Wir haben viel gemeinsam.	*We have a lot in common.*
Laß es uns gemeinsam tun.	*Let's do it together.*
Der Laden ist heute geschlossen.	*The shop is closed today.*
Georg ist ein harter Bursche.	*George is a tough guy.*
Ich fühle mich in Form.	*I feel fit.*
Peter kam als Letzter.	*Peter came last.*
Ich bin satt.	*I'm full.*
Das war ein schrecklicher Unfall.	*It was an awful accident.*
Es ist ziemlich spät.	*It's fairly late.*

NOCH MAL!

● *Activity:* Choose any twelve words from the list and write them down. Then write down their opposites beside them. Use arrows as shown, for example:

gut → schlecht

Adverben *Adverbs*

auch	*also*	mindestens	*at least*
besonders	*especially*	natürlich	*of course*
durchschnittlich	*on average*	nur	*only*
etwa, ungefähr	*about, approximately*	sehr	*very*
fast	*almost*	sogar	*even*
ganz	*completely, quite*	tatsächlich	*indeed, certainly*
genug	*enough*	vielleicht	*perhaps*
immer	*always*	wahrscheinlich	*probably*
kaum	*hardly*	wenig	*less, little*
leider	*unfortunately*	wirklich	*really*
mehr	*more*	ziemlich	*fairly, rather*

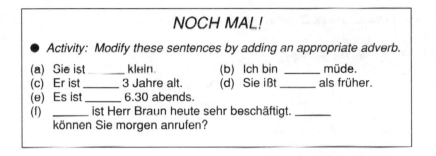

NOCH MAL!

● *Activity: Modify these sentences by adding an appropriate adverb.*

(a) Sie ist _____ klein.   (b) Ich bin _____ müde.

(c) Er ist _____ 3 Jahre alt.   (d) Sie ißt _____ als früher.

(e) Es ist _____ 6.30 abends.

(f) _____ ist Herr Braun heute sehr beschäftigt. _____
    können Sie morgen anrufen?

Wo und Wohin? *Where and Where to?*

In German, certain prepositions are always used with the **accusative** case, for example:

Sie geht **durch den** Garten.	*She goes **through** the garden.*
Er kommt **auf mich zu**.	*He comes **towards** me.*

durch	*through*	um ... herum	*around*
... entlang	*along*		

Certain other prepositions are always used with the **dative** case.

Sie geht **zur** Post.	*She goes **to the** post office.*
Er kommt mir **entgegen**.	*He comes **towards** me.*

aus	*out of*	... vorbei	*past*
gegenüber	*opposite*	weit von	*far from*
nach	*after, to* (a town)	zu	*to* (place/person)
nach dem Essen	*after the meal*	nach Hause	
nach Freiburg	*to Freiburg*	gehen	*to go home*
von	*from*	zu Hause sein	*to be at home*
in der Nähe	*near*		

Certain prepositions may be used with **either** the accusative or the dative case. The **accusative** case expresses **movement towards** a person, place or object. It answers the question *Where ... to?* The **dative** case shows **position**. It answers the question *Where ... ?*

Ich gehe **in den** Garten.	*I go **into the** garden.* (accusative – where to?)
Der Hund spielt **im** Garten.	*The dog is playing **in the** garden.* (dative – where?)

an	*on / at / to* (a place)	über	*over*
auf	*on* (top of)	hinter	*behind*
herauf, rauf	*up*	in	*in, into*
herunter, runter	*down*	neben	*beside*

Wo und Wohin? *Where and Where to?*

unter	*under*
über	*above*
unter	*below*
vor	*in front of*
zwischen	*between*

Andere Präpositionen
Other prepositions

da, dort	*there*
draußen	*outside*

drinnen, innen	*inside*
hier	*here*
irgendwo	*somewhere*
nirgendwo	*nowhere*
überall	*everywhere*
weg, fort	*away*
zurück	*back*
Ich lehne mich vor.	*I lean forward.*

Contractions

When **der, das** and **dem** are used with certain prepositions, it is common to combine the two:

an dem → am	in dem → im	zu der → zur
an das → ans	in das → ins	zu dem → zum
bei dem → beim	von dem → vom	

NOCH MAL!

● Activity: Where is he?

(a)   (b)

(c) MGM   (d)

Wann? *When?*

Temporale Ausdrücke
Expressions of time

ab und zu	*now and again*
am Wochenende	*at the weekend*
bald	*soon*
bis	*until*
dann	*then*
das nächste Mal	*next time*
der Nächste, bitte!	
	next, please!
den ganzen Tag	*all day*
diese Woche	*this week*
diesen Monat	*this month*
dieses Jahr	*this year*
einmal	*once*
endlich	*finally*
erst	*not until, only*
erst morgen	*not until tomorrow*
Er war erst zehn	*He was only ten.*
früh	*early*
gestern	*yesterday*
gewöhnlich	*usually*
gleich	*in a moment*
heute	*today*
heutzutage	*nowadays*
immer	*always*

in der Zwischenzeit	
	meanwhile
jeden Tag	*every day*
letzten Sommer	*last summer*
manchmal	*sometime(s)*
nach	*after*
nachher	*afterwards*
nächstes Jahr	*next year*
nie, niemals	*never*
noch	*still*
noch nicht	*not . . . yet*
oft	*often*
regelmäßig	*regularly*
schon	*already*
selten	*rarely*
sobald	*as soon as*
sofort	*immediately*
spät	*late*
später	*later*
von Zeit zu Zeit	*from time to time*
vor	*before*
vor 8 Uhr	*before 8 o' clock*
vor ...	*ago*
vor drei Wochen	*three weeks ago*
vor kurzem, in letzter Zeit	
	recently
wieder	*again*
zuerst	*first*

NOCH MAL!

● *Activity: Complete the sentences with appropriate time expressions.*

(a) **Letztes Jahr** bin ich nach Rom gefahren. ____ ____ fahre ich nach Paris.
   ***Last year** I went to Rome.* ____ ____ *I'm going to Paris.*
(b) Ich spiele ____ Tennis. ____ spiele ich am Donnerstag abend.
(c) Klaus fährt ____ mit dem Auto zur Arbeit aber ____ fährt er mit dem Zug.
(d) ____ habe ich meine Freundin besucht. ____ werde ich meine Mutter besuchen.
(e) Ich habe ____ keine Zeit. Ich kann es ____ machen.

Fragewörter *Questions words*

zur Zeit, jetzt	*at the moment, now*	Was für . . . ?	*What kind of . . . ?*
Wie?	*How?*	Wann?	*When?*
Wie viele?	*How much / many?*	Wo?	*Where?*
Wieviel kostet das?	*How much is it?*	Welche?	*Which?*
Wie heißt er?	*What is he called?*	Wer?	*Who?*
Was?	*What?*	Warum?	*Why?*

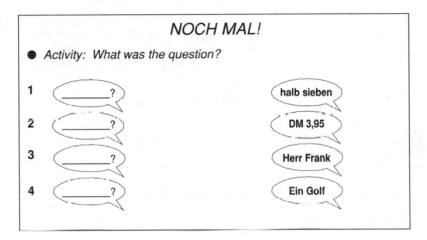

NOCH MAL!

● *Activity: What was the question?*

1 _____ ?   halb sieben

2 _____ ?   DM 3,95

3 _____ ?   Herr Frank

4 _____ ?   Ein Golf

Artikeln, Pronomen und Konjunktionen
Articles, pronouns and conjunctions

Der bestimmte Artikel
The definite article

der, die, das   *the*

Nouns in German are **masculine**; (Maskulinum – der); **feminine**
(Femininum – die); or **neuter** (Neutrum – das).

Der Schwarzwald ist wunderschön	*The Black Forest is lovely.*
Die Putzfrau kommt heute nicht.	*The cleaning lady isn't coming today.*
Das Auto ist neu.	*The car is new.*
Die Touristen besuchen die Kirche.	*The tourists are visiting the church.*

Cases

There are **four cases** in German: nominative, accusative, dative and
genitive. The case, or form, a noun takes depends on its role in the sentence.

Nominativ The noun is in the nominative case when it is the subject of the
sentence.

Die Katze jagt die Maus. ***The cat*** *chases the mouse.*

Akkusativ The noun is in the accusative case when it is the **direct object**
of the sentence.

Die Katze jagt **die Maus**. *The cat chases **the mouse**.*

Genitiv The noun is in the genitive case when it shows **possession**.

Die Katze **des Bauers** jagt die Maus. *The **farmer's** cat chases the mouse.*

Dativ The noun is in the dative case when it is the **indirect object** of the
sentence.

Die Katze bringt **dem Bauern** die tote Maus. *The cat takes the dead
mouse **to the farmer**.*

	Masculine	Feminine	Neuter	Plural
Nominative	der	die	das	die
Accusative	den	die	das	die
Genitive	des	der	des	der
Dative	dem	der	dem	den

Artikeln, Pronomen und Konjunktionen
Articles, pronouns and conjunctions

Der unbestimmte Artikel   *The indefinite article*

ein, eine ein   *a*

> **Ein** Mann geht über die Straße.   *A man is crossing the road.*
> Claudia hat **eine** neue Wohnung.   *Claudia has a new flat.*
> **Ein** Kind spielt im Garten.   *A child is playing in the garden.*
>
> *Note*: There is no plural form of **ein**.

| kein | *not a, no* | keine | *not any (plural)* |

Kein uses the same endings as ein and gives a noun a negative meaning.

Ich habe **kein** Auto.   *I don't have a car.*
Er hat **keine** Papiere.   *He doesn't have any papers.*

	Masculine	Feminine	Neuter	Plural
Nominative	ein	eine	cin	keine
Accusative	einen	eine	ein	keine
Genitive	eines	einer	eines	keiner
Dative	einem	einer	einem	keinen

NOCH MAL!

● *Activity: In the office.*

Name these items. Are they **der**, **die** or **das** words?
Now make a sentence with each item, for example:
Ich habe **einen/keinen** PC.   *(I have/haven't got a PC.)*

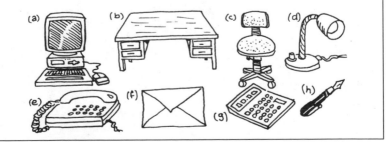

Artikeln, Pronomen und Konjunktionen
Articles, pronouns and conjunctions

Possessivpronomen
Possessive pronouns

In German mein (*my*), dein (*your*), etc., change according to the noun they describe. They take the same endings as **ein** when the pronoun stands **before** the noun. (See the **ein** table above.)

mein	my	**unser**	our
dein	your (singular, familiar)	**euer**	your (plural of dein)
sein	his/its (masculine nouns)	**Ihr**	your (formal)
ihr	her/its (feminine nouns)	**ihr**	your (plural)

Examples: Das ist **mein** Buch.
Sie fährt zu **ihrem** Freund.

When the pronoun comes **after** the noun it describes, you add the following endings to **mein**, **dein**, etc.

Masculine	Feminine	Neuter	Plural
-er	**-e**	**-s**	**-e**
mein**er**	mein**e**	mein**s**	mein**e** *mine*

Example: Er ist **meiner**.

jeder, dieser etc., use the same endings as **der**.

jeder (einzelne)	*each*	jener	*that*
jeder	*every*	jene	*those*
dieser	*this*	dieser, erster	*the former*
diese	*these*	jener, letzter	*the latter*
		jeder, der ...	*whoever*

Artikeln, Pronomen und Konjunktionen
Articles, pronouns and conjunctions

Personalpronomen
Personal pronouns

Singular				Plural			
ich	mich	mir	*I / me / to me*	wir	uns	uns	*we / us / to us*
du	dich	dir	*you / you / to you*	ihr	euch	euch	*you / you / to you*
er	ihn	ihm	*he / him / to him*	Sie	Sie	Ihnen	*you / you / to you*
sie	sie	ihr	*she / her / to her*	sie	sie	ihnen	*they / them / to them*
es	es	ihm	*it / it / to it*				

Ralf hat **mir** einen Brief geschrieben. *Ralf has written a letter **to me**.*
Sie ist ein Freund von **ihm**. *She is a friend of **his**.*
Anna will **uns** morgen treffen. *Anna wants to meet **us** tomorrow.*

für uns	*for us*	daß	*that*
gegen mich	*against me*	denn	*for*
ohne sie	*without them*	ob	*if (whether)*
		obwohl	*although*
außer mir	*except me*	oder	*or*
bei ihr	*at her house*	sonst	*or else*
mit ihm	*with him*	trotz	*in spite of*
von dir/euch/		trotzdem	*nevertheless*
Ihnen	*from you*	und	*und*
zu mir	*to me*	weil	*because*
		wenn, falls	*if*
Konjunktionen *Conjunctions*		wenn ... nicht	*unless*
		wie	*how*
aber	*but*		

Es tut mir leid, aber er ist nicht da. *I'm sorry, but he isn't there.*
Er hat es gekauft, weil es billig war. *He bought it because it was cheap.*

Artikeln, Pronomen und Konjunktionen
Articles, pronouns and conjunctions

NOCH MAL!

● *Activity: Put the right form for (i) the (i) this/these (iii) my (iv) her (v) your in front of these words:*

Example: (i) der Hund

(ii) dieser Hund (iii) mein Hund (iv) _____ (v) _____

Verben *Verbs*

Here is some brief information about verbs. See 16 Coda for other irregular verbs. For more information about verbs please read *Teach Yourself German Verbs*.

PRÄSENZ *PRESENT TENSE*

Ich kaufe jeden Tag Brötchen.	*I buy bread rolls every day.*
Ich spiele Tennis.	*I play / I'm playing tennis.*

Regelmäßige Verben *Regular verbs*

kaufen *to buy*

(singular)		(plural)	
ich kaufe	*I buy*	wir kaufen	*we buy*
du kaufst	*you buy*	ihr kauft	*you buy*
er/sie/es kauft	*he / she / it buys*	Sie kaufen	*you buy*
		sie kaufen	*they buy*

Unregelmäßige Verben *Irregular verbs*

haben *to have*

ich habe	*I have*	wir haben	*we have*
du hast	*you have*	ihr habt	*you have*
er/sie/es hat	*he / she / it has*	Sie haben	*you have*
		sie haben	*they have*

sein *to be*

ich bin	*I am*	wir sind	*we are*
du bist	*you are*	ihr seid	*you are*
er/sie/es ist	*he / she / it is*	Sie sind	*you are*
		sie sind	*they are*

du is the familiar form of *you* and is singular; **ihr** is the plural form of **du**; **Sie** is the polite form of *you* and is used in the singular and the plural.

Verben *Verbs*

The **infinitive** of a verb in German ends in **-en**: kauf**en**, fahr**en**
This is the form which you find in the dictionary.
Er will das Buch **kaufen**.   *He wants **to buy** the book.*

Vergangenheit *Past*

In German the perfect tense (**Perfekt**) is used when you talk about the past. It is made up of the present of haben or sein + the past participle of the verb.

Regular (weak) verbs: Ich habe **ge**kauft   *I bought, I have bought*

Irregular (strong) verbs: Ich habe gesehen   *I saw, I have seen*
                               Ich bin gegangen   *I went, I have gone*

The imperfect tense is used mainly for reports and descriptions:

Regular verbs: er **kaufte**   *he bought*
Irregular verbs: er **ging**   *he went*

Futur *Future tense*

The future is made up of part of the verb **werden** + **the infinitive**.
The present tense can also be used to talk about future plans.

Ich **werde** ein Auto **kaufen**.   ***I'm going to buy** a car.*

Ich **spiele** morgen Tennis.   ***I'm playing** tennis tomorrow.*

Modalverben *Modal verbs*

Infinitive

dürfen	*to be allowed to*	ich darf	*I may*
können	*to be able to*	ich kann	*I can*
mögen	*to like*	ich mag	*I like*
müssen	*to have to*	ich muß	*I must*
sollen	*to be supposed to*	ich soll	*I should*
wollen	*to want to*	ich will	*I want*

Verben *Verbs*

Ich muß zur Arbeit gehen.	*I must go to work.*
Ich will in die Stadt fahren.	*I want to go to town.*

Unpersönliche Verben *Impersonal verbs*

Some verbs in German use **es** as a neutral subject. The real subject or person referred to is therefore a pronoun: mir, dir, etc.

Es gefällt **mir.**	*I like it (literally, it is pleasing to me)*
Es geht mir gut.	*I'm well.*
Es gelingt mir.	*I succeed.*
Es gibt . . .	*There is . . .*
Es regnet.	*It's raining.*
Es tut mir leid.	*I'm sorry.*
Es tut mir weh.	*It hurts (me).*
Mir ist kalt/warm.	*I'm cold / warm.*
Mir ist schlecht.	*I feel sick.*

Trennbare Verben *Separable verbs*

Separable verbs are made up of two parts: a prefix and a verb, which you separate from each other when you make a sentence, for example:
    an + kommen = ankommen (*to arrive*).

In the present tense the prefix goes to the end of the sentence:
    ankommen   Ich komme um 9 an.   *I arrive at 9.*

In the perfect tense it goes to the front of the past participle:
    aufstehen   Ich bin spät aufgestanden.   *I got up late.*

Some other common prefixes are: ab; her; hin; zu
    abfahren   *to depart*

Verbs *Verben*

NOCH MAL!

● *Activity: (a) Was hat er gestern gemacht? (b) Was macht er heute? (c) Was wird er morgen machen?* (d) Und sie?

● And you?

Was hast du gestern gemacht ?
Was machst du heute?
Was wirst du morgen machen?

TOPIC
VOCABULARY

1 Zur Person *Personal Matters*

AUSSEHEN
PERSONAL APPEARANCE

(Also see 12 *At the hairdressers*, p.165)

Ich bin ...	*I am ...*
Er/Sie ist ...	*He / she is ...*
groß	*tall*
klein	*short*
dünn	*thin*
schlank	*slim*
dick	*fat*
gut gebaut	*well built*
mittelgroß	*medium height*

Ich habe ... Haar *I have ... hair*
blondes	*blond*
dunkles/	
hellblondes	*dark / fair*
graues/weißes	*grey / white*
rotbraunes	*auburn*
rotes/braunes/ kastanienbraunes	
	red / brown / chestnut
glattes/lockiges	*straight / curly*
langes/kurzes	*long / short*
meliertes	*streaked*
welliges/schütteres	
	wavy / thinning
eine Glatze	*a bald head*

und ... Augen	*and ... eyes*
blaue	*blue*
blaugraue	*blue-grey*
grüne	*green*
braune	*brown*

Ich bin kurz-/weitsichtig.   *I am short / long sighted.*
Ich trage eine Brille/Kontaktlinsen.   *I wear glasses / contact lenses.*

Ich bin ... groß *I am ... tall*   Ich wiege ...   *I weigh ...*

Ich sehe blaß aus.   *I'm pale.*
Ich bin sonnengebräunt,
   braun gebrannt.   *I am suntanned.*

Ich habe ...	*I am ...*
eine helle Hautfarbe	
	fair skinned
eine dunkle Hautfarbe	
	dark skinned
eine trockene Haut	
	I have dry skin
empfindliche Haut	
	sensitive skin
Er hat/trägt ...	*He has ...*
einen Bart (¨e)	*a beard*
Koteletten	*sideboards*

einen Schnurbart (¨e),	
Schnauzer (-)	*a moustache*
einen Vollbart (¨e)	
	full beard
einen Zwirbelbart (¨e)	
	handlebar moustache
Er/Sie hat ...	*He / She has ...*
Akne	*acne*
Falten, Runzeln	*wrinkles*
Grübchen	*dimples*
einen Leberfleck (-e)	
	a mole

1 **Zur Person** *Personal Matters*

ein süßes Lächeln
    a nice smile
ein Muttermal (-e) *a birth mark*
eine Narbe (-n) *a scar*
einen Pickel (-n) *a spot*
Sommersprossen *freckles*
eine große Nase (-n)
    a big nose
eine Boxernase (-n)
    a boxer's nose
eine gebrochene Nase (-n)
    a broken nose
eine Hakennase (-n)
    a hooked nose
einen Riechkolben,
  Höcker (umg.) *a hooter, conk (sl.)*
eine Säufernase (umg.)
    a boozer's nose (sl.)
eine Stupsnase (-n)
    a snub nose

abstehende Ohren
    ears that stick out
Boxerohren *cauliflower ears*
Segelohren *big, flapping ears*

dicke/schmale
  Lippen *thick / thin lips*
einen Schmollmund ("er)
    pouting lips
einen breiten/
  schmalen Mund
    a wide / narrow
    mouth
buschige
  Augenbrauen *bushy eyebrows*
Pausbacken *chubby cheeks*
rote Wangen *rosy cheeks*

einen Bierbauch ("e)
    a beer belly
Plattfüße *flat feet*
Quadratlatschen (umg.)
    feet like barges (coll.)

Er/Sie ist . . . *He / she is . . .*
rechtshändig/linkshändig
    right / left-handed

häßlich *ugly*
hübsch *pretty*
niedlich *cute*
süß *sweet*

Er sieht gut aus.	*He is good-looking.*
Er/Sie sieht schmuddelig, verlottert aus.	*He / She looks scruffy*
Er/Sie sieht gepflegt aus.	*He / She looks well-groomed*
Mann-o-Mann, die sieht ja stark aus!	*Wow, she's a good looker!*
Er sieht (auch) nicht übel aus!	*He's not bad (either)!*

---

behindert *handicapped*
beidseitig
  gelähmt *paraplegic*
blind *blind*
die Prothese (-n) *artificial limb*
der Rollstuhl ("e) *wheel chair*

geistig/körperlich behindert
    mentally / physically
    handicapped
gelähmt *lame*
stumm *dumb*
taub *deaf*

NOCH MAL!

● *Activity 1: What does he/she look like? Describe these people to your German friends.*

● *Activity 2: What do you look like? Describe yourself.*

1 **Zur Person** *Personal Matters*

EMPFINDUNGEN UND GEFÜHLE
FEELINGS AND EMOTIONS

die Stimmung (-en) *mood*
das Gefühl (-e)   *emotion*
die Empfindung (-en)
       feeling

Wie fühlst du dich?
How are you feeling?

Ich fühle mich ... *I feel ...*
abgewiesen, zurückgewiesen
       rejected
beschämt   *ashamed*
besser   *better*
ekelhaft   *disgusting*
furchtbar, schrecklich
       awful
gelangweilt *bored*
niedergeschlagen,
  deprimiert *depressed*
sagenhaft/klasse
  /unwahrscheinlich gut
       terrific
super/top/erstklassig/astrein!
       great!
total gelassen/cool !
       cool !
unwohl   *uneasy*

Ich bin ...   *I am ...*
angeturnt, high *high*
besorgt   *worried,*
               apprehensive
auf Touren   *turned on*
               (sexually)
ausgelaugt,
  ausgepowert *drained*
begeistert   *switched on*
begeistert, enthusiastisch
               enthusiastic
betrübt   *distressed*
durstig   *thirsty*
entsetzt   *appalled*
entspannt   *relaxed*
enttäuscht   *let down*
erfreut   *delighted*
erledigt   *shattered* (tired)
erschöpft   *exhausted*
fit/topfit   *fit / very fit*
freundlich   *friendly*
gefräßig   *greedy* (food)
gelassen   *laid-back*
glücklich   *happy*
gut/schlecht gelaunt
               in a good / bad mood
hoffnungsvoll/voller Hoffnung
               hopeful
lebhaft   *lively*
müde   *tired*

46

1 Zur Person *Personal Matters*

neugierig	*curious*	überrascht	*surprised*
optimistisch	*optimistic*	unglücklich	*unhappy*
pessimistisch	*pessimistic*	unzufrieden	*dissatisfied*
redselig/		verärgert	*annoyed*
gesprächig	*talkative*	verletzt	*upset*
satt	*full*	völlig erschöpft/unglaublich	
sexy	*sexy*	kaputt	*tired out*
traurig	*sad*	zerrüttet	*shattered* (nerves)
überglücklich	*overjoyed*	zufrieden	*satisfied*

Ich habe Angst	*I'm afraid*
Ich habe keine Lust	*I can't be bothered / I don't want to*

Charaktereigenschaften *Characteristics*

Was für ein Mensch bist du?	*What sort of a person are you?*
Ich bin (er/sie ist) . . .	*I am (he / she is). . .*

neidisch	*envious*	boshaft	*spiteful*
		damenhaft	*ladylike*
albern	*silly*	dumm, blöd	*stupid*
arrogant	*arrogant*	ehrgeizig	*ambitious*
artig	*well-behaved*	ehrlich	*honest*
aufgeschlossen	*open-minded*	eifersüchtig	*jealous*
aufgeweckt	*sharp, bright*	eiskalt, kaltschnäuzig	
aufmerksam	*attentive*		*unfeeling*
aufmüpfig (umg.)	*rebellious*	entzückend, liebenswürdig	
aus grobem Holz			*charming*
geschnitzt	*insensitive*	ernst	*serious*
ausgebufft	*shrewd*	feinfühlig	*sensitive*
ausgeglichen	*even-tempered,*	fleißig	*hard-working*
	well-balanced	flink	*nimble, bright*
ausgeschlafen (umg.)		frech	*cheeky*
	on the ball	freundlich	*friendly*
begabt, gescheit,		fröhlich	*cheerful*
klug	*clever*	gastfreundlich	*hospitable*
bescheiden	*modest*	gebildet	*well-educated*

47

1 Zur Person *Personal Matters*

geduldig	*patient*	selbstbewußt	*self-confident*
geizig	*miserly*	selbstsüchtig	*selfish*
gemein	*nasty*	seltsam,	
gesellig	*sociable*	eigenartig	*funny* (strange)
grob/ungehobelt	*coarse / uncouth*	sensibel	*sensitive*
gierig	*greedy*	stolz	*proud*
grausam	*cruel*	streng	*strict*
großherzig	*generous*	stur	*stubborn*
hilfsbereit	*helpful*	tyrannisch	*bullying*
hinterlistig	*crafty, cunning*	unbedarft	*simple-minded*
hochnäsig	*snooty*	unbeherrscht	*wild*
intelligent	*intelligent, smart*	unbeholfen	*clumsy*
kühl	*cool*	undankbar	*ungrateful*
kultiviert	*sophisticated*	ungeduldig	*impatient*
launisch	*moody*	ungezwungen	*casual*
liebevoll, zärtlich	*affectionate*	unglaubwürdig	*unreliable*
link (umg.)	*malicious, a real*	unschuldig	*innocent*
	swine	unverschämt	*rude, insolent*
lustig, komisch	*funny* (amusing)	unvorsichtig	*careless / clumsy*
miesepetrig (umg.)	*miserable, grouchy*	unwissend, ignorant	
mißtrauisch	*suspicious*		*ignorant*
mutig, tapfer	*brave, courageous*	verantwortungslos	
naiv	*naive*		*irresponsible*
neidisch	*envious*	verdorben (umg.)	*spoilt*
nervös	*nervous*	vernünftig	*reasonable, sensible*
neugierig	*inquisitive*	verschlossen	*reserved, secretive*
offen, ehrlich	*sincere*	verschmitzt	*mischievous*
patzig	*insolent*	verschwiegen	*discreet*
reserviert	*reserved*	verständnisvoll	*sympathetic*
roh	*rough*	vertrauenswürdig	*trustworthy*
rücksichtsvoll	*considerate*	verträumt	*a dreamer*
sanft, zart	*gentle*	vornehm	*distinguished, refined*
sarkastisch	*sarcastic*	vorsichtig	*cautious*
scheu	*timid*	widerspenstig	*wilful*
schlagfertig	*quick-witted*	zerstreut	*absent-minded*
schlampig (umg.)	*sloppy, slovenly*	zornig, ungehalten	
schüchtern	*shy*		*angry*

1 **Zur Person** *Personal Matters*

VORLIEBEN UND ABNEIGUNGEN
LIKES AND DISLIKES

(See 8 *Arts* p. 110, and 9 *Hobbies and sports*, p. 121 for more vocabulary)

Ich habe . . . gern, Ich mag . . .	*I like . . .*
Ich spiele gern Tennis.	*I like playing tennis.*
Ich möchte . . .	*I'd like to . . .*
Ich möchte heute abend ins Kino gehen.	*I'd like to go to the cinema this evening.*
Ich . . . lieber . . .	*I prefer . . .*
Ich gehe lieber zur Ausstellung.	*I prefer to go to the exhibition.*
Ich . . . nicht gern, Ich mag . . . nicht	*I don't like . . .*
Ich hasse . . .	*I hate . . .*
Ich hasse Schlangen.	*I hate snakes.*
Ich kann . . . nicht ausstehen.	*I can't stand . . .*

zurückhaltend	*reticent*	gern haben, mögen	*to be fond of . . .*
zuverlässig	*reliable*	lieben	*to love*
über alles/abgöttisch lieben,		sich in etwas/jdn.	
anbeten	*to adore*	verlieben	*to fall in love with sth / sb*
bewundern	*to admire*		
ein Fan/Bewunderer			
von . . . sein	*to be a fan of . . .*		

Ich mag jdn. (nicht)	*I like (dislike) someone*
Ich verstehe mich gut/schlecht mit jdm	*I get on well / badly with someone*
Ich kann jdn. nicht ausstehen	*I can't stand someone*

1 **Zur Person** *Personal Matters*

DIE FAMILIE   *FAMILY*

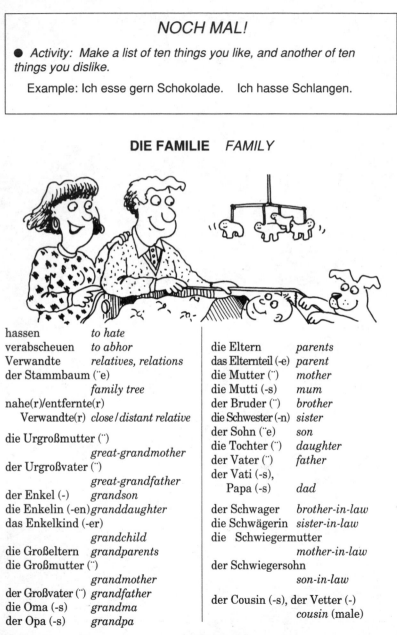

hassen	*to hate*	die Eltern	*parents*
verabscheuen	*to abhor*	das Elternteil (-e)	*parent*
Verwandte	*relatives, relations*	die Mutter (¨)	*mother*
der Stammbaum (¨e)		die Mutti (-s)	*mum*
	family tree	der Bruder (¨)	*brother*
nahe(r)/entfernte(r)		die Schwester (-n)	*sister*
Verwandte(r)	*close / distant relative*	der Sohn (¨e)	*son*
die Urgroßmutter (¨)		die Tochter (¨)	*daughter*
	great-grandmother	der Vater (¨)	*father*
der Urgroßvater (¨)		der Vati (-s),	
	great-grandfather	Papa (-s)	*dad*
der Enkel (-)	*grandson*		
die Enkelin (-en)	*granddaughter*	der Schwager	*brother-in-law*
das Enkelkind (-er)		die Schwägerin	*sister-in-law*
	grandchild	die Schwiegermutter	
die Großeltern	*grandparents*		*mother-in-law*
die Großmutter (¨)		der Schwiegersohn	
	grandmother		*son-in-law*
der Großvater (¨)	*grandfather*		
die Oma (-s)	*grandma*	der Cousin (-s), der Vetter (-)	
der Opa (-s)	*grandpa*		*cousin* (male)

1 Zur Person *Personal Matters*

die Cousine (-n) *cousin* (female)
der Neffe (-n) *nephew*
die Nichte (-n) *niece*
der Onkel (-) *uncle*
die Tante (-n) *aunt*

der Stief-/ Halbbruder (¨)
    step / half-brother
die Stiefmutter (¨) *step-mother*

das Baby (-s) *baby*
das Kleinkind (-er) *toddler*
das Kind (-er) *child*
der Teenager (-) *teenager*
der/die Jugendliche(r)
    adolescent(f / m)
der Erwachsene (-n)
    adult

die jüngere Schwester (-n)
    younger sister
der älterer Bruder *older brother*

das Einzelkind (-er)
    only child
der Zwilling (-e) *twin*
die eineiigen Zwillinge
    identical twins
adoptiert *adopted*
das Waisenkind (-er)
    orphan

mütterlicherseits *maternal*
väterlicherseits *paternal*
meine Großmutter mütterlicherseits
    my maternal
    grandmother
das Foto (-s), Bild (-er)
    photograph
das Fotoalbum (-alben)
    photograph album
Hier ist ein Foto
  von meiner/ *Here is a photo*
  meinem . . . *of my . . .*

NOCH MAL!

● *Activity: Complete the family tree:*

1 **Zur Person** *Personal Matters*

HAUSTIERE
PETS

der Hamster (-) *hamster*
das Kaninchen (-) *rabbit*
das Karnickel (-) *bunny*
die Katze   *cat*

die Maus (¨e)   *mouse*
das Meerschweinchen (-)
                  guinea pig
der Papagei (-en) *parrot*
die Schildkröte *tortoise*

WARNUNG VOR DEM HUND!

VORSICHT BISSIGER HUND!

Platz!
Braver Hund!

der Hund *Dog*

die Hündin (-nen) *bitch*
die Promenadenmischung (-en)
                  mongrel
reinrassig   *pedigree*
der Welpe (-n)   *puppy*
der Collie (-s)   *collie*
der Dackel (-)   *dachshund*
der Pudel (-)   *poodle*
der Schäferhund (-e)
                  Alsatian
der Blindenhund (-e)
                  guide dog
der Wachhund (-e) *guard dog*

der Freßnapf (¨e) *bowl*
das Futter   *food*
das Halsband (¨er) *collar*
der Hundekorb (¨e) *dog box / basket*
der Knochen (-)   *bone*
der Kuchen (-)   *biscuit*
die Leine (-n)   *lead*
das Kotschäufelchen (-)
                  poop scoop

die Katze *Cat*

die Hauskatze (-n) *domestic cat*
der Kater (-)   *tom cat*
die Mietze (-n)   *kitty*
das Kätzchen (-)   *kitten*

1 **Zur Person** *Personal Matters*

der Vogel *Bird*

der Käfig (-e)   *cage*
der Kanarienvogel (¨)
          canary
der Piepmatz (¨e) *dickybird*
das Vogelfutter *birdseed*
der Wellensittich (-e)
          budgie

der Fisch *Fish*

das Aquarium
   (Aquarien) *aquarium*
der Goldfisch (-e) *goldfish*
das Goldfischglas (¨er)
          goldfish bowl
der Teich (-e)   *pond*
der tropische
   Fisch (-e)   *tropical fish*

ausmisten   *to clean out*
bellen   *to bark*
fangen   *to catch*
futtern   *to feed*
knurren   *to growl*
kratzen   *to scratch*
miauen   *to mew*
schnüffeln   *to sniff*
schnurren   *to purr*

Gassi gehen   *to go walkies*
mit dem Hund spazieren
   gehen   *to take the dog for a
                 walk*
spazierenführen *to exercise*
tränken   *to give water to*

*Herzlichen Glückwünsch
zu Eurem
kleinen Sohn!*

*Herzlichen Glückwünsch
zu
Eurer Tochter!*

DIE GEBURT
CHILDBIRTH

das Baby (-s) *baby*
das Geburtsdatum (-daten)
  date of birth
der Geburtstag (-e)
  birthday
der Junge (-n) *boy*
das Mädchen (-) *girl*

die Schwangerschaft (-en)
Pregnancy

Sie ist schwanger *She's pregnant*

Frauenarzt/-in *gynaecologist*
die Hebamme (-n) *midwife*
fruchtbar *fertile*
die Ultraschall-
  untersuchung (-en)
  scan

die Umstandskleidung
  *maternity
  clothes*
über der Zeit sein
  to be overdue

die Geburt (-en) *Birth*

die Entbindung (-en)
  delivery
der Fötus (-se) *foetus*
der Kaiserschnitt (-e)
  caesarian
der Kreißsaal (-säle)
  delivery room
die Zange(-n) *forceps*
die Fehlgeburt (-en)
  miscarriage
die Frühgeburt (-en)
  premature birth
die natürliche
  Geburt (-en) *natural birth*

Hallo, da bin ich!
Christina
23.9.95
mit 3,460g und 49 cm
Wir freuen uns riesig
Rainer und Petra Keller

2 Geburt, Hochzeit und Tod *Birth, Marriage and Death*

Die Taufe (-n)	*Christening, baptism*	der Pate (-n)	*godfather*
das Geschenk (-e)	*present, gift*	meine Patentante	*my godmother*
das Patenkind (-er)	*godchild*	die Patin (-nen)	*godmother*
die Paten	*godparents*	taufen	*to christen*
mein Patenonkel	*my godfather*		

DAS BABY
BABY

das Au-pair (Mädchen)
    au pair
der Babysitter (-) *baby-sitter*
die Eltern   *parents*
die Tagesmutter (¨)
    child-minder

die Babynahrung (-)
    baby food
das Babypuder (-) *baby powder*
die Muttermilch *mother's milk*
das Milchpulver (-)
    powdered milk
die Nuckelflasche (-n)
    baby's bottle
der Schnuller (-) *dummy*
das Töpfchen (-) *potty*
 Pampers, die
    Einwegwindel (-n)
    disposable nappy
die Windel (-n) *nappy, diaper*
der Zwieback (¨e) *rusk*
die Babytragetasche (-n)
    carrycot
der Buggy (-s) *pushchair*
das Kinderbett (-en)
    cot
der Kinderhochstuhl (¨e)
    high chair
der Kinderwagen (-)
    pram
die Wiege (-n) *cradle*
die Wolldecke (-n) *blanket*

das Kinderzimmer (-)
    nursery
der Laufstall (¨e) *playpen*
das Mobile (-) *mobile*
die Rassel (-n) *rattle*
die Spieluhr (-en) *musical box*
der Teddybär (-en) *teddy bear*
das Wiegenlied (-er)
    lullaby

die Babyschuhe (-n)
    bootees
das Kinderhemdchen (-)
    vest
das Lätzchen (-) *bib*
das Mützchen (-) *bonnet*
der Schlafanzug (¨e)
    sleeping suit
der Strampelanzug (¨e),
    Strampler (-) *rompers*

abwischen,
    abputzen *to wipe*
aufwachen *to wake up*
baden *to bath*
einschlafen *to go to sleep*
füttern *to feed*
geboren werden *to be born*
ein Kind bekommen
    to have a baby
mit dem Baby spazierengehen
    to take for a walk
mit der Flasche füttern
    to bottle feed
nuckeln *to suck*
plärren *to howl*

2 Geburt, Hochzeit und Tod *Birth, Marriage and Death*

stillen	*to breast feed*	Windel wechseln	*to change a nappy*
wachsen	*to grow*	zahnen	*to teethe*
weinen	*to cry*		

Er/Sie wurde am . . . geboren.
Das Baby nuckelt am Daumen.

He / she was born on . . .
The baby is sucking its thumb.

Babysprache *Baby talk*

Heia machen	*to have a sleep*	Pipi/Aa machen	*to have a wee wee /*
ab in die Heia!	*off to beddy-byes*		*do a number two*

Er/Sie . . .
    hat einen wunden Po.
    schreit viel.
Ich brauche etwas
    für das Zahnen.

Ich brauche etwas gegen . . .
    Durchfall
    eine Magenverstimmung

He / She . . .
    has a sore bottom.
    cries a lot.

I need something for teething.

I need something for . . .
    diarrhoea
    indigestion

NOCH MAL!

● *Activity: Help the babysitter! What can't she find?*

AUFWACHSEN *GROWING UP*

Herzlichen Glückwunsch zum
  Geburtstag!   *Happy Birthday*

Lieber Markus!

Herzlichen Glückwunsch
zum Geburtstag
Alles Liebe
Nicole

Spielzeuge *Toys*

der Ball ("e) *ball*
der Bauklotz ("e) *building brick*
das Dreirad ("er) *tricycle*
das Fahrrad ("er) *bicycle*
die Handpuppe (-n)
           puppet
das Kinderbuch ("er)
           children's story book
die Modelleisenbahn (-en)
           model train
die Puppe (-n) *doll*
das Puzzlespiel (-e)
           jigsaw
der Roller (-) *scooter*
das Spielzeugauto (-s)
           toy car
die Spielzeugkiste (-n)
           toy box

Der Kinderspielplatz
           children's playground
Gibt es . . . ? *Is there a . . . ?*
ein Klettergerüst (-e)
           climbing frame
einen Kreisel (-) *roundabout*
eine Rutsche (-n),
    Rutschbahn (-en)
           slide
einen Sandkasten (")
           sandpit
eine Schaukel (-n) *swing*
eine Wippe (-n) *seesaw*

Ist es . . . ?   *Is it . . . ?*
für (Drei)jährige geeignet
           suitable for (3) year olds
gefährlich/
    ungefährlich *dangerous / safe*

aufwachsen   *to grow up*
sich hinsetzen *to sit up*

2 Geburt, Hochzeit und Tod *Birth, Marriage and Death*

hinfallen	*to fall*
krabbeln	*to crawl*
laufen/sprechen	
lernen	*to learn to walk/talk*
spielen	*to play*

LIEBE UND HEIRAT
LOVE AND MARRIAGE

Beziehungen *Relationships*

der (feste) Freund	*(steady) boyfriend*
die (feste) Freundin	
	(steady) girlfriend
der/die Geliebte (-n)	
	lover
erste Liebe	*first love*
Partner/in	*partner*
bisexuell	*bisexual*
heterosexuell	*heterosexual*
homosexuell	*homosexual*
lesbisch	*lesbian*
schwul	*gay*

Karin hat einen festen Freund.	*Karin has a steady boyfriend.*

---

mit jdm. gehen	*to go out with someone*
sich in jdn. verlieben	
	to fall in love with someboby
in jdn. verliebt sein	
	to be in love with somebody
miteinander schlafen	
	to sleep together

mit jdm. Geschlechtsverkehr haben	
	to have sex
die Verlobung	*engagement*
der (Heirats)antrag (¨e)	
	proposal
der Polterabend (-e)	
	hen party/stag night
die Verlobte	*fiancée*
der Verlobter	*fiancé*

Wir verloben uns

Lisa Baumann   *Philipp Scherer*

19. 9. 95

die Hochzeit *Marriage*

Wir heiraten

Gudrun Ritter
Daniel Meier

5.7.95
Kirchliche Trauung
am 6.7.95
in Bremen

die Blumenkinder	*flower children*
die Braut (¨e)	*bride*
der Bräutigam (-e)	*bridegroom*
die Ehefrau (-en)	*wife*
der Ehemann (¨er)	*husband*
das (Ehe)paar (-e)	*(married) couple*
die Frischvermählten	*newly-weds*
der Trauzeuge/die Trauzeugin	*best man / maid of honour*
der Brautstrauß (-sträuße)	*bride's bouquet*
die Einladung (-en)	*invitation*
die Flitterwochen	*honeymoon*
die kirchliche Hochzeit	*church wedding*
die standesamtliche Hochzeit	*civil marriage*
das Hochzeitskleid (-er)	*wedding dress*
das Hochzeitsmahl (-e)	*wedding breakfast, reception*
der Hochzeitstag (-e)	*wedding day / wedding anniversary*
die Hochzeitstorte (-n)	*wedding cake*
das Standesamt (¨er)	*registry office*

Herzlichen
Glückwunsch zu
Eurer Hochzeit!
Congratulations on
your wedding day!

2 Geburt, Hochzeit und Tod *Birth, Marriage and Death*

Silberhochzeit/
Goldene
Hochzeit *silver / golden
wedding
anniversary*

sich verloben *to get engaged*
einen Heiratsantrag
machen *to propose*
heiraten *to get married*
verheiratet sein *to be married*

Wir werden im Juni heiraten. *We are getting married in June.*

In Germany the civil marriage ceremony is obligatory. The couple can have a second wedding in church if they wish.

der Familienstand
Marital status

Ich bin . . . *I am . . .*
ledig *single*
verheiratet *married*
geschieden *divorced*
verwitwet *widowed*

der Junggeselle (-n)
  a bachelor
der/die Alleinstehende, Single
  a single person
unverheiratet *a spinster*
alleinerziehende(r) Mutter(Vater)
  *single mother
  (father)*

Ich lebe getrennt. *I'm separated.*
Ich wohne mit meinem Lebensgefährten/
  meiner Lebensgefährtin zusammen. *I'm living with my partner.*
Wir leben in wilder Ehe. *We live in sin.*

der Mädchenname (-n)
  maiden name
der Familienname (-n)
  married name
die Trennung (-en) *separation*

die Scheidung (-en)
  divorce
sich trennen *to separate*
sich scheiden lassen
  to divorce

2 Geburt, Hochzeit und Tod *Birth, Marriage and Death*

TOD *DEATH*

Mein Mann/Meine Frau/Mein(e) Freund(in) is gestorben.	*My husband / wife / friend has died.*
Er/Sie ist tot.	*He / She is dead.*
Ich bin Witwe/r.	*I am a widow / er.*

die Beisetzung *Funeral*

die Beerdigung (-en),
    das Begräbnis (se) *burial*
die Einäscherung (-en)
    cremation
der Fricdhof ("e) *cemetery*
das Krematorium
    (Krematorien) *crematorium*

der Trauergottesdienst (-e)
    funeral service

das Grab ("er) *grave*
der Grabstein (-e) *gravestone*
das Kranz ("e) *wreath*
der Leichenschmaus *funeral meal*
der Sarg ("e) *coffin*
die Trauer *mourning*
die Trauergemeinde (-n)
    mourners

Mein herzliches Beileid.	*I would like to convey my condolences.*
Mein tiefstes Mitgefühl.	*In deepest sympathy.*
In tiefer Anteilnahm am Tod Ihrer Mutter.	*I was very sorry to learn of your mother's death.*

Testament *Will*

der Erbe/die Erbin
    heir / heiress
die Testamentseröffnung (-en)
    reading of the will
erben *to inherit*

hinterlassen *to leave*
jdm. etwas vermachen
    *to bequeath something
    to somebody*

Er hat alles seiner Frau vermacht.	*He left everything to his wife.*

begraben/beerdigen	*to bury*
einäschern	*to cremate*
trauern	*to mourn*

Selbstmord begehen	*to commit suicide*
sterben	*to die*
bei einem Unfall umkommen	*to be killed in an accident*

3 Kleidung und Mode *Clothes and Fashion*

KLEIDUNG
CLOTHES

der Anzug (¨e)   *suit*
die Hose (-n)   *trousers*
die Jeans (-)   *jeans*
die Latzhose (-n) *dungarees*
die Lederhose(-n) *leather trousers*
der Morgenmantel (¨)
　　　　　dressing gown
der Overall (-s)   *overalls*
der Blaumann (¨er)
　　　　　boiler suit (work)
das Polohemd (-en)
　　　　　polo shirt
der Pullover (-)   *pullover*
der Rollkragenpullover (-)
　　　　　roll neck sweater
der Schlafanzug (¨e)
　　　　　pyjamas
die Shorts (pl.)   *shorts*
die Socke (-n)   *sock*
die Strickjacke (-n) *cardigan*
das Sweatshirt (-s)
　　　　　sweat shirt
das T-Shirt (-s)   *T-shirt*
die Uniform (-en) *uniform*

Damenbekleidung
Ladieswear

das Abendkleid (-er)
　　　　　evening dress
die Bluse (-n)   *blouse*
das Kostüm (-e) *suit (jacket and
　　　　　skirt)*
die Leggings (pl.) *leggings*
der Minirock (¨e) *mini skirt*
das Nachthemd (-en)
　　　　　nightie
der Rock (¨e)   *skirt*
die Schürze (-n) *apron*

Herrenbekleidung
Menswear

die Fliege (-n)   *bow tie*
der Frack (¨e)/(-s) *tails*
das Halstuch (¨er) *cravat*
das Hemd (-en)   *shirt*
der Hosenträger (-)
　　　　　braces
das Jackett (-s) *jacket*
die Kniebundhose (-n)
　　　　　knickerbockers, breeches
die Kombination (-en)
　　　　　*matching jacket
　　　　　and trousers*
die kurze(n)
　　Lederhose (-n) *Lederhosen (shorts)*
der Nadelstreifenanzug (¨e)
　　　　　pinstriped suit
der Schlips (-e), die Kravatte (-n)
　　　　　tie
der Smoking (-s) *dinner jacket*
die Weste (-en)   *waistcoat*

Damenunterwäsche
Lingerie

der Body (-s)   *'body' top*
der BH (-s) (*Büstenhalter*)
　　　　　bra
der Halbunterrock (¨e)
　　　　　waist slip
die Miederhose (-n)
　　　　　girdle
der Petticoat (-s) *petticoat*
der Slip (-s)   *pants, knickers*
der Straps (-e)   *suspender belt*
der Strumpf (¨e) *stocking*
die Strumpfhose (-n)
　　　　　tights
die Tanga (-s)   *tanga*
das Unterhemd (-en)   *vest*
der Unterrock (¨e) *underskirt*

3 Kleidung und Mode *Clothes and Fashion*

Unterwäsche *Underwear*

die Boxershorts (pl.)
　　　　boxer shorts
der Slip (-s)　　*briefs*

Oberbekleidung *Outerwear*

der Anorak (-s)　*anorak*
der Blazer (-s)　*blazer*
der/das Blouson (-s)
　　　　bomber jacket
die Jacke (-n)　*jacket*
der Mantel (¨)　*coat*
der Pelzmantel (¨) *fur coat*
der Regenmantel (¨)
　　　　raincoat

der Hut (¨e)　　*hat*
die Baseballmütze (-n)
　　　　baseball cap
die Kapuze (-n)　*hood*
das Kopftuch (¨er) *headscarf*
die Mütze (-n)　*cap*
die Pudelmütze (-n)
　　　　woolly hat

der Zylinder (-)　*top hat*

Sportkleidung *Sportswear*

die Fußballschuhe
　　　　football boots
der Gymnastikanzug (¨e)
　　　　leotard and tights
der Jogginganzug (¨e)
　　　　tracksuit
die Sporthose (-n) *shorts*
das Trikot (-s)　*sports shirt*
die Turnschuhe　*trainers*

Bademode *Swimwear*

der Badeanzug (¨e)
　　　　swimsuit
die Badehose (-n) *trunks*
die Badekappe (-n)
　　　　swimming cap
der Bikini (-s)　*bikini*

Schuhe *Footwear, shoes*

ein Paar ...　*a pair of...*
ein Paar Stiefel *a pair of boots*

die Badelatschen *flip-flops*
die Cowboystiefel *cowboy boots*
die Gummistiefel *rubber boots,*
　　　　wellingtons
die hochhackigen Schuhe
　　　　high heeled shoes
die Pantoffeln, die Hausschuhe
　　　　slippers
die Sandalen　*sandals*
die Schnürschuhe *lace-ups*
die Stiefel　　*boots*

3 Kleidung und Mode *Clothes and Fashion*

NOCH MAL!

● *Activity: What are they packing?*

TRENDS, MUSTER UND KLEIDUNG KAUFEN
STYLES, PATTERNS AND BUYING CLOTHES

Wie sieht es aus?	*What does it look like?*

die Fetzen (pl.)	*scruffy togs (coll.)*	leger	*casual*
die Lumpen (pl.)	*tatty rags (coll.)*	modisch	*fashionable*
abgetragen	*shabby*	schick	*smart*
altmodisch	*old-fashioned*	stilvoll	*stylish*
elegant, vornehm		zerknittert	*crumpled*
	elegant	(zu) weit	*(too) baggy*
eng	*tight*		
förmlich	*formal*	nicht harmonieren,	
klassisch	*classical*	nicht zusammen passen	
(zu) lang/kurz	*(too) long / short*		*to clash*

Sie ist leger gekleidet.	*She's dressed casually.*

3 Kleidung und Mode *Clothes and Fashion*

gemustert	*patterned*	absetzen	*to take off (hat,*
bedruckt	*printed*		*glasses)*
einfarbig, uni	*plain*	anprobieren	*to try on*
geblümt	*floral*	anziehen	*to put on*
gestreift	*striped*	aufsetzen	*to put on (hat,*
gesprenkelt	*spotted*		*glasses)*
kariert	*checked, tartan*	binden, schnüren	*to tie*
		sich an/ausziehen	*to get dressed /*

Sich anziehen
Getting dressed

			undressed
		tragen	*to wear*
		umziehen	*to change*
ausziehen, ablegen		von der Stange,	
(form.)	*to take off*	Konfektion	*off-the-peg*

Rolf setzt seinen Hut auf.	*Rolf is putting his hat on.*
Zieh dir deinen Mantel über. Es ist	*You ought to put a coat on.*
kalt draußen.	*It's cold outside.*

Kleidung kaufen *Buying clothes*

Kann ich . . . anprobieren?	*Can I try . . . on?*
Er /Sie /Es ist zu groß/zu klein/	
zu weit/zu eng.	*It's too big / small / wide / narrow.*
Haben Sie eine Nummer	
größer/kleiner?	*Have you got a bigger / smaller size?*
Ich hätte es gern etwas weiter/enger/	*I'd like it wider / narrower*
länger/kürzer.	*longer / shorter.*
Gibt es das auch billiger/in besserer	*Have you got anything*
Qualität?	*cheaper / better?*
Ich mag es/mag es nicht.	*I like it / don't like it.*
Er/Sie/Es paßt/paßt nicht.	*It fits / doesn't fit.*
Ich nehme der/die/das.	*I'll take it.*

3 Kleidung und Mode *Clothes and Fashion*

NOCH MAL!

● *Activity: What's wrong with it?*

KLEIDUNGSTEILE
PARTS OF THE GARMENTS

der Ärmel (-)	sleeve
das Bund (-e)	waist-band
der/das Revers (-)	
	lapel
die Falte (-n)	pleat
das Knopfloch (-er)	
	buttonhole
der Kragen (-)	collar
die Manschette (-n)	
	cuff
die Naht ("e)	seam
der Saum ("e)	hem
die Tasche (-n)	pocket

Stoff, Material *Material*

die Baumwolle	cotton
der Filz (-e)	felt
der Jeansstoff (-e)	
	denim
das Leder (-)	leather
das Leinen (-)	linen

das Nylon	nylon
der Pelz (-e)	fur
das Polyester (-)	polyester
der Samt (-e)	velvet
der Satin (-s)	satin
die Seide (-n)	silk
die Spitze (-n)	lace
der Tweed (-s)	tweed
das Wildleder (-)	suede
die Wolle (-n)	wool

Nähen *Sewing*

> Was du heute kannst besorgen,
> das verschiebe nicht auf morgen.
> *A stitch in time saves nine.*

Schneider (meister)/in	
	(master)tailor / dressmaker
die Häkelnadel (-n)	
	crochet hook
der Knopf ("e)	button
die Nadel (-n)	needle

3 Kleidung und Mode *Clothes and Fashion*

das Nähgarn (-e)	*cotton, thread*
die Nähmaschine (-n)	*sewing machine*
der Reißverschluß (-verschlüsse)	*zip*
die Schere (-n)	*scissors*
die Sicherheitsnadel (-n)	*safety pin*
die Stecknadel (-n)	*pin*
die Stricknadel (-n)	*knitting needle*
der Stich (-e)	*stitch*
das Stoffband ("er)	*ribbon*

abnähen	*to take in*
flicken	*to mend*
häkeln	*to crochet*
kürzen	*to shorten*
nähen	*to sew*
schneidern	*to make clothes*

sticken	*to embroider*
stricken	*to knit*
umändern	*to alter*
zuschneiden	*to cut out*

KLEIDERPFLEGE
CLOTHES CARE

der Aufhänger (-)	*hook (on clothes)*
das Bügeleisen (-)	*iron*
das Dampfbügeleisen (-)	*steam iron*
der Fleck (-en)	*stain*
der Kleiderbügel (-)	*coat hanger*
aufhängen	*to hang up (a suit)*
bügeln	*to iron*
reinigen lassen	*to dry clean*
waschen	*to clean, wash*
zerreißen	*to tear*

Waschen oder reinigen lassen?
Wash or dry clean?

Handwäsche	
Waschgang bei max. 60∞	
Trocknen im Wäschetrockner	
heiß, stark bügeln	
Chemischereinigung	
Nicht bleichen, Chlorbleiche nicht möglich	
Nicht waschen	

3 Kleidung und Mode *Clothes and Fashion*

Buntwäsche	*Coloureds*	Vorwäsche	*Prewash*
Feinwäsche	*Delicates*	Waschpulver	*washing powder*
Kochwäsche	*Whites*	Weichspüler	*softener*
Sparwäsche	*Economy*		

Dunkle Farben separat waschen	*Wash dark colours separately*
Links waschen	*Wash inside out*
Nass in Form ziehen	*Spread flat to dry*
Nicht schleudern	*Do not spin*
Nicht stärken	*Do not use starch*
Spülen	*Rinse*

ZUBEHÖR
ACCESSORIES

die Brieftasche (-n)
    wallet
der Gürtel (-) *belt*
die Handschuhe (-n)
    glove
die Handtasche (-n)
    handbag
das Portemonnaie(s)/der
  Geldbeutel (-) *purse*
der Regenschirm (-e)
    umbrella
der Schal (-e)/(-s) *scarf*
die Schultertasche (-n)
    shoulder bag
das Umhängetuch ("er)
    shawl

Schmuck *Jewellery*

das Armband ("er)
    bracelet
das Kreuz (-e) *cross*
der Manschettenknopf ("e)
    cuff link
der Modeschmuck
    costume jewellery
der Anhänger (-) *pendant*

die Armbanduhr,
    die Uhr (-en) *watch*
die Brosche (-n) *brooch*
die Halskette (-n) *necklace*
die Kette (-n) *chain*
die Perlenkette (-n)
    pearl necklace

der Ring (-e) *ring*
der Nasenring (-e)
    nose ring
der Trauring (-e) *wedding ring*
der Verlobungsring (-e)
    engagement ring

der Ohrring (-e) *earring*
der Clip (-s) *clip-on earring*
der Stecker (-) *pierced earring*

die Tätowierung (-en)
    tattoo

Edelsteine und Halbedelsteine und Edelmetalle
Precious and semi-precious stones and metals

der Amethyst (-en)
    amethyst
die Bronze *bronze*

der Diamant (-en)
diamond
die Emaille — *enamel*
das Gold — *gold*
die Jade — *jade*
die Koralle (-n) — *coral*
das Kristall (-e) — *crystal*
das Kupfer — *copper*
der Opal (-e) — *opal*

die Perle (-n) — *pearl*
das Platin — *platinum*
der Rubin (-e) — *ruby*
der Saphir (-e) — *sapphire*
das Silber — *silver*
der Smaragd (-e) — *emerald*
das Titan — *titanium*
der Topas (-e) — *topaz*

NOCH MAL!

● *Activity: Describe what Sylvia and Jens are wearing, from the pictures below. You can choose the colours!*

4 Essen und Trinken *Food and drink*

NAHRUNGSMITTEL
FOODSTUFFS

das Protein (-e),
  das Eiweiß (-e) *protein*
das Kohlenhydrat (-e)
     carbohydrate
das Vitamin (-e) *vitamin*

das Rezept (-e) *recipe*
die Zutaten *ingredients*

die Hefe *yeast*
das Mehl (-e) *flour*
die Speisestärke *corn flour*

der Zucker ( ) *sugar*
der braune Zucker
     brown sugar
der Puderzucker *icing sugar*
der Süßstoff (-e) *sweetner*

die Margarine *margarine*
das Schmalz *dripping / lard*

das Öl (-e) *oil*
das Olivenöl *olive oil*

die Milchprodukte
Dairy products

die Butter *butter*
der Quark *quark*
die Sahne *cream*
der Yoghurt (-s) *yoghurt*
die Milch *milk*
die Dickmilch *sour milk*
die Fitmilch *low fat / skimmed
     milk*
die H-Milch *long-life milk*

der Käse (-) *cheese*
der Frischkäse *cream cheese*
der Hüttenkäse *cottage cheese*
der Schafskäse *sheep's cheese*

das Ei (-er) *egg*
das Frühstücksei (-er)
     boiled egg
der Pfannkuchen (-)
     pancake
das Omelett (-s) *omelette*
das verlorene Ei (-er)
     poached egg

die getrockneten Früchte
     dried fruit
die Datteln *dates*
die Feigen *figs*
die Rosinen *raisins*
die Sultaninen *sultanas*
die kandierten
  Kirschen *glacé cherries*

die Nüsse *nuts*
die Cashewnüsse *cashew nuts*
die Erdnüsse *peanuts*
die Haselnüsse *hazel nuts*
die Kokosnuß (-nüsse)
     coconut
die Mandeln *almonds*
die Walnüsse *walnuts*

die Teigwaren *pasta*
die Makkaroni *macaroni*
die Nudeln *noodles*
die Spaghetti *spaghetti*

der Reis *rice*
die Haferflocken *porridge oats*
das Müsli (-s) *müsli*
die Corn Flakes *corn flakes*
der Honig *honey*
die Marmelade (-n)
     jam
die Orangenmarmelade (-n)
     marmalade

das Brot (-e) *bread, a loaf*
das Gersterbrot *barley bread*
das Graubrot *rye and wheat bread*

4 Essen und Trinken *Food and drink*

das Nußbrot *walnut bread*
das Pumpernickel *pumpernickel*
das Roggenbrot *rye bread*
das Schwarzbrot *wholemeal rye bread*
das Vollkornbrot *wholemeal bread*
das Weißbrot *white bread*

das Brötchen bread roll
das Baguette (-s) *baguette*
das Butterbrot (-e)
    sandwich
das Knäckebrot *crispbread*
der Toast (-s) *toast*

die Kräuter herbs
das Basilikum *basil*
der Dill *dill*
der Fenchel *fennel*
der Knoblauch *garlic*
das Lorbeerblatt *bay leaf*
der Majoran *marjoram*
die Minze *mint*
das Oregano *oregano*
die Petersilie *parsley*
der Rosmarin *rosemary*
das Salbei *sage*
der Schnittlauch *chives*
der Thymian *thyme*

die Gewürze spices
der Curry *curry*
der Ingwer *ginger*
der Kümmel *cumin*
das Muskat *nutmeg*
die Nelken *cloves*
das Paprika *paprika*
die Vanille *vanilla*
das Zimt *cinnamon*

das Würzen seasoning
die Bratensoße (-n)
    gravy
der Ketchup *tomato sauce*
die Mayonnaise *mayonnaise /*
    salad cream
der Meerrettich *horseradish sauce*
der Pfeffer *pepper*
die Salatsoße (-n)
    salad oil, dressing
das Salz *salt*
die Soße (-n) *sauce*
der Senf *mustard*
die Sojasoße (-n) *soya sauce*
der Weinessig *wine vinegar*

UTENSILIEN UND KÜCHENGERÄTE
UTENSILS AND KITCHEN EQUIPMENT

die Bratpfanne (-n)
    frying pan
das Brett (-er) *board*
der Dosenöffner (-)
    tin-opener
der Flaschenöffner (-)
    bottle opener
der Kochlöffel (-) *wooden spoon*
der Kochtopf (-töpfe)
    pan

der Korkenzieher (-)
    corkscrew
die Küchenwaage (-n)
    kitchen scales
das Küchenmesser (-)
    kitchen knife
das Nudelholz (-hölzer)
    rolling pin
der Quirl (-e) *whisk*
die Schüssel (-n) *bowl*

4 **Essen und Trinken** *Food and drink*

das Sieb (-e) *sieve*
der Stieltopf (-töpfe)
   saucepan
der Topflappen (-)
   oven gloves / cloth

abgießen *to strain*
backen *to bake*
braten *to fry, to roast*
dünsten *to steam*
grillen *to grill*
kochen *to boil, to cook*
köcheln *to simmer*
pellen *to peel* (orange,
   banana)
reiben *to grate*
schälen *to peel* (potatoes,
   onions, apples)
schlagen *to beat*
schmoren *to braise, to stew*
schneiden *to cut*
verrühren,
   unterheben *to mix*

Küchengeräte
Kitchen equipment

der Backofen (¨) *oven*
der Grill (-s) *grill*
der Herd (-e) *cooker*
die Kaffeemaschine (-n)
   coffee percolator
der Kessel (-) *kettle*
das Kochfeld (-er) *hob*
die Küchenmaschine (-n)
   food processor
der Mixer (-) *mixer, blender*

der Schnellkochtopf (-töpfe)
   pressure cooker
der Toaster (-) *toaster*

Mahlzeiten *Meal times*

das Frühstück *breakfast*
das Mittagessen
   lunch
Kaffee und Kuchen
   *coffee and cake
   (afternoon tea)*
das Abendbrot *tea*
das Abendessen *dinner*

**den Tisch
   decken** ***laying the table***
das Besteck (-e) *cutlery*
die Gabel (-n) *fork*
der Löffel (-) *spoon*
das Messer (-) *knife*
der Servierlöffel (-)
   serving spoon
der Teelöffel (-) *teaspoon*

das Geschirr *crockery*
das Frühstücksbrett (-er)
   breakfast board
der Krug (¨e) *jug*
das Milchkännchen (-)
   milk jug
die Schüssel (-n) *dish*
die Tasse (-n) *cup*
die Teekanne (-n) *teapot*
der Teller (-) *plate*
die Untertasse (-n)
   saucer
die Zuckerdose (-n)
   sugar bowl

4 Essen und Trinken *Food and drink*

FLEISCH, OBST UND GEMÜSE
MEAT, FRUIT AND VEGETABLES

der Aufschnitt   *cooked meats*
die Boulette (-n),
  die Frikadelle (-n) *beefburger*
das Hackfleisch, das Gehacktes,
  das Mett   *minced meat*
das Hammelfleisch
           mutton
das Kalbfleisch *veal*
das Kaninchen *rabbit*
das Kasseler (-) *smoked pork chop*
das Kotelett (-s) *chop / cutlet*
das Lammfleisch *lamb*
die Leber   *liver*
das Lendchen (-) *pork / veal fillet steak*
die Nieren   *kidneys*
das Rindfleisch *beef*
der Schinken *ham*
der Schinkenspeck
           bacon
das Schweinfleisch
           pork
die Schweinshaxe (-n), das Eisbein (-e)
           knuckle of pork
das Steak (-s) *steak*
die Sülze   *brawn / jellied pork*

die Wurst (¨e) *sausage*
die Fleischwurst/die Jagdwurst
           cooked pork sausage
die Leberwurst *liver sausage*
die Mettwurst *pork / beef sausage*
die Rotwurst   *black pudding*
die Salami (-s) *salami*
das Wiener, heiße Würstchen
           frankfurter
die Weißwurst *veal sausage*

das Geflügel *poultry*
die Ente (-n)   *duck*
die Gans (¨e)   *goose*
das Hähnchen (-) *chicken*
die Pute (-n)   *turkey*

Wild   *game*
das Reh, der Hirsch
           venison
das Wildschwein *wild boar*

Fisch   *fish*
(for types of fish see *Hobbies*, p. 123)
Räucherfisch smoked fish

Obst *Fruit*

die Ananas (-)   *pineapple*
der Apfel (¨)   *apple*
die Apfelsine (-n) *orange*
die Aprikose (-n) *apricot*
die Banane (-n)   *banana*
die Birne (-n)   *pear*
die Brombeere (-n) *blackberry*
die Erdbeere (-n) *strawberry*
die Himbeere (-n) *raspberry*
die Kirsche (-n)   *cherry*
die Kiwi (-s)   *kiwi*
die Limette (-n)   *lime*
die Mango (-s)   *mango*
die Maracuja (-s) *passion fruit*
die Melone (-n)   *melon*
die Mirabelle (-n) *mirabelle*
           (yellow plum)
die Nektarine (-n) *nectarine*
die Pampelmuse (-n),
  die Grapefruit (-s) *grapefruit*
der Pfirsich (-e) *peach*
die Pflaume (-n) /
  die Zwetschge (-n) *plum*
die Preiselbeere (-n)
           cranberry
die rote Johannisbeere (-n)
           redcurrant

4 Essen und Trinken *Food and drink*

die schwarze Johannisbeere (-n)
    blackcurrant
die Stachelbeere (-n)
    gooseberry
die Süßkirsche (-n)/Sauerkirsche (-n)
    sweet / sour cherry
die Weintraube (-n)
    grape
die Zitrone (-n) *lemon*

Gemüse *Vegetables*

die Kartoffel (-n) *potato*
die Folienkartoffeln
    baked potatoes
die Bratkartoffeln *fried potatoes*
der Kartoffelpuffer (-),
  der Reibekuchen (-)
    potato fritters
das/der Kartoffelpüree/-brei
    creamed, mashed
    potatoes
die Kroketten *croquettes*
die Pellkartoffeln *potatoes boiled (in*
    their skins)
die Pommes (frites)
    chips
die Röstis *potato cakes*
die Salzkartoffeln
    boiled potatoes
die Kartoffelklöße
    potato dumplings
die Kartoffelchips
    crisps

Rohkost *raw vegetables*

die Bohne (-n) *beans*
dicke Bohnen *broad beans*
grüne Bohnen *green beans, French*
    beans
Stangenbohnen *runner beans*
der Brokkoli *broccoli*
die Erbse (-n) *pea*

der Fenchel *fennel*
die Frühlingszwiebeln
    spring onions
die Gurke (-n) *gherkin*
der (Rot) Kohl (-köpfe)
    (red) cabbage
der Kohlrabi (-s) *kohlrabi*
der Kopfsalat *lettuce*
die Kresse *watercress*
der Lauch *leek*
die Linsen *lentils*
der Mais *sweetcorn*
der Maiskolben (-) *corn on the cob*
die Möhre (-n), die Karotte (-n)
    carrot
die Olive (-n) *olive*
die Paprika *pepper*
der Pastinak (-e) *parnip*
das Radieschen (-) *radish*
der Rosenkohl *Brussels sprouts*
die rote Beete *beetroot*
die Salatgurke (-n) *cucumber*
die Schalotte (-n) *shallot*
der Spargel *asparagus*
der Spinat *spinach*
die Steckrübe (-n) *turnip*
die Tomate (-n) *tomato*
die Zucchini (-s) *courgettes*
die Zwiebel (-n) *onion*

der Pilz (-e) **mushroom**
der Champignon (-s)
    button mushroom
die Morchel (-n) *morel*
der Pfifferling (-e) *chanterelle*

der Salat (-e) **salad**
der gemischte Salat (-e)
    mixed salad

die Suppe (-n) **soup**
Erbsensuppe *pea soup*
Fleischbrühe/
  -bouillon *bouillon*

4 Essen und Trinken *Food and drink*

Ich hätte gern...
zwei Stangen Lauch
zwei Kohlköpfe

I'd like...
two leeks
two cabbages

Gulaschsuppe	*goulash soup*	fettig	*fatty*
klare Hühnerbrühe		gut gewürzt	*tasty*
	clear chicken soup	heiß	*hot*
		kalt	*cold*
Ich esse gern...	*I like...*	salzig	*salty*
Ich mag...nicht	*I don't like...*	sauer	*sour*
Ich bin satt.	*I'm full.*	trocken	*stale, dry*
Es schmeckt gut.	*It tastes good.*	süß	*sweet*
Es ist zu...	*It's too...*	viel	*much*
scharf	*hot and spicy*	zäh	*tough*
bitter	*bitter*	zart	*tender*

NOCH MAL!

● *Activity: Follow the clues and find the missing vegetable.*

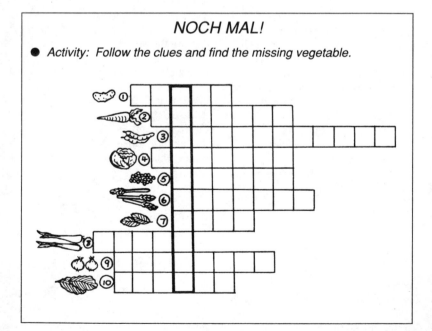

76

4 Essen und Trinken *Food and drink*

ESSEN GEHEN UND SPEZIALITÄTEN
EATING OUT AND SPECIALITIES

Guten Appetit! *Enjoy your meal!*
Danke gleichfalls. *And you, too.*

die Bar (-s)	*bar*
das Café (-s)	*café*
die Cafeteria	*cafeteria*

die Gaststätte (-n);
    das Lokal (-e) *pub serving food*
die Kantine (-n) *canteen*
die Kneipe (-n) *pub*
das Restaurant (-s)
           restaurant
der Schnellimbiß (-bisse)
           snack bar
das Stehcafé (-s) *self-service cafe*
           (standing only)

Im Restaurant
In the restaurant

der Koch (Köche) *chef*
die Küchenhilfe (-n)
           cook
der Tellerwäscher (-)
           washer-upper
der Kellner (-)/der Ober (-)
           waiter
die Kellnerin (-nen)
           waitress

der Tisch (-e)	*table*
das Gedeck (-e)	*place setting*
die Kerze (-n)	*candle*
die Serviette (-n)	*serviette*
der Stuhl (Stühle)	*chair*

die Speisekarte (-n) **menu**
das Tagesmenü (-s)
           set meal of the day

das Tagesgericht (-e)
           dish of the day
die Vorspeise (-n) *hors d'oeuvre*
das Fischgericht (-e)
           fish course
der erste Gang ("e)*first course*
der Hauptgang ("e)
           main course
die Nachspeise (-n),
  der Nachtisch (-e)
           dessert
die Bedienung *service charge*
das Kleingeld,
  das Wechselgeld *change*
die Mehrwertsteuer
           VAT
die Rechnung (-en)
           bill
das Trinkgeld (-er) *tip*

Typische Gerichte und Spezialitäten
Typical Dishes and Specialities

Auflauf, Gratin *savoury dish baked*
           in the oven
Eintopf *stew*
Grünkohl mit *kale and spicy*
  Pinkel *pork sausages*
Hühnerfrikassee *chicken fricassee*
Königsberger
  Klopse *meatball dish*
Rinderroulade *rolled beef with*
           mince stuffing
Sauerkraut *sauerkraut*
Schwarzwälder *smoked bacon*
  Schinken *speciality*
Wiener Schnitzel *pork steak in*
           breadcrumbs
Wurst mit *sausage with*
  Kartoffelsalat *potato salad*

4 **Essen und Trinken** *Food and drink*

NOCH MAL!

● *Activity: Complete the menu with your own choice of dishes:*

Vorspeisen

Fisch

Hauptgerichte

Desserts

KUCHEN UND GETRÄNKE
CAKES AND DRINKS

die Torten *gateaux*
die Quarktorte (-n)
    quark gateau
die Sachertorte (-n)
    Viennese chocolate
    gateau
die Sahnetorte (-n)
    cream gateau
die Schwarzwälderkirschtorte (-n)
    black forest gateau

der Kuchen (-) *cake*
der Amerikaner (-) *small, flat iced cake*
der Apfelkuchen (-)
    apple cake

der Berliner (-),
    der Krapfen (-) *doughnut*
die Biskuitrolle (-n)
    Swiss roll
der Käsekuchen (-)
    cheesecake
die Nußecke (-n) *nut slice*
das Plätzchen (-) *biscuits*

Teig *pastry*
der Apfelstrudel (-)
    apple strudel
die Apfeltasche (-n)
    apple turnover
der Bienenstich (-e)
    honey and almond
    slice

4 Essen und Trinken *Food and drink*

das Eis (-)   *ice cream*
der Eisbecher (-) *sundae*
der Eiskaffee   *iced coffee*
die Eisschokolade *iced chocolate*

Getränke *Drinks*

ein Becher   *a mug of . . .*
ein Kännchen   *a pot of . . .*
eine Tasse   *a cup of . . .*
mit Kaffeesahne *with evaporated milk*
mit Milch   *with milk*
mit Sahne   *with cream*
mit Zitrone   *with lemon*

Heiße Getränke *Hot drinks*

der Tee   *tea*
der Früchtetee *fruit tea / tisane*
der Kräutertee   *herbal tea*
der Teebeutel (-) *tea-bag*

der Kaffee   *coffee*
der Cappuccino *cappuccino*
der Espresso   *espresso*
der Filterkaffee *filter coffee*
der koffeinfreie Kaffee
      decaffeinated coffee
der Pulverkaffee *instant coffee*
die heiße Schokolade
      hot chocolate

Kalte Getränke *Cold drinks*

die Dose (-n)   *a can*
die Flasche (-n)/
   halbe Flasche *a bottle / half bottle*
das Glas ("er)   *a glass*
das Maß (-e)   *1-litre beer glass*

alkoholfreie Getränke
      soft drinks, minerals
der Apfelsaft   *apple juice*
die Cola   *coca cola*

der Fruchtsaft ("e) *fruit juice*
das Mineralwasser,
   der Sprudel   *mineral water*
der Orangensaft *orange juice*
der Spezi   *coke and orange*
      fanta
die Sprite   *lemonade*
ein stilles Wasser *still water*

Alkoholische Getränke
Alcoholic drinks

das Bier   **beer**
das Alster, das Radler
      shandy
das Alt   *type of bitter*
das Bier vom Faß,
   das Faßbier   *draught beer*
das Bockbier   *stout*
der Maibock   *strong dark beer*
das Pils   *lager (light)*
das Weizenbier *wheat beer*

der Wein (-e)   **wine**
der Champagner (-s)
      champagne
der Hauswein (-e) *house wine (table*
      wine)
der Rosé (-s)   *rosé*
der Rotwein (-e) *red wine*
der Sekt (-e)   *sparkling wine*
      (German
      champagne)
der Schoppen (-) *quarter litre of wine*
der Weißwein (-e) *white wine*

Spirituosen   **spirits**
der Brandy (-s) *brandy*
der Gin (-s)   *gin*
der Grog (-s)   *hot rum toddy*
der Kümmerling (-e)
      herbal digestive

der Rum (-s)   *rum*
der Schnaps (¨e)   *schnapps*
der Wodka (-s)   *vodka*
der Whisky (-s)   *whisky*

trinken   *to drink*
in kleinen Schlucken trinken
     to sip

NOCH MAL!

● *Activity: What would you say to order these teas?*

Ich möchte ... ./einen/eine/ein...   I would like a.../some... .

5 Das Zuhause *At home*

WOHNEN UND UNTERKUNFT
HOUSING AND ACCOMMODATION

das Haus   *the house*
der Bungalow (-s) *bungalow*
das Doppelhaus (¨er)
    semi-detached house
das Einfamilienhaus (¨er)
    detached house
das Reihenhaus (¨er)
    terraced house house

der Bauernhof (¨e) *farm*
das Ferienhaus (¨er)
    holiday cottage
das Gebäude (-) *building*
das gemietete Haus (¨er)
    rented house
das schweizerische Landhaus (¨er)
    chalet
die Villa (-en)   *villa*
das Hochhaus (¨er)
    multi-storey building

das Wohnsilo (-s) *concrete block of houses*
der Wolkenkratzer (-)   *skyscraper*
die Wohnung (-en) *flat*
die (Ein) zimmerwohnung (-en)
    (one-room) flat
die Etage (-n), das Stockwerk (-e)
    floor
die Mietwohnung (-en)
    rented flat
die Sozialwohnung (en)
    council flat
der Wohnblock (¨e) *block of flats*

ein Haus mit . . . *a house with a/an . . .*
einem Garten   *garden*
einer Garage (-n)   *garage*
einer Doppelgarage (-n)
    double garage
einer Einliegerwohnung (-n)
    adjoining flat

Ich /Wir besitzen unser eigenes Haus. *I / we own our own house.*

---

der Hauskauf
Buying a house

Käufer/in (Immobilien)
    buyer
Makler/in   *(estate) agent*
Verkäufer/in   *seller*

3-Zi.-Whg. in Breisach
ab sofort zu vermieten, Küche, Bad, sep. WC, Balkon, Keller, Kfz-Stellpl., 87 m², KM 1.450,-- DM + NK + Kaution, Anfragen unter Tel. 07631/798500

1-Fam.-Hs. Kirchzarten
DHH, Ortsteil Burg-Höfen, in herrlicher, ruh., naturverbundener Wohnlage, 6½ Zi. + ELW, insges. ca. 205 m² Wfl., 3 Bäder, Kachelofen, Garage, alles in absolutem Neuzustand. Freistellung kann binnen 3 Monaten erfolgen. Erleben Sie das herrliche Klima im Dreisamtal! Kaufpreis DM 895.000,-.

die Anzeige (-n) *advertisement*
das Gründstuck (¨e)
    plot of land
die Hypothek (-en) *mortgage*

die Miete (-n)   *rent*
die Kaltmiete (-n) *rent (excl.rates and heating)*

5 Das Zuhause *At home*

die Mietsicherheit (-en)/Kaution (-en)	*deposit*
die Nebenkosten (-)	*rates*
bezahlen	*to pay*
borgen	*to borrow*
kaufen	*to buy*
mieten	*to rent*
vermieten	*to let*
ruhig/zentrale Lage	*quiet / central location*
günstig für ...	*convenient for ...*
ländlich/auf dem Land	*rural situation*
Nähe ...	*near to ...*
die Heizung (-en)	*heating*

die Elektrik	*electicity*
das Erdgas	*gas*
das Holz	*wood*
der Kamin (-e)	*fireplace*
die Kohle	*coal*
der Ofen (¨)	*stove*
das Öl	*oil*
die Zentralheizung (-en)	*central heating*
die Isolierung	*insulation*
die Doppelverglasung	*double glazing*
die Fußbodenheizung (-en)	*underfloor heating*
die Klimaanlage (-en)	*air conditioning*
schallgedämmt	*soundproofed*

BESTANDTEILE EINES HAUSES
PARTS OF THE HOUSE

der Balkon (-e)	*balcony*
das Dach (¨er)	*roof*
die Einfahrt (-en)	*drive*
das Fenster (-)	*window*
die Haustür (-en)	*front door*
die Mauer (-n)	*(garden) wall*
der Schornstein (-e)	*chimney*
die Terrasse (-n)	*terrace*
das Tor (-e)	*gate*
die Tür (-en)	*door*
der Vorgarten (¨)	*front garden*
die Wand (¨e)	*wall (house)*
der Windfang (¨e)	*porch*
der Wintergarten (¨)	*conservatory*

der Briefkasten (¨)	*letter box*
die Klingel (-n)	*bell*
der Schlüssel (-)	*key*
die Treppe (-n)	*stairs*
das Erdgeschoß	*ground floor*
oben/unten	*upstairs / downstairs*
das Obergeschoß/1. Etage/ erster Stock	*first floor*
das Unter-/Kellergeschoß, das Souterrain	*basement*

die Zimmer (-) *Rooms*

das Arbeitszimmer (-)	*study*
das Badezimmer (-)	*bathroom*
der Dachboden (¨)/Speicher (-)	*attic*

5 Das Zuhause *At home*

die Dusche (-n) *shower*
die Eingangshalle (-n)
    entrance hall
das Eßzimmer (-) *dining room*
der Flur (-e)   *hall*
das Gästezimmer (-)
    guest room / spare
    room
der Hauswirtschaftsraum ("e)
    utility room
der Keller (-)   *cellar*
die Küche (-n) *kitchen*

das Schlafzimmer (-)
    bedroom
das Spielzimmer (-)
    playroom, nursery
die Toilette (-n), das Klo (-s)
    toilet, loo
der Treppenabsatz ("e)
    landing
das Wohnzimmer (-)
    living room, lounge,
    sitting room

NOCH MAL!

● *Activity 1: Label each room.*

● *Activity 2: Describe the flat and the house in these adverts.*

a) 3-Zi-Whg, 93m²
Kü, Bad, ZH, BK,
KM DM 1050,. +NK 150,- +KT
Tel 0761 44682

b) 1-Fam-.Haus
ca. 210m² Bj.'93
zentrumnah. Einbaukü, 2Bäder,
Ölzentralhzg,Wi.-Garten,
Sauna,Garten
VHB 800.000,-DM Tel 0762 74134

5 Das Zuhause *At home*

MÖBEL UND EINRICHTUNGEN
FURNITURE, FURNISHINGS AND FITTINGS

Im Wohnzimmer
In the living room

das Bild (-er)   *picture*
das Bücherregal (-e)
  bookcase
der Fernseher (-) *television*
die Gardine (-n),
  der Vorhang ("en)
    curtain
der Heizkörper (-) *radiator*
die Hi-Fi-Anlage (-n)
    hi-fi system
der Kaffeetisch (-e)
    coffee table
das Kissen (-)   *cushion*
die Lampe (-n)   *lamp*
das Parkett (-s) *parquet*
das Regal (-e)   *shelf*
der Schalter (-) *switch*
der Schaukelstuhl ("e)
    rocking chair
der Sessel (-)   *armchair*
das Sofa (-s)   *sofa, settee*
die Tapete (-n) *wallpaper*
der Teppich (-e)/ der Läufer (-)/
  die Brücke (-n)   *rug*
der Teppichboden (")
    fitted carpet
der Übertopf ("e)*plant pot*
die Vase (-n)   *vase*
das Video (-s)   *video*

Im Eßzimmer
In the dining room

der Stuhl ("e)   *chair*
der Eßtisch (-e) *dining table*
das Sideboard (-s) *sideboard*

In der Küche *In the kitchen*

die Abzugshaube (-n)
    extractor
der Backofen (") *oven*
der Geschirrtuch ("er)
    teatowel
der Hängeschrank ("e)
    wallcupboard
der Herd (-e)   *cooker*
der Hocker (-)   *stool*
der Kühlschrank ("e)
    fridge
die Spüle (-n)   *sink*
die Spülmaschine (-n)
    dishwasher
die Waschmaschine (-n)
    washing machine

Im Badezimmer
In the bathroom

das Bad ("er)   *bath*
die Dusche (-n) *shower*
das Handtuch ("er)/
  das Badetuch ("er)
    hand / bath towel
der Spiegel (-) *mirror*
die Toilette (-n) *toilet*
das Toilettenpapier
    toilet paper
das Waschbecken (-)
    washbasin

Im Schlafzimmer
In the bedroom

das Bett (-en)   *bed*
das Doppelbett   *double bed*
das Wasserbett   *water bed*
die Bettdecke (-n) *duvet, quilt*
der Bettbezug ("e) *quilt cover*
das Bettlaken (-) *sheet*
der Kleiderschrank ("e)
    wardrobe

5 Das Zuhause *At home*

NOCH MAL!

● *Activity: How would you furnish each room?*

Ich möchte einen neuen/eine neue/ein neues . . . für . . .

**das Schlafzimmer die Küche das Badezimmer
das Wohnzimmer das Eßzimmer**

die Kommode (-n) *chest of drawers*
das Kopfkissen (-) *pillow*
der Nachttisch (-e) *bedside table*

HAUSARBEIT
HOUSEWORK

der Besen (-) *broom*
die Bürste (-n) *brush*
der Eimer (-) *bucket*
der Mop (-s) *mop*
die Politur (-en) *polish*
das Putztuch (¨er)
    cleaning cloth
das Spülmittel (-) *washing-up liquid*
der Staubsauger (-)
    vacuum cleaner

das Staubtuch (¨er)
    duster
die Putzfrau (-en) *cleaning lady*

(ab)wischen *to wipe*
abwaschen *to wash up*
aufräumen *to tidy up*
das Bett machen *to make the bed*
fegen *to sweep*
die Fenster putzen
    to clean the windows
polieren *to polish*
putzen *to clean*
Staub wischen *to dust*
staubsaugen *to vacuum*
Wäsche waschen *to do the washing /
    laundry*

5 Das Zuhause *At home*

BAUEN UND RENOVIEREN
BUILDING AND RENOVATING

Berufe *Jobs*

Arbeiter/in	*labourer*
Bauunternehmer/in	*builder*
Dachdecker/in	*roofer / slater*
Elektriker/in	*electrician*
Glaser/in	*glazier*
Installateur/in, Klempner/in	*plumber*
Maler/in	*painter and decorator*
Tischler/in, Schreiner/in	*carpenter*

Baumaterialien und Werkszeuge
Building materials and tools

der Gips (-e)	*plaster*
das Holz ("er)	*wood*
der Kies (-e)	*gravel*
der Mörtel (-)	*mortar*
der Sand (-e)	*sand*
der Stein (-e)	*stone*

der Zement (-e) *cement*
der Ziegelstein,
der Backstein (-e) *brick*

der Rohbau (-e) *Shell*

die Gründung (-en), das Fundament (-e)	*foundations*
die Isolierung (-en), die Dämmung (-en)	*insulation*

das Dach ("er) *roof*
das Dachflächenfenster (-) *skylight*

das Glas *glass*
die Doppelverglasung *double glazing*
die Wärmeschutzverglasung *triple glazing*

Fußböden und Wände *floors and walls*

die Fliese (-n)	*tile*
die Kachel (-n)	*glazed tile*
der Fußbodenbelag ("e)	*floor covering*
das Parkett (-e)	*parquet*

Außen-/Innenwände	*outside / inside walls*
die Mauer (-n)	*wall*
Die Innenwand muß noch verputzt werden.	*The inside wall needs plastering.*
Das Haus befindet sich im Bau.	*The house is under construction.*
Der Kölner Dom besitzt eine kühne Konstruktion.	*Cologne cathedral is a daring construction.*

Werkzeuge und Ausrüstung
Tools and equipment

das (die) Werkzeug *tool kit*

die (Schrauben) mutter (-n) *nut*
die Axt("e) *axe*
die Bohrmaschine (-n) *drill*

5 Das Zuhause *At home*

der Bolzen (-) *bolt*
der Hammer (-) *hammer*
der Meißel (-) *chisel*
der Nagel (¨) *nail*
die Säge (-n) *saw*
die Schleifmaschine (-n)
   sander
die Schraube (-n) *screw*
der Schraubenschlüssel (-)
   spanner
der Schraubenzieher (-)
   screwdriver
die Spitzhacke (-n)
   pick
das Kabel (-) *cable*
die Werkbank (¨e) *workbench*
die Zange (-n) *pliers*

die Kelle (-n) *trowel*
der Kran (¨e) *crane*
die Leiter (-n) *ladder*
die Schaufel (-n) *shovel*
die Schubkarre (-n)
   wheelbarrow
das Seil (-e) *rope*
die Wasserwaage (-n)
   spirit level

bohren   *to drill*
festdrehen, anziehen
   to tighten
hämmern *to hammer*
los-, abschrauben, lösen
   to undo, loosen, unscrew
sägen   *to saw*

die Installation *Plumbing*

der Hahn (¨e) *tap*
der Heizkörper (-) *radiator*
die Heizung (-en) *heating*
der Kessel (-) *boiler*
das Rohr (-e) *pipe*

installieren *to install*

die Elektrik *Electrics*

die Birne (-n) *light bulb*
die Leitung (-en) *wire*
der Schalter (-) *switch*
die Sicherung (-en)
   fuse
die Steckdose (-n) *socket*
der Stecker (-) *plug*

Die Sicherung ist durchgebrannt. *A fuse has blown.*

Malen und Tapezieren
Painting and decorating

die Farbe (-n) *paint*
die Farbrolle (-n) *paint roller*
der Lack (-e), die Firnis (-se)
   varnish
die Leiter (-n) *ladder*
die Tapete (-n) *wallpaper*

bauen   *to build*
reparieren *to mend, repair*
nageln   *to nail*
streichen, anstreichen
   to paint
schleifen *to sand*
abziehen, abkratzen
   to strip (wallpaper /
   paint)

5 Das Zuhause *At home*

DER GARTEN *THE GARDEN*

(For trees, see 14 *The Natural World*, page 193. For fruit and vegetables and herbs, see 4 *Food and Drink*, page 74.)

die Gartenarbeit *horticulture / gardening*
das Blumenbeet (-e)
    flower bed
der Blumenkasten (¨)
    window box
die Zwiebel (-n) *bulb*

der Gartenstrauch (¨er) *bush/shrub*

die Azalee (-n) *azalea*
die Forsythie (-n) *forsythia*
die Heide *heather*
die Magnolie (-n) *magnolia*
der Rhododendron
  (Rhododendren) *rhododendron*

die Blume (-n) *flower*

die Chrysantheme (-n)
    chrysanthemum
das Edelweiß (-e) *edelweiss*
der Fingerhut (¨e) *foxglove*
das Gänseblümchen (-),
  das Tausendschön (-s)
    daisy
der Lavendel (-) *lavender*
die Lilie (-n) *lily*
die Nelke (-n) *carnation*
die Osterglocke (-n)
    daffodil
die Rose (-n) *rose*
die Sonnenblume (-n)
    sunflower
das Vergißmeinnicht (-)
    forget-me-not

die Zimmerpflanze (-n) *house plant*

das Alpenveilchen (-)
    cyclamen
die Geranie (-) *geranium*
die Hyazinthe (n) *hyacinth*
der Weihnachtsstern (-e)
    poinsettia

der Efeu (-s) *ivy*
der Farn (-e) *fern*
der Gummibaum (¨e)
    rubber plant
der Kaktus (Kakteen)
    cactus
die Palme (-n) *palm*
die Yukkapalme (-n)
    yucca

das Unkraut (¨er) *weed*

die Brennessel (-n)
    stinging nettle

der Baum (¨e) *tree*
der Blumentopf (¨e)
    plant pot
der Gemüsegarten (¨)
    vegetable garden
das Gewächshaus (¨er)
    greenhouse
das Gras (¨er) *grass*
der Obstbaum (¨e) *fruit tree*
der Rasen *lawn*
die Vogeltränke (-n)
    bird bath
der Weg (-e) *path*

der Samen (-) *seed*

der Geräteschuppen (-) *garden shed*

das Gartengerät (-e)
    gardening tool

die Heckenschere (-n)
shears
die Gartenschere (-n)
secateurs
die Gießkanne (-n) *watering can*
der Rasenmäher (-)
lawn mower
die Harke (-n)   *rake*
der Schlauch (¨e) *hose-pipe*
die Schubkarre (-n)
wheelbarrow
der Spaten (-)   *spade*

die Gartenmöbel *garden furniture*

der Grill (-s)   *barbecue*
das Planschbecken (-)
paddling pool
der Sonnenschirm (-e)
sunshade

umgraben   *to dig*
den Rasen mähen *to cut the grass*
pflanzen   *to plant*
beschneiden   *to prune*
gießen   *to water*
Unkraut jäten   *to weed*
düngen   *to fertilise*
wachsen   *to grow*

Im Herbst müssen die Rosen beschnitten werden.	*The roses must be pruned in autumn.*

6 Berufe und Arbeit *Jobs and work*

BERUFE *JOBS*

(See also 7 *The company*, page 97.)

Ich bin ...	*I am a/an ...*
Er/Sie ist ...	*He/She is a/an ...*
Ich bin Arzt/Ärztin.	*I am a doctor.*

Architekt/in	*architect*
Arzt/Ärztin	*doctor*
Bäcker/in	*baker*
Bankangestellte/r	*bank employee*
Bankier	*banker*
Beamter/Beamtin	*civil servant*
Bergmann	*miner*
Bibliothekar/in	*librarian*
Briefträger/in	*postman*
Buchhalter/in	*accountant*
Busfahrer/in	*bus driver*
Chirurg/in	*surgeon*
Direktor/in,	
Firmenchef/in	*company director*
Dozent/in	*lecturer*
Drogist/in,	
Apotheker/in	*pharmacist*
Drucker/in	*printer*
EDV Fachmann/-frau	
	computer operator
Fahrer/in	*driver*
Fensterputzer/in	*window cleaner*
Feuerwehrmann/-frau	
	fireman
Florist/in	*florist*
Förster/in	*forester*
Fotograf/in	*photographer*
Friseur/Friseurin	*hairdresser*
Gärtner/in	*gardener*
Gemüsehändler/in	
	greengrocer
Geschäftsmann/-frau	
	businessman/woman

Grafiker/in, Graphik Designer	
	graphic designer
Hausfrau/	
Hausmann	*housewife/houseman*
Industrie Designer/in	
	industrial designer
Informatiker/in	*computer scientist*
Innenarchitekt/in	*interior designer*
Kaufmann/-frau	*shop keeper*
Kellner/in	*waiter/waitress*
Koch/Köchin	*cook*
Krankengymnast/in	
	physiotherapist
Krankenschwester	*nurse*
Künstler/in	*artist*
Landarbeiter/in	*agricultural worker*
Landwirt/in, Bauer/Bäuerin	
	farmer
Lastwagenfahrer/in	
	lorry driver
Lebensmittelhändler/in	
	grocer
Lehrer/in	*teacher*
Lieferant/in	*delivery man/woman*
Lok(omotiv)führer//in	
	engine driver
Matrose	*sailor*
Mechaniker/in	*mechanic*
Metzger/in, Fleischer/in	
	butcher
Milchmann	*milkman*
Modezeichner/in	*fashion designer*
Müllwerker/in	*dustman*

6 Berufe und Arbeit *Jobs and work*

Optiker/in	*optician*	Schuhmacher/in,	
Polizist/in	*policeman*	Schuster/in	*shoemaker, cobbler*
Portier	*doorman, porter*	Soldat/in	*soldier*
Programmierer/in		Sprechstundenhilfe	*dental / doctor's*
	computer programmer		*receptionist*
Psychologe		Steuerberater/in	*tax consultant*
/Psychologin	*psychologist*	Steward/eß	*cabin attendant,*
Putzfrau	*cleaning lady*		*stewardess*
Rechtsanwalt		Taxifahrer/in	*taxi driver*
/-anwältin	*solicitor, lawyer*	Techniker/in,	
Reiseleiter/in,		Ingenieur/in	*engineer*
Kurier	*courier*	Textil Designer/in	
Reporter/in	*reporter*		*textile designer*
Sänger/in	*singer*	Verkäufer/in	*salesman / woman*
Schaufensterdekorateur/in		(Laden) verkäufer/in	
	window dresser		*shop assistant*
Schauspieler/in	*actor / actress*	Volkswirt/in	*economist*
Schlosser/in	*fitter, metalworker*	Wirt/in	*landlord / landlady*
Schneider/in	*tailor, dressmaker*	Zahnarzt	
		/Zahnärztin	*dentist*

Most job titles have both a masculine and feminine form in German. In most cases you add **-in** to the noun for the feminine form. For example: der Pilot/die Pilot**in** – *the pilot.*

A few nouns have only one form: **der/die** Angestellte – *the clerk.* But after **ein** (masculine) you must add an **r** to the noun: **ein** Angestellte**r** – *a clerk.*

Bewerbungen *Applications*

Beruflicher Werdegang	Lebenslauf *curriculum vitae*
experience	Schulausbildung *education*
besondere Kenntnisse	das Zeugnis (-se) *certificate, reference*
special skills	

Lebenslauf

Persönliche Daten

Name: Gerhardy
Vorname: Simone
Wohnort: 30459 Hannover
Talstraße 8
Tel.: 0511 76142
Geburtsdatum: 17.05.1975
Geburtsort: Hannover
Familienstand: ledig
Staatsangehörigkeit: deutsch

Schulbildung

1981 - 1985   St. Elisabeth Grundschule, Hannover
1985 - 1990   Käthe-Kollwitz Gymnasium, Hannover
Juni 1990   Allgemeine Hochschulreife

Beruflicher Werdegang

Nov 1990 - Mai 1992   kaufmännische Lehre
                       Schulze GmbH, Hannover

Juni 1992 - Sept 1994 Sekretärin des Verkaufsleiters
                       Pfeiffer AG, Peine

Okt 1994 -   Direktions-Sekretärin
                       Habermann AG, Hannover

Besondere Kenntnisse:
Englisch in Wort und Schrift
EDV-Kenntnisse

Hannover, den 01.02.96

6 Berufe und Arbeit *Jobs and work*

NOCH MAL!

● *Activity: Write your own c.v. in German.*

DER ARBEITSPLATZ
THE WORKPLACE

Ich arbeite . . .
I work in/on . . .

am Band	*assembly line*
in einer Bank	*bank*
in einem Büro	*in an office*
in einer Fabrik	*factory*
in einem Hotel	*hotel*
in einer Praxis	*surgery*
an einer Schule	*school*

in einer Werkstatt	*workshop*
zu Hause	*at home*
arbeiten	*to work*
Feierabend machen, Schicht machen	*to finish work*
pendeln	*to commute*
Schichtarbeit machen	*to work shifts*
stechen, stempeln	*to clock in and out*
Überstunden machen	*to do overtime*
verdienen	*to earn*

Ich arbeite Teilzeit.	*I work part-time.*
Ich bin freiberuflich tätig.	*I'm freelance.*
Ich bin selbstandig.	*I am self-employed.*
Ich mache um 17 Uhr Feierabend.	*I finish work at 5 o'clock.*

SICHERHEIT AM ARBEITSPLATZ
SAFETY AT WORK

Achtung, Lebensgefahr!	*Danger!*
Eintritt verboten!	*No entry!*
Rauchen verboten	*Smoking forbidden*
Vorsicht!	*Caution!*

6 Berufe und Arbeit *Jobs and work*

Alarm	*Alarm*
Ausfahrt	*Exit for vehicles*
Ausgang	*Exit*
Feuerlöscher	*Fire extinguisher*
Notausgang	*Emergency exit, Fire exit*
Sammelplatz	*Assembly point*

Tragen Sie . . . *Wear . . .*
Handschuhe   *gloves*
Schutzkleidung *protective clothing*
eine Maske   *a mask*
eine Schutzbrille *goggles*

der Arbeitsunfall (¨e)
         industrial accident

(For hospital and first aid vocabulary see also 10 *Health and sickness*, page 140.)

der Brand (¨e)   *fire*

die Erste Hilfe   *first aid*
der Feuerlöscher (-)
         fire extinguisher
die Feuerwehr (-en)
         fire brigade
der Krankenwagen (-)
         ambulance
der Notarzt (¨e) *emergency doctor*
der Notdienst (-e) *emergency services*
der Notfall (¨e)   *emergency*
der Schlag (¨e)   *electric shock*
der Sturz (¨e)   *fall*

einen Unfall haben
         to have an accident
sich schneiden   *to cut oneself*
einen Schlag bekommen,
   einen gewischt kriegen (umg.)
         to suffer an electric shock
stürzen   *to fall*

Ich habe mich verletzt.   *I'm injured.*
Er/Sie steht unter Schock.   *He/She is suffering from shock.*

Arbeitslosigkeit unemployment
das Arbeitsamt (¨er)
         employment office
das Arbeitslosengeld (-er)
         earnings-related benefit
das Stempelgeld (-er)
         dole money

die Umschulung (-en)
     re-training

Ich bin arbeitslos *I am unemployed*
stempeln gehen *to be on the dole*

NOCH MAL!

● *Activity 2: Write a list of ten jobs and say where each person works, for example:*

Ein **Mechaniker** arbeitet in einer **Werkstatt**.

6 Berufe und Arbeit *Jobs and work*

Die Gewerkschaften   unions

Delegierte(r)   *delegate*
Dienst nach
    Vorschrift   *work to rule*
die Gewerkschaft (-en)
                trade union
der Gewerkschaftler (-)
                trades union member
der Streik (-s)   *strike*
der Streikposten (-)
                pickets
der Vertrauensmann (-"er)
                shop steward

in den Streik treten
                to go on strike
streiken   *to be on strike*

PRODUKTION UND DIENSTLEISTUNGSGEWERBE
MANUFACTURING AND SERVICE INDUSTRIES

Ich arbeite   *I work in (the) ...*
Ich bin
Auszubildende /r ...
                I am a trainee in (the) ...

in der Atomindustrie
                nuclear power industry
in der Autoindustrie
                the motor industry
im Bankwesen   *banking*
in der Bauindustrie
                construction industry

Besoldung *Pay*

das Einkommen (-),
    der Verdienst *earnings*
das Gehalt ("er) *salary*
der Lohn ("e)   *wage*
netto   *net*
brutto   *gross*

die Abzüge   *deductions*
direkt einbehaltene
    Lohnsteuer *equivalent of P.A.Y. E.
                (in UK)*
die Einkommensteuer *income tax*

der Ruhestand retirement

die Rente (-n)   *pension*
Rentner/in   *pensioner*
im Ruhestand sein
                to be retired
in den Ruhestand gehen
                to retire
Vorruhestand   *early retirement*

in der Landwirtschaft
                agriculture
in der Elektroindustrie
                the electronics industry
im Gartenbau   *horticulture*
im Hoch-/Tiefbau *civil engineering*
im Hotel- und
    Gaststättengewerbe
                catering
in der Kohleindustrie
                the coal industry
in der Lebensmittelbranche
                food industry
in der Ölindustrie *oil industry*
in der Pharmaindustrie
                pharmaceutical industry
in der Stahlindustrie
                the steel industry

6 Berufe und Arbeit *Jobs and work*

im Verlagswesen *publishing*

Ich bin . . . tätig. *I work in (the) . . .*
im Design   *design*
in der Elektrotechnik
                electrical engineering
in der Nachrichten
                communications
    technik   *technology*
in der Stromversorgung
            the electricity industry

in der Telekommunikation
                telecommunications

entwerfen	*to design*
entwickeln	*to develop*
vorführen	*to demonstrate*
koordinieren	*to co-ordinate*
herstellen	*to manufacture*
verkaufen	*to sell*

Ich mache Buchführung	*I do the accounting*
Ich entwerfe Autos	*I design cars*
Ich führe . . . vor	*I demonstrate . . .*

7 Die Firma *The Company*

DIE FIRMA
THE COMPANY

der Betrieb (-e) ⎱
das Geschäft (-e) ⎰ *firm, company*

die Gesellschaft (-en) ⎱
das Unternehmen (-) ⎰ *firm, company*

die AG (-s)
  (Aktiengesellschaft (-en))
    *Public Limited
    Company*
die Agentur (-en) *agency*
die Fabrik (-en) *factory*
die GmbH (-s) (Gesellschaft mit
  beschränkter Haftung)
    Limited company
die Hauptgeschaftsstelle (-n),
  der Hauptsitz (-e)
    head office
das Privatunternehmen (-)
    private business
die Tochtergesellschaft (-en)
    subsidiary
die Zweigstelle (-n) *branch*

der Dienstwagen (-)
    company car

die Firmenpolitik
    company policy
der Geschäftsbericht (-e)
    company report
die Sitzung (-en) *meeting*
das Geschäft (-e) *deal*
der Gewinn (-e)/Verlust (-e)
    profit / loss
der Vermögenswert (-e)
    assets

die Anmeldung (-en)
    reception
das Betriebsgelände (-),
  der Geschäftsraume (¨e)
    premises
das Büro (-s)   *office*
das Lager (-)   *store*
das Lagerhaus (¨er)
    warehouse
die Produktionsstätte (-n)
    shop floor
der Sitzungssaal (-säle)
    *boardroom, meeting
    room*
die Werkstatt (¨en) *workshop*

DIE BELEGSCHAFT (-EN)
THE WORKFORCE

**die Geschäftsleitung (-en)
  management**
Direktor/in, das Vorstandsmitglied
    company director
Finanzdirektor/in, der Leiter des
  Finanzwesens *financial director*
Geschäftsführer/in, Manager/in,
  Präsident/in *managing director*
Prokurist/in   *company secretary*

der Aufsichtsrat (¨e),
  Betriebsrat (¨e) *works council*
Pressesprecher/in *press officer*
Vorsitzende/r   *Chairwoman,
    Chairman*
der Vorstand (¨e),
  Verwaltungsrat (¨e)
    Board of directors
Vorstandsvorsitzende/r
    Chairman of the Board

Abteilungsleiter/in *head of department*
Assistent/in   *assistant*
Berater/in   *consultant, adviser*

7 Die Firma *The Company*

Büroleiter/in   *office supervisor,*
manager
Direktionsassistent/in
personal assistant
Gruppenleiter/in, Bereichsleiter/in
group leader
das mittlere Managment
middle management

das Büropersonal
Office staff

der Arbeitgeber *employer*
Arbeitnehmer/in, Angestellte/r,
   Beschäftigte/r *employee*
Auszubildende/r, Praktikant/in
trainee

Büroangestellte/r
office, white-collar worker
Chef/in   *boss*
Empfangssekretär/in
receptionist

Handelsvertreter/in
commercial traveller
kaufmännische/r Angestellte/r
clerk
Kurier/in   *courier*
Mitarbeiter/in   *colleague*
Sekretär/in   *secretary*
Vertreter/in   *(sales) representative,*
agent

die Produktionsstätte (-n)
on the shop floor
Arbeiter/in   *worker, blue-collar*
worker
der Hausmeister (-)
caretaker
Auszubildende/r,
   der Lehrling (-e) *apprentice*
Techniker/in   *technician*
Vorarbeiter/in   *foreman*
die Wartungsmannschaft (-en)
maintenance crew
der Wachmann (¨er)
security guard

---

die Früh-/Spät-/Nachtschicht (-en)   *early / late / nightshift*
ganztags/Teilzeit/Gleitzeit   *full time / part-time / flexitime*
Ich arbeite in Schichten   *I work shifts.*
Pendler/in   *commuter*

Ich arbeite in der (... abteilung.)
I work in (the
... department.)
Buchhaltung   *accounts*
EDV   *data-processing*
Export   *export*
Import   *import*
Kundendienst   *service*
Personal   *personnel*
PR-   *Public Relations*
Rechts   *legal*
Schulungs   *training*

Verwaltung   *administration*
Werbe   *publicity*
befördern   *to promote*
beschäftigen   *to employ*
einstellen   *to appoint*
entlassen   *to make redundant*
feuern, rausschmeißen (umg.)
to sack (inf.)
fristlos   *without notice*
kündigen   *to give in one's notice*

7 Die Firma *The Company*

VERKÄUFE, BUCHHALTUNG UND VERSAND
SALES, ACCOUNTS AND DESPATCH

Verkäufe *Sales*

der Einzelhändler (-)
 retailer
der Großhändler (-)
 wholesaler
der Händler (-) *dealer*
die Konkurrenz *rival, competitor, competition*
der potentielle Kunde (-n)
 prospective buyer

Verbraucher/in *consumer*
das Verkaufsteam (-s)
 sales team
das Geschäft (-e) *business*
die Geschäftsreise (-n)
 business trip
die Leistung (-en) *performance*
Angebot und Nachfrage
 supply and demand
der Prozentsatz (¨e)
 percentage
der Vertrag (¨e) *contract*

kaufen *to buy, purchase*
verkaufen *to sell*
ein Vertrag unterschreiben
 to sign a contract

Nächste Woche fahre ich auf Dienstreise.   *I'm going on a business trip next week.*

die Anfrage (-n) enquiry, inquiry
das Muster, die
 Probe *sample*
der Lieferant (-en) *supplier*
die (allgemeinen)
 Geschäftsbedingungen
  terms and conditions

das Heft (-e), das Faltblatt (¨er)
 booklet
die Broschüre (-n) *brochure*
der Katalog (-e) *catalogue*
der Ausstellungsraum (¨e)
 showroom

sich etwas erkundigen   *to enquire about*
Wir interessieren uns für ...   *We are interested in ...*

das Angebot (-e) *offer*
der Kostenvoranschlag (¨e)
 estimate
das Preisangebot *quotation*
unverbindlich *without any obligation*

der Rabatt (-e), das Skonto (-s)
 discount

der Händlerrabatt (-e)
 trade discount
der Mengenrabatt (-e)
 quantitiy discount

einen Nachlaß
 gewähren *to grant a discount*
garantieren *to guarantee*

7 Die Firma *The Company*

**die Bestellung (-en),
   der Auftrag (¨e)** *order*
der Begleitbrief (-e)
   covering letter
das Bestell-/
   Auftragsformular (-e)
   order form
der Liefertermin (-e)
   delivery date
der Probeauftrag (¨e)
   trial order

das Versandgeschäft (-e)
   mail order

bestellen   *to order*
einen Auftrag erteilen
   to place an order
sich beschweren *to complain*
stornieren   *to cancel*

Konten *Accounts*

(See also *11: Institutions – Banking
and Finance*, page 142.)

die Ausgaben (-) *expenditure*
der Ausgleich (-),
   der Schadensersatz (-),
   die Erstattung (-en)
      compensation
die Gebühr (-en) *fee*
das Konto (Konten),
   die Rechnung (-en)
      account
die Kosten, der Aufwand
      costs
kostenlos   *free*
die Kreditbedingungen *credit terms*
die Ratenzahlung (-en)
   payment by instalments

der Termin (-e),
   die Frist (-en) *deadline*
**die Bezahlung (-en),
   Zahlung (-en) *payment***
per Nachnahme *COD (cash on delivery)*
der Gutschein (-e) *voucher*
die Gutschrift-/Belastungsanzeige (-n)
      credit / debit note
die Proforma-Rechnung (-en)
      pro-forma invoice
die Quittung (-en),
   der Beleg (-e) *receipt*
die Rechnung (-en) *invoice, bill*
das Saldo (Saldi), der Restbetrag (¨e),
   die Bilanz (-en)
      balance
die Zahlungsbedingungen
      payment terms

7 Die Firma *The Company*

die Zahlungsdokumente
  payment documents
der Bankscheck (-s),
  die Banktratte (-n)
    bank draft
der Wechsel (-) *bill of exchange*
der (die) Sichtwechsel/-tratte
    sight draft

das Dokumentenakkreditiv (-e)
  documentary letter
    of credit

bar zahlen	*to pay in cash*
bestätigen	*to confirm*
erhalten	*to receive*

eine Rechnung ausstellen
    to make out an invoice

Wir danken für Ihre Rechnung.
Bitte begleichen Sie den Betrag
  gemäß beiliegender Rechnung.
Wir haben den Betrag von DM ...
  auf Ihrem Konto bei der ...
  Bank überwiesen.

Thank you for your invoice.
Please send us your remittance for
  the amount of the enclosed invoice.
We have transferred the sum
  of DM ... to your account
  at the ... bank.

---

der Versand dispatch
die Fracht (-en) *freight*
die Sendung (-en),
  die Lieferung (-en)
    consignment
der Spediteur (-e) *freight forwarder,*
    shipper
der Transport (-e),
  die Beförderung (-en)
    transport
der Versand, die Verschiffung
    shipment
der Vertrieb (-e) *distribution*

die Waren   goods
der Behälter (-) *container*

das Gewicht (-e) *weight*
die Größe (-n)   *size*
die Kiste (-n)   *case*
die Ladung (-en) *load*
(nicht) lieferbar *(not) available*
vorrätig/nicht vorrätig
    in / out of stock

die Lieferung (-en) delivery
die Lieferbedingungen *delivery terms*
die Genehmigung (-en)
    permit

die Beschwerde (-n), die Mängelrüge (-n),
  die Reklamation (-en)
    complaint

Incoterms

CIF (Kosten,Versicherung, Fracht)	*CIF (cost, Insurance and Freight)*
EXW (ab Werk ...)	*EXW (Ex-works ...)*
FOB (Frei an Bord)	*FOB (Free On Board)*
FAS (Frei Längsseite Seeschiff ...)	*FAS (Free Alongside Ship ...)*

101

7 Die Firma *The Company*

frei Haus   *carriage paid*

die Versandpapiere *shipping documents*
das Konnossement (-s)
    bill of lading, B/L
der Versicherungsschein (-e)
    insurance certificate
die Versicherungspolice (-n)
    insurance policy

der Lieferschein (-e)
    delivery note

absenden   *to dispatch*
laden   *to load*
liefern   *to deliver*
schicken, senden *to send, to forward*
transportieren, befördern
    to transport

Unsere Preise gelten CIF Hamburg.
Wir freuen uns, Ihnen mitteilen zu
    können, daß wir die Waren aus
    Ihrem Auftrag Nr. . . ., an Sie
    abgesandt haben.
Wir müsssen Ihnen leider mitteilen,
    daß wir Artikel Nr. . . . nicht
    auf Lager haben.

Our prices are quoted CIF Hamburg.
We are pleased to inform you that
    the goods of your order No. . . .
    have been dispatched.

We are sorry to inform you that
    article No. . . . is out of stock

MARKETING UND PRODUKTION
MARKETING AND PRODUCTION

das Marketing *marketing*
die Analyse (-n) *analysis*
der Bericht (-e) *report*
der Haushaltsplan ("e)
    budget
lang-/kurzfristig *long/short term*
das Logo (-s),
    Emblem (-e) *logo*
der Markenname (-n)
    brand name
die Marktentwicklung (-en)
    market trends
die Marktforschung (-en)
    market research
das Projekt (-e), Vorhaben (-)
    project
die Verhandlungen
    negotations

die Verkaufskampagne (-n)
    sales campaign
die Verkaufszahlen *sales figures*
das Warenzeichen (-)
    trademark
die Werbung (-en) *advertising, promotion*
der Zeitplan ("e) *schedule*
das Ziel (-e)   *target*

die Produktion (-en)
Production

die Anlage (-n) *plant (machinery)*
die Fabrik (-en) *plant (factory)*
die Handarbeit (-en)
    handmade
die Produktionsmenge (-n)
    output
der Bestandteil (-e)
    component
der Überschuß (-schüsse)
    surplus

7 **Die Firma** *The Company*

der Handel
Commerce, trade

das Bruttosozialprodukt (-e)
    gross national product
der Einfuhrzoll ("e)
    import duty
der Export (-e) *export*
der Handel *trade*
die Handelskammer (-n)
    chamber of commerce
die Handelsschranke (-n)
    trade restrictions
der Hersteller (-) *manufacturer*
der Import (o) *import*
die Lizenz (-en) *licence*
der europäische Markt ("e)
    European market
der Inlandsmarkt/Auslandsmarkt
    home / export markets
die Menge (-n) *quantity*

ALLES UMS BÜRO
IN THE OFFICE

Maschinen, Geräte
Equipment

die Akte (-n) *file, document*
der Aktenordner *file*
der Aktenschrank ("e),
    filing cabinet
der Bleistift (-e) *pencil*
die Briefmarke (-n) *stamp*
der Briefumschlag ("e)
    envelope
die Büroklammer (-n)
    paper clip
das Diktiergerät (e)
    dictaphone
die Eingangsablage/
  die Ausgangsablage (-n)
    in-tray / out-tray

die Qualität (-en) *quality*
die Rezession (-en)*recession*
der Umsatz ("e) *turnover*
die Vorschrift (-en) *regulation*
die Wirtschaft *economics*

die Handelsmesse (-n)
trade fair
der Aussteller (-) *exhibitor*
die Ausstellung (-en)
    exhibition
der Messestand ("e)
    stand
das Plakat (-e) *poster*
Dolmetscher/in *interpreter*
Übersetzer/in *translator*

exportieren/ausführen
    to export
importieren/einführen
    to import

das Fax (-e) *fax machine*
der Fotokopierer (-)
    photo copier
die Frankiermaschine (-n)
    franking machine
das Gummiband ("er)
    elastic band
der Hefter(-)/Tacker (-)
    stapler / staples
der Kalender (-) *calendar*
das Klebeband ("er) *sticky tape*
der Klebstoff (-e) *glue*
der Kugelschreiber (-)
    biro
die Lampe (-n) *lamp*
das Lineal (-e) *ruler*
der Locher (-) *hole punch*
das Papier (-e) *paper*
der Papierkorb ("e) *waste-paper bin*

7 Die Firma *The Company*

der PC (-s), der Computer (-)
    PC, computer
das Radiergummi (-s)
    rubber, eraser
die Rechenmaschine (-n)
    calculator
die Reißzwecke (-n) *drawing pin*
die Schere (-n) *scissors*
die Schreibmaschine (-n)
    typewriter
der Schreibtisch (-e)
    desk
die Schublade (-n) *drawer*

die selbstklebenden Etiketten
    sticky labels
der Stift (-e) *pen*
der Stuhl (¨e) *chair*
der Taschenrechner (-)
    pocket calculator
das Telefon (-e) *telephone*
das Tesafilm ® *sellotape*
das Tippex ® *correction fluid*
der Ventilator *ventilator*
das Wörterbuch (¨er)
    dictionary
die Zerkleinerungsmaschine (-n)
    shredder

Darf ich eine Fotokopie machen?
Darf ich Ihr Fax benutzen?
Macht es Ihnen etwas aus, wenn
ich das Fenster auf-/zumache?

Can I make a photocopy?
Can I use the fax machine?
*Do you mind if I open / close
the window?*

Am Computer
Using the Computer

die Hardware *hardware*
das Band (¨er) *tape*
der Bildschirm (-e) *screen*
die CD (-s) *CD*
der Computer (-),
    der Rechner (-) *computer*
der Drucker (-) *printer*
die Druckkopfpatrone (-n)
    print cartridge
die Festplatte (-n) *hard disk*
der Laserdrucker (-)
    laser printer
die Lautsprecherboxen
    sound system
die Maus (-¨e) *mouse*
der Nadeldrucker (-)
    dot-matrix printer

der PC (-s) *PC*
der Scanner (-) *scanner*
der Schalter (-) *switch*
der Stecker (-) *plug*
die Tastatur (-en) *keyboard*
der Terminal (-s) *terminal*
der Tintenstrahldrucker (-)
    ink-jet printer
das Anwendungsprogramm (-e)
    application programme
Benutzer/in *user*
benutzerfreundlich *user-friendly*
das Betriebssystem (-e)
    operating system
der Bildschirmtext (-e)
    teletext
das Bit (-s) *bit*
das Byte (-s) *byte*
das CAD (computerunterstütes
    Zeichnen) *CAD (computer-
    aided design)*

7 Die Firma *The Company*

die Datenbank (-en)
    database
die Diskette (-n) *diskette, floppy disk*
elektronische Post *electronic mail*
die Funktionstaste (-n)
    function key
der Großrechner (-)
    mainframe
das Handbuch (¨er) *manual*
das Ikon (-en) *icon*
das Laufwerk (-e) *drive*
das Lernprogramm (-e)
    tutorial
der Mikroprozessor (-en)
    microprocessor
das Modem (-s) *modem*
der Pfad (-e) *path*
das Programm (-e) *programme*
Programmierer/in *programmer*
die Software *software*
der Speicher (-) *memory*
die Tabellenkalkulation (-en)
    spreadsheet analysis
die Textverarbeitung *word processing*
der Virus (Viren) *virus*
der Zugriff (-e) *access*

das Absatzlineal (-e)
    ruler
die Ansicht (-en) *view*
der Befehl (-e) *command*
der Cursor (-) *cursor*
die Datei (-en) *file*
der Datei-Manager (-)
    Program Manager
der Dateiname (-n) *file name*
das Dialogfeld (-er), das Pull Down
  Menü (-s) *dialogue box,*
    pull-down menu
die Eingabetaste (-n)
    enter key
die Extras *tools*

das Fenster (-) *window*
das Format (-e) *format*
die Menüleiste (-n)
    menu bar
das Paßwort (¨er) *password*
das Sonderzeichen (-)
    special character
die Steuerung (-en), Strg
    control, (Ctrl)
die Symbolleiste (-en)
    toolbar
die Sicherheitskopie (-n)
    back up
die Tabelle (-n) *table*
die Taste (-n) *key*
?   *Help symbol*

ausschalten *to switch off*
ausschneiden *to cut*
bearbeiten *to edit*
beenden *to exit, to quit*
doppelklicken *to double-click*
drucken *to print*
eine Taste drücken
    to press a key
einfügen *to paste*
eingeben, eintippen
    to key in
einschalten *to switch on*
formatieren *to format*
installieren *to set up, to install*
klicken *to click*
kopieren *to copy*
laden *to load*
markieren *to mark*
öffnen *to open*
das Programm starten
    to get into the
    programme
speichern *to save*
tippen *to type*
unterstreichen *to underline*

Es funktioniert nicht.
Wie kannst du ...?　　　　*It doesn't work. How do you ... ?*

NOCH MAL!

● *Activity: Give the German headings for the menu bar:*

Eile Edit View Insert Format Tools Table Window Help

Das Telefonieren *Telephoning*

Deutsche **T** ·
Telekom

das Telefon *telephone*
der Anrufbeantworter (-)
　　　　answering machine
das Autotelefon (-e) *car phone*
das Fax (-e)　*fax*
der Funkrufempfänger (-)
　　　　pager
das Handy (Handies)　*mobile phone*
die Münztelefonzelle (-n)
　　　　pay phone
das tragbares Telefon
　　　　portable telephone
die Telefonauskunft ("e)
　　　　directory enquiries

die Auslandsauskunft ("e)
　　　　international directory enquiries
die Gelben Seiten *Yellow Pages*
das Telefonbuch ("er)
　　　　directory
die Vermittlung (-en)
　　　　operator
die Zentrale (-n) *switchboard*

das Telefongespräch (-e)
　　　　telephone conversation
das Ferngespräch (-e)
　　　　long-distance call
das Ortsgespräch (-e)
　　　　local call

7 Die Firma *The Company*

das R-Gespräch (-e)
    reverse charge call
das Freizeichen (-) *dialling tone*
der Hörer (-)   *receiver*
die Nachricht (-en) *message*
die Telefonnummer (-n)
    telephone number
die Verbindung (-en)
    connection
die Vorwahl (-en) *dialling code*

die Gebühren   *charges*

die Grundgebühr (-en)
    rental
die Telefonkarte (-n)
    phonecard
die Telefonzelle (-n)
    telephone box

besetzt   *engaged*
defekt   *out of order*
verbinden   *to connect*
wählen   *to dial*

Ich möchte ...	*I would like ...*
telefonieren.	*to make a telephone call.*
eine Telefonkarte mit ...	*a telephone card with ...*
Einheiten, bitte.	*units, please.*
Können Sie mir bitte wechseln?	*Can you give me some change?*

Am Telefon *On the phone*

Hallo?	*Hello!*
Guten Morgen/Guten Tag.	*Good morning / Good afternoon.*
Kann ich Ihnen helfen?	*Can I help you?*
Könnte ich bitte mit ... sprechen?	*Can I speak to ...?*
Könnten Sie mich bitte mit ... verbinden?	*Can I have extension ...?, Can you put me through to ...?*
Bleiben Sie bitte dran.	*Hold on, please.*
Ich verbinde (Sie).	*I'll put you through.*
Mein Name ist ...	*My name is ...*
... am Apparat.	*... here.*
Er/Sie ist nicht da.	*He / she is not there.*
Er/Sie spricht gerade auf der anderen Leitung.	*He / she is on the other line.*
Möchten Sie, daß er/sie Sie zurückruft?	*Would you like him / her to call you back?*
Soll ich ihm/ihr eine Nachricht hinterlassen?	*Can I take / leave a message?*
Danke für Ihren Anruf.	*Thank you for calling*
Bitte.	*Don't mention it.*
Es tut mir leid, ich habe mich verwählt.	*I'm sorry, I've got the wrong number.*

Können Sie (uns) zurückrufen?	*Can you call (us) back?*
Würden Sie das bitte buchstabieren?	*Could you spell it, please?*
Würden Sie das bitte wiederholen?	*Could you repeat it?*
Hinterlassen Sie eine Nachricht nach dem Pfeifton.	*Leave a message after the tone.*

telefonieren, anrufen	*to phone, to call, to ring*	faxen	*to send a fax*
		zurückrufen	*to call back*

Terminvereinbarung und Ausreden
Making arrangements and excuses

Wo sollen wir uns treffen?   ***Where shall we meet?***
Treffen wir uns . . . .
   Laß uns doch . . . treffen.   *Let's meet . . .*
   in meinem/Ihrem Büro   *in my / your office*
   bei mir   *at my house*
Ich hole dich/Sie ab.   *I'll pick you up.*
Wann wollen wir uns treffen?   *When shall we meet?*
Mir wäre . . . lieber.   *I'd prefer to meet . . .*
   in einer halben Stunde   *in half an hour*
   morgen   *tomorrow*

Können wir einen Termin
   vereinbaren?   ***Can we make an appointment?***
Würde Ihnen . . . zusagen?   *Would . . . be convenient for you?*
Welcher Tag würde Ihnen passen?   *Which day would suit you?*

Tut mir leid . . .   *I'm sorry . . .*
Am Montag geht es bei mir nicht.   *I can't manage Monday.*
Ich habe (leider) keine Zeit.   *(Unfortunately) I haven't got the time.*
Ich habe zuviel zu tun.   *I have too much work.*
Ich habe schon einen Termin.   *I have another appointment.*
Ich bin (sehr) beschäftigt.   *I'm (very) busy.*
Ich möchte nicht./Ich will nicht.   *I don't want to.*
Ich kann nicht.   *I can't.*
Ich muß zum Zahnarzt.   *I have to go to the dentist.*

Tut mir leid, ich habe es nicht geschafft.	*I'm sorry I couldn't make it.*
Tut mir leid, ich bin spät dran.	*Sorry I'm late.*
Mein Auto wollte nicht anspringen.	*My car wouldn't start.*

NOCH MAL!

● *Activity: You want to arrange a meeting with a friend or business client, but you have already made the following arrangements. How would you make your excuses?*

8 Kunst und Medien *Art and the Media*

KUNST UND KÜNSTLER
ART AND ARTISTS

die Kunstausstellung (-en)
art exhibition
die Kunstsammlung (-en)
art collection
Designer/in   *designer*
die Galerie (-n)   *gallery*
Grafiker/in   *graphic artist*
Illustrator/in   *illustrator*
die abstrakte Kunst
abstract art
die Kunstgeschichte
history of art
die schönen Künste
fine arts

Zeichnen und Malen
Drawing and painting

das Bild (-er)   *picture*
der Bleistift (-e)   *pencil*
der Buntstift (-e)   *crayon*
die Leinwand ("e)   *canvas*
der Pinsel (-)   *paintbrush*
die Skizze (-n)   *sketch*
die Staffelei (-en)   *easel*
die Wasserfarbe (-n)
water colour paint

das Gemälde (-n) *painting*
das Aquarell (-e) *water colour*
das Landschaftsgemälde (-)
landscape
das Ölgemälde (-)
oil
das Porträt (-s) *portrait*
das Stilleben (-) *still life*

Töpferei, Bildhauerei und Architektur
Pottery, sculpture and architecture

der Topf ("e)   *pot*
Töpfer/in   *potter*
die Töpferei (-en) *pottery*
der Töpferofen (˙) *kiln*
die Töpferscheibe (-n)
potter's wheel

Bildhauer/in   *sculptor*
die Figur (-en)   *figure*
der Meißel (-)   *chisel*
das Modell (-e)   *model*
die Skulptur (-en),
die Plastik (-en) *sculpture*
die Statue (-n)   *statue*
das Atelier (-s)   *studio*

das Material (-ien)
material
die Bronze   *bronze*
der Gips   *plaster*
das Holz   *wood*
der Kunststoff   *plastic*
der Marmor   *marble*
der Stein   *stone*
der Ton   *clay*

**die Architektur,
die Baukunst** *architecture*
der Entwurf ("e) *design*
der Denkmalschutz
*protection of
historical
monuments*

der Architekturstil (-e)
**architectural
style**
die Griechische/Römische Antike
ancient Greek / ancient Roman

8 Kunst und Medien *Art and the Media*

die Frühen
    Christen — *early Christian*
die Romanik — *romanesque*
die Gotik — *gothic*
die Renaissance — *renaissance*
das Barock — *baroque*
das Rokoko — *Rococo*
die Romantik — *Romanticism*
der Klassizismus — *classicism*
der Jugendstil — *Art Nouveau, Art deco*
der Impressionismus
    impressionism

die moderne
    Kunst — ***modern art***
Dadaismus — *dadaism*
Expressionismus — *expressionism*

Kubismus — *cubism*
Fauvismus — *fauvism*
Surrealismus — *surrealism*
Realismus — *realism*

bildhauern (umg.), sich als
    Bildhauer betätigen
    to sculpt
drucken — *to print*
hauen — *to chisel*
malen — *to paint*
modellieren — *to model*
schnitzen, meißeln
    to carve
skizzieren — *to sketch*
töpfern — *to throw (in clay)*
zeichnen — *to draw*

DAS GESCHRIEBENE WORT
THE WRITTEN WORD

Bücher *Books*

Schriftsteller/in *writer*
Autor/in — *author*
Biograph/in — *biographer*
Dichter/in — *poet*
Dramatiker/in — *playwright*
Romanschriftsteller/in,
    Romancier — *novelist*

das Abonnement (-s)
    subscription
Bibliothekar/in — *librarian*
Buchhändler/in — *bookseller*
Herausgeber/in — *editor (books)*
Journalist/in — *journalist*
Redakteur/in — *editor (newspapers)*
die Tantiemen — *royalties*
Verleger/in — *publisher*

das Sachbuch (¨er) *non fiction*
die Autobiographie (-n)
    autobiography

die Biographie (-n)
    biography
die Broschüre (-n) *brochure*
das Dokument — *document*
das Handbuch (¨er)
    manual, handbook
das Kinderbuch (¨er)
    children's book
das Lehrbuch (¨er) *textbook*
das Lexikon (Lexika)
    encyclopaedia
das Nachschlagewerk (-e)
    reference book
das Rätselbuch (-er)
    puzzle book
die Reisebeschreibung (-en)
    travel book
der Reiseführer (-)
    guidebook
der Sprachführer (-)
    phrasebook
das Wörterbuch (¨er)
    dictionary

Fiktion, erzählende Literatur, Belletristik *Fiction*

die Geschichte (-n)
    story
der Geschichtsroman (-e),
  historischer Roman (-e)
    historical novel
der Krimi (-s)   *crime, detective story*
das Märchen (-) *fairy tale*
der Roman (-e) *novel*
die Sage (-n)   *legend*
der Science-fiction Roman (-e)
    sci-fi novel
der Thriller (-)   *thriller*

die gebundene Ausgabe (-n)
    hardback
das Band (¨e)   *volume*
das Exemplar (-e) *copy*
der Einband (¨e),
  der Umschlag (¨e)
    cover
die Illustration (-en)
    illustration
der Inhalt (-e)   *contents*
das Kapitel (-)   *chapter*
das Register (-) *index*

die Seite (-n)   *page*
das Taschenbuch (¨er)
    paperback

der Text (-e)   ***text***
der Buchstabe (-n) *letter*
die Phrase (-n)/
  Satzteil (-e) *phrase*
der Satz (¨e)   *sentence*
die Zeile (-n)   *line*
der (Text)absatz (¨e)
    paragraph
der Textabschnitt (e)
    passage
das Wort (¨er) *word*
das Zitat (-e)   *quotation*
der Abriß (Abrisse) *outline*
die Fußnote (-n) *footnote*

die Lyrik, Dichtung *poetry*

die Ballade (-n) *ballad*
das Gedicht (-e) *poem*
das Kindergedicht (-e)
  /-lied (-er)   *nursery rhyme*
der Limerick (-s) *limerick*
die Strophe (-n), der Vers (-e)
    verse, stanza

Zeitungen und Zeitschriften *Newspapers and magazines*

8 Kunst und Medien *Art and the Media*

die Auflagenhöhe (-n)
    circulation figures
die Ausgabe (-n),
  die Nummer (-n)
    issue, edition
die Boulevardpresse
    popular press,
    'yellow press'
Journalist/in   *journalist*
die seriösen Zeitungen
    quality papers
die Tageszeitung (-en)
    daily paper
das Wochenblatt (¨er)
    weekly paper
die Zeitschrift (-en)
    magazine

Rubriken   ***sections***
Anzeigen   *Advertisements*
Aus dem Ausland *International news*
Aus dem Inland *Home, national news*
Börse   *Stock market report*
Cartoons   *Cartoons*
Feuilleton, Bericht
    Feature
Funk und Fernsehen
    Radio & TV
Horoskop (-e)   *Horoscope*
Inhalt   *Contents*
Kleinanzeigen *Small ads, classifieds*
Kreuzworträtsel *Crossword*
Kultur   *Culture*
Leitartikel   *Editorial*
Lokalseite   *Local news*
Politik   *Politics*
Reise, Touristik *Travel*
Rezensionen   *Reviews*
Soziales   *Social*
Sport   *Sport*
standesamtliche Nachrichten
    Births, Marriages
    and Deaths

Stellenanzeigen *Situations Vacant*
Wetter   *Weather*
Wirtschaft   *Financial news*

das Layout (-s) *layout*
die Schlagzeile (-n)
    headline
die Titelseite (-n) *front page*
die letzte Seite *back page*

die Zeichensetzung
Punctuation

der Akzent (-e) *accent*
das Anführungszeichen (-)
    inverted commas
das Apostroph (-e) *apostrophe*
das Ausrufezeichen (-)
    exclamation mark
der Bindestrich (-e),
  Gedankenstrich (-e)
    hyphen
der Doppelpunkt (-e)
    colon
das Fragezeichen (-)
    question mark
die Klammer (-n) *bracket*
das Komma (-s) *comma*
der Punkt (-e) *full stop*
das Semikolon (-s),
  der Strichpunkt (-e)
    semi-colon
Umlaut   *umlaut*

die Schrift   ***font***
der Fettdruck *bold print*
kursiv   *italic*
handgeschrieben *handwritten*
die Blockschrift (-en),
  der Großbuchstaben (-)
    block capitals,
    capital letters
der Kleinbuchstabe (-n)
    small letter

8 Kunst und Medien *Art and the Media*

Bitte das Formular in Druckschrift ausfüllen.	*Please fill out the form in block capitals.*

drucken	*to print*	schreiben	*to write*
herausgeben	*to edit*	tippen	*to type*
korrigieren	*to correct*	veröffentlichen	*to publish*

Meinungen *Opinions*

Der Umfrage nach . . .	*According to the polls . . .*
Kein Kommentar.	*No comment.*
Meiner Meinung nach . . .	*In my opinion . . .*
Erstens . . . / Zweitens . . .	*Firstly . . . / Secondly . . .*
Es handelt sich um . . .	*It's about . . ., It is concerned with . . .*
Das kommt darauf an, (ob . . .)	*It depends (whether . . .)*
einerseits . . ., andererseits . . .	*on the one hand . . .*
	on the other hand . . .

die Umfrage (-n)	*survey, questionnaire*	der Grund ("e)	*reason*
zum Beispiel	*for example*		
angenommen	*supposing*	argumentieren	*to argue*
natürlich	*of course*	behaupten	*to claim*
nicht nur . . ., sondern auch . . .		denken, meinen	*to think*
	not only . . . but also . . .	erwähnen	*to mention*
vor allem	*above all*	erzählen	*to tell*
trotzdem	*all the same,*	glauben	*to believe*
	nevertheless	recht/unrecht	
auf jeden Fall	*in any case*	haben	*to be right / wrong*
zum Schluß	*in conclusion, finally*	schätzen	*to reckon, to estimate*
		unterbrechen	*to interrupt*
der Vorteil (-e)	*advantage*	vorschlagen	*to suggest*
der Nachteil (-e)	*disadvantage*	zweifeln	*to doubt*

8 Kunst und Medien *Art and the Media*

KINO UND THEATER
CINEMA AND THEATRE

Produzent/in — *producer*
Regisseur/in — *director*
Toningenieur/in — *sound engineer*
Schauspieler/
  Schauspielerin — *actor / actress*
Hauptdarsteller/in
     main actor
der Star (-s) — *star*
Kritiker/in — *critic*
Theaterbesucher/in
     play, theatregoer
die Zuschauer/in *(a member of the)*
     audience

die Garderobe (-n) *cloakroom*
das Foyer (-s) — *foyer*
die Karte (-n) — *ticket*
die Kasse (-n) — *box-office*
das Matinee (-s), die
  Frühvorstellung (-en)
     matinée

der Zuschauerraum (¨e)
     auditorium
der Gang (¨e) — *aisle*
der dritte Rang, die Galerie
     gallery
der erste Rang — *dress circle*
die Loge (-n) — *box*
das Parkett (-s) — *stalls, front stalls*
der Rang (¨e) — *circle*
der zweite Rang *upper circle*
die (Sitz)Reihe (-n)
     row
der Sitzplatz (¨e) *seat*

die Pause (-n) — *interval*
das Programm (-e)
     programme

DAS KINO
THE CINEMA

der Film (-e) *film*
die Aufnahme — *take*
die Filmmusik (-en)
     soundtrack
der Filmstar (-s) *film star*
das Filmstudio (-s)
     film studio
Kameramann/-frau
     cameraman / woman
die Leinwand (¨e) *screen*
die Rolle (-n) — *part*
der Spezialeffekt (-e)
     special effect

... film — **... film**
der zensierte — *censored*
der Horror — *horror*
der Kriegs — *war*
der Kriminal — *detective*
der Liebes — *romance, love story*
der Porno — *pornographic*
der Science-fiction *science fiction*
der Stumm — *silent*

der Thriller (-) — *thriller*
der Western (-) — *western*
die Werbung (-en) *advertisements*

schneiden — *to cut*
frei ab ... Jahren — *not suitable for*
     persons under ... years

DAS THEATER
THE THEATRE

Das Theaterstück (-e),
  das Schauspiel (-e)
     play
der Applaus, der Beifall
     applause
die Aufführung (-en)
     performance, show

erster Akt, dritte
   Szene   *act 1, scene 3*

hinter den Kulissen
       behind the scenes
Intendant/in   *theatre manager*
das Kostüm (-e) *costume*
die Maske (n)   *make-up*
die Probe (-n)   *rehearsal*
die Requisiten   *props*
die Schauspielergarderobe (-n)
       dressing room
Regisseur/in   *producer*
Souffleur/Souffleuse
       prompter

die Oper (-n)   ***opera***
Dirigent/in   *conductor*
der Opernchor (¨e) *chorus*
das Orchester (-) *orchestra*
Solist/in   *soloist*

das Ballett (-s) *ballet*
Ballettänzer/in   *ballet dancer*
die Balletttruppe (-n)
       corps de ballet
Choreograph/in *choreographer*
die Primaballerina
       prima ballerina

die Tanzgruppe (-n)
       chorus

der Zirkus (-se)
       circus
(Zirkus) Direktor/in
       ringmaster
Akrobat/in   *acrobat*
Artist/in   *artist*
der Clown (-s)   *clown*
die Dressurtiere *performing animals*
der Jongleur (-e) *juggler*
die Manege (-n) *ring*
Trapezkünstler/in
       trapeze artist

auspfeifen   *to boo*
Beifall klatschen *to applause*
inszenieren   *to stage*
klatschen   *to clap*
in der Rolle der ...
       to play the role of ...
spielen, aufführen
       to act, to perform
tanzen   *to dance*
proben   *to rehearse*
anschauen   *to watch*
Zugabe!   *Encore!, More!*

Ich möchte ... reservieren.   *I would like to book ...*
Es ist ausverkauft.   *It's sold out.*
Es handelte von ...   *It was about ...*
Ich würde es (nicht) empfehlen.   *I would (not) recommend it.*

8 Kunst und Medien *Art and the Media*

DIE MUSIK *MUSIC*

das Instrument (-e)
    instrument
Musiker/in   *musician*
Sänger/in   *singer*
Spieler/in   *player*

die Popmusik *Pop music*

die Band   *band*
der Diskjockey *DJ*
das Freiluftkonzert (-e)
    open-air concert
die Gitarre (-n) *guitar*
Gitarrist/in   *guitarist*
die Gruppe (-n) *group*
die Klaviatur (-en),
   die Tastatur (-en) *keyboard*
die Lautsprecherbox (-en)
    loudspeaker
der Liedtext (-e) *lyrics*
die Melodie (-n) *melody, tune*
das Mikrofon (-e) *microphone*
der Popstar (-s), der Schlagerstar (-s)
    pop star
der Schlager (-) *hit*
die Schlagerparade (-n)
    top ten, charts
der Verstärker (-) *amplifier*

die Blaskapelle (-n)
    brass band
der Blues   *blues*
die Country- und Westernmusik
    country and western
der Jazz   *jazz*
die Kirchenmusik
    church music
der Rock, der Rock and Roll
    rock, rock'n'roll
der Soul   *soul*
die Volksmusik *folk*

Klassische Musik
Classical music

der Chor ("e)   *choir*
Komponist/in   *composer*
das Orchester (-) *orchestra*
Pianist/in   *pianist*

Sänger/in   ***singer***
Alt   *alto*
Baß   *bass*
Oberstimme   *treble*
Sopranist/in   *soprano*
Tenor   *tenor*

die Instrumente *instruments*
Saiten-, Streich-
   instrumente *strings*
die Baßgeige (-n), das Kontrabaß
   (-basse)   *double bass*
die Bratsche (-n) *viola*
das Cello (-s) *cello*
die Harfe (-n) *harp*
die Violine (-n) *violin*

Holzblasinstrumente
    woodwind
das Fagott (-s) *bassoon*
die Klarinette (-n) *clarinet*
die Oboe (-n) *oboe*
die Piccolo (-s) *piccolo*
die Querflöte (-n) *flute*
das Saxophon (-e) *saxophone*

Blechblasinstrumente
    brass
das Horn ("er) *horn*
die Posaune (-n) *trombone*
die Trompete (-n) *trumpet*
die Tuba (-s) *tuba*
das Waldhorn ("er) *French horn*

Schlaginstrumente
    percussion
das Cymbel (-s), das Becken (-)
    cymbals

8 Kunst und Medien *Art and the Media*

die kleine Trommel (-n)
side drum
die Pauke (-n)   *kettledrum*
die Triangel (-n) *triangle*
die Trommel (-n) *drum*
das Xylophon (-e) *xylophone*

Volksmusikinstrumente
popular musical instruments
das Akkordeon (-s)
accordion
das Banjo (-s) *banjo*
die Bongos   *bongo drums*
der Dudelsack (¨e) *bagpipes*
die Gitarre (-n) *guitar*
die Mundharmonika (-s)
mouth organ, harmonica
das Tamburin (-s) *tambourine*

Dirigent/in   *conductor*
Musiker/in   *player*
Solist/in   *soloist*
das Solo (-s)   *solo*

das Klavier (-e) *piano*
der Flügel (-) *grand piano*
die Orgel (-n) *organ*

eine gute/schwache Stimme
a good / poor voice

richtig/falsch singen
to sing in / out of tune
zu tief singen/spielen
to sing / play flat
die Note (-n) *note*
der Takt (-e) *time*

die (Schall)Platte (-n)
record
die Bildplatte (-n) *video disc*
die CD (-s), die Compact-Disc
CD
der CD-Spieler (-)
CD player
die Hi-Fi-Anlage (-n)
hi-fi system
die Kassette (-n) *cassette*
der Kassettenrekorder (-)
cassette recorder
der Plattenspieler (-)
record player

aufnehmen   *to record*
auf Band aufnehmen
to tape
eine Disc machen *to cut a disc*
klimpern   *to strum*
singen   *to sing*
spielen   *to play*
stimmen   *to tune*

8 Kunst und Medien *Art and the Media*

RADIO UND FERNSEHEN *RADIO AND TELEVISION*

ARD   ZDF

der Fernseher (-)
    television
die Antenne (-n) *aerial*
der Bildschirm (-e) *screen*
der Farbfernseher (-)
    colour television
die Fernbedienung (-en)
    remote control
das Kabel (-)   *cable*
das Kabelfernsehen (-)
    cable television
das Radio (-s) *radio*
das Satellitenfernsehen (-)
    satellite television
die Satelliten-
  schüssel (-n) *satellite dish*
das Videoband ("er) *video tape*
die Videokamera (-s)
    video camera
der Videorekorder (-)
    video recorder

Fernsehzuschauer/in
    viewer
der Kameramann ("er)
    cameraman
Moderator/in *presenter*
Produzent/in *producer*
Radiohörer/in *listener*

das (Fernseh-) Programm (-e),
  der Kanal ("e)
    channel
die Aufnahme (-n) *recording*
das Interview (-s) *interview*

die Kurzmeldung (-en)
    news flash
die Nachrichten *news*
die Sendung (-en) *broadcast*
der Ton ("e)   *sound*

die Sendung (en) *programme*
der Dokumentarfilm (-e)
    documentary
das komische
  Fernsehspiel (-e)
    comedy
die Seifenoper (-n) *soap opera*
die Serie (-n) *series, serial*
die Spielshow(-s) *game show*
der Werbespot (-s) *commercial*
die Wiederholung (-en)
    repeat
die Wettervorhersage (-n)
    weather forecast
der Zeichentrickfilm (-e)
    cartoon

abspielen *to play back*
aufnehmen *to record*
ausschalte/einschalten
    to switch off / on
einen Ausfall haben
    to break down
einstellen *to tune*
löschen   *to wipe off*
senden,
  ausstrahlen *to broadcast*
umschalten *to change channels*

8 Kunst und Medien *Art and the Media*

Hast Du/Haben Sie . . . gesehen?
Was hast Du/haben Sie von . . .
    gehalten?

Did you see . . .?, Have you seen . . .?

What did you think of . . .?

NOCH MAL!

● *Activity: Name the different types of programme.*

ZDF

Vormittagsprogramm (siehe ARD).
5.00 länderjournal.
13.00 Tennis: Daviscup: Rußland – Deutschland, live. Halbfinale, 1. Einzel: Becker – Tschesnokow hard Figgemeier (Übertragung aus Moskau).
16.00 heute.
16.05 Heartbreak High (46). Jugendserie.
16.55 Sport heute.
17.00 heute.

17.08 länderjournal. U. a.: 50 Jahre Münchner Symphoniker.
17.55 Zwei Münchner in Hamburg. Serie.
19.00 heute. 19.20 Wetter.
19.25 Forsthaus Falkenau. Serie.
20.15 Faust. ✳ Krimiserie.
21.15 Der Untergang der Estonia. Nichts gelernt aus der Katastrophe? – Bericht von Dietmar Barsig und Horst Danker.
21.45 heute-journal.
22.15 Aspekte. ✳ 1500. Ausgabe des Kulturmagazins – Thema: Kultur von oben und unten – U. a.: Hans-Dietrich Genscher berichtet aus der Kulturstadt Halle; Fürstin

Gloria von Thurn und Taxis trifft „Die Prinzen"; Schauspieler Mathieu Carrière besucht die Malerin Anna Blessmann; Astronaut Thomas Reiter gratuliert aus dem Weltall.
23.15 Willemsens Woche. Talkshow live aus Hamburg – Gäste u. a.: Heino, Muriel Baumeister (Schauspielerin), Fahrad Fad (Jungfilmer).
0.15 heute nacht.
0.30 Verbotene Nächte. ✳ Melodram, USA 1990; R: Waris Hussein; D: Melissa Gilbert, Robin Shou, Victor K. Wong u. a.
2.00 Text aktuell. 2.10 Straßenfeger.

SAT 1

5.30 Deutschland heute morgen.
Serien: 9.00 Cannon. 10.00 Fantasy Island. 11.00 Hallo, Onkel Doc! (Wh.). 12.00 Love Boat. 13.00 Falcon Crest. 14.00 Cagney & Lacey. 15.00 Raumschiff Enterprise. 16.00

Baywatch.
17.00 Riskier was! Quiz.
17.30 Sat 1 Regional Report.
18.00 Geh aufs Ganze! Gewinnpoker.
19.00 Sat 1 Newsmagazin. Nachrichten.
19.15 täglich ran. Sport.
19.30 Glücksrad. Gewinnshow.
20.15 Der Tag des Falken. Fantasyfilm, USA 1984; R: Richard Donner; D: Rutger

Hauer, Matthew Broderick fer u. a.
22.30 ran: Fußball.
23.20 Scharfe Girls auf Achse. Erotikfilm, Schweiz/Frankr. 1985; R: Michel Leblanc.
Nachtprogramm: 0.30 McGee, der Tiger. Kriminalfilm, USA 1969; R: Robert Clouse. 2.05 Raumschiff Enterprise. 2.55 Baywatch. 3.55 Cannon. 4.45 Riskier was! 5.10 ran: Fußball.

9 Hobbys und Sport *Hobbies and Sports*

(For likes and dislikes see section 1
Personal Matters, page 49.)

Aktivitäten *Activities*

Sport- und Vergnügungsstätten
        Venues
die Bowlingbahn (-en)
        bowling alley
der Club (-s)   *club*
die Disco (-s)   *disco*
die Eisbahn (-en) *ice rink*
der Festplatz (¨e) *fairground*
die Fete (-n)/die Party(-s)/das Fest (-e)
        party
das Freibad (¨er) *outdoor swimming
        pool*
der Jugendklub (-s)
        youth club
das Kasino (-s) *casino*
das Konzert (-e) *concert*
das Nachtlokal (-e)
        night club
der Park (-s)   *park*
die Rennbahn (-en)
        racecourse
das Schwimmbad (¨er)
        *indoor swimming
        pool*
das Stadion (Stadien)
        stadium
der Vergnügungspark (-s)
        amusement park

angeln   *to go fishing*
basteln   *to do DIY*
essen gehen   *to go out for a meal*
Fahrrad fahren *to go for a cycle ride*
im Garten arbeiten
        to do the gardening
Golf spielen   *to play golf*
joggen   *to go jogging*

lesen   *to read*
malen   *to paint*
Musik hören   *to listen to music*
reiten   *to go horseriding*
schwimmen   *to swim*
spazieren gehen *to go for walks*
stricken   *to knit*
tanzen   *to dance*
Tennis spielen   *to play tennis*
Theater spielen *to act*
wandern   *to hike*

sammeln   ***to collect***
Briefmarken (-) *stamps*
Modellautos   *model cars*
Münzen   *coins*
Postkarten   *postcards*

Ich gehe gern . . . *I like going*
in die Disko   *to the disco*
ins Kino   *to the cinema*
zu einer Fete   *to a party*
zum Fußballspiel *to a football match*

HOBBYS *HOBBIES*

Fotografie   ***photography***
das Fotoalbum (-alben)
        photo album
der Fotoapparat (-e),
  die Kamera (-s) *camera*
Fotograf/in   *photographer*
die Polaroid/
  die Sofortbildkamera (-s)
        Polaroid
die Schwarzweißfotografie
        *black-and-white
        photography*
die Spiegelreflex (-kamera)
        *single lens reflex
        (camera)*
die Videokamera (-s)
        video camera
die vollautomatische Kamera
        automatic camera

9 Hobbys und Sport *Hobbies and Sports*

Objektiv (-e) *lens*
das Teleobjektiv (-e)
    telephoto lens
das Weitwinkelobjektiv (-e)
    wide angle lens

Film (-e)   *film*
Farb-   *colour*
Schwarzweiß-   *black-and-white*
Super-8-   *super-8-*
geringempfindlich
    slow
hochempfindlich *fast*

die Batterie (-n) *battery*
das Blitz(licht) *flash*
das Dia (-s)   *slide*

Bild (-er)/Abzug (¨e)
    print

das Negativ (-e) *negative*
seidenmatt/hochglanz
    matt / glossy
unter-/überbelichtet
    under- / overexposed
die Vergrößerung (-en)
    enlargement

Abzüge machen *to print*
die Brennweite einstellen
    to focus
ein Bild machen *to take a photo*
entwickeln   *to develop*
vergrößern   *to enlarge*
zurückspulen   *to rewind*

Karten *Cards*

das Brettspiel (-e) *board game*
das Kartenspiel (-e)
    card game
Schach   *chess*
das Kartenspiel *pack of cards*
die Farben   *suits*
Herz   *hearts*
Karo   *diamonds*
Kreuz   *clubs*
Pik   *spades*
das As (-se)   *ace*
der Bube (-n)   *jack*
die Dame(-n)   *queen*
der Joker (-)   *joker*
der König (-e)   *king*
der Trumpf (¨e) *trump*
Bridge   *bridge*
Doppelkopf   *German card game*
Mau Mau   *German card game*
Poker   *poker*
Rommé   *rummy*
Siebzehnundvier *blackjack, pontoon*
Skat   *'skat'*
Tarockkarte   *tarot card*
Whist   *whist*

Karten spielen *to play cards*
reizen   *to bid*

Die Rückspule/der Blitz
    funktioniert nicht.   *The winder / flash doesn't work.*
Du bist an der Reihe/dran.   *It's your turn.*
Ich habe ein gutes Blatt.   *I've got a good hand.*

9 Hobbys und Sport *Hobbies and Sports*

Schach *Chess*

Spieler/in	*player*
das Schachbrett (-er)	
	chessboard
die weißen/schwarzen Schachfiguren	
	white / black chess pieces
der Bauer (-n)	*pawn*
der Läufer (-)	*bishop*
der Turm ("e)	*castle, rook*
Schach	*check*
Schachmatt	*checkmate*
der Springer (-)	*knight*
rochieren	*to castle*
Schach!	*check!*
matt!	*check mate!*
Es ist dein Zug/Du bist am Zug.	
	It's your move

Spiele *Games*

Backgammon	*backgammon*
das Spielbrett (-er)	
	board
Damespiel	*draughts*
(Spiel)Stein	*draught*
die Dame	*king*
Domino	*dominoes*
der Dominostein (-e)	
	domino
Halma	*Chinese checquers*
Mühle	*nine men's morris*
Würfeln/Knobeln	*dice game*
der Würfel (-)	*dice*

Tanzen *Dancing*

Cha-Cha-Cha	*cha-cha (-cha)*
Foxtrott	*foxtrot*
Jazz	*jazz*

Jive	*jive*
Lateinamerikanischer Tanz ("e)	
	Latin-American dancing
Quickstep	*quick-step*
Rock and Roll	*rock and roll, jive*
Rumba	*rumba*
Samba	*samba*
Standardtanz ("e)	*standard dancing*
Tango	*tango*
Volkstanz	*folk / country dancing*
Walzer	*waltz*

Angeln *Fishing*

Süßwasserfische	***fresh water fish***
die Forelle (-n)	*trout*
der Flußbarsch (-e)	
	perch
der Lachs (-e)	*salmon*
der Karpfen (-)	*carp*

Hochseefische *sea fish*	
der Hai (-e)	*shark*
der Hering (-e)	*herring*
der Kabeljau (-s)/(-e)	
	cod
die Makrele (-n)	*mackerel*
die Scholle (-n)	*plaice*
der Thunfisch (-e)	*tuna*
der Tintenfisch (-e)	
	octopus, squid

Schalentiere	***shellfish***
die Auster (-n)	*oyster*
die Garnele (-n)	*prawn, shrimp*
die Herzmuschel (-n)	
	cockle
der Hummer (-)	*lobster*
die Jakobsmuschel (-n)	
	scallop
die Krabbe (-n)	*crab*
die Languste (-n)	*crayfish*

die Miesmuschel (-n)
 mussel

das Sportangeln *angling*
das Fliegenfischen
 fly fishing
das Hochseeangeln
 deep-sea fishing
das Süßwasserangeln
 coarse fishing

Angelgeräte *fishing tackle*
die Angelschnur (¨e)
 fishing line
die Fliege (-n) *fly*
der Haken (-) *hook*
der Hocker (-) *stool*
der Köder (-) *bait*
der Korb (¨e) *basket*
das Netz (-e) *net*
die Rolle (-n) *reel*
das Ruderboot (-e) *fishing, rowing boat*
die Rute (-n) *rod*
der Schwimmer (-)
 float
der Watstiefel (-) *waders*

angeln gehen *to go fishing*
auswerfen *to cast*
fangen *to catch*
fischen, angeln *to fish*

Pferde und Reitsport
Horses and riding

das Fohlen (-) *foal*
der Gaul (¨e) *nag*
der Hengst (-e) *stallion*
das Pferd (-e) *horse*
das Pony (-s) *pony*
die Stute (-n) *mare*
der Vollblüter (-) *thoroughbred*
der Wallach (-e) *gelding*

der Apfelschimmel (-)
 dapple-grey
der Fuchs (¨e) *chestnut*
der Rappe (-n) *black horse*
der Rotfuchs (¨e) *bay*
der Schecke (-n) *piebald*
der Schimmel (-) *white horse*

Reitzeug *riding gear*
das Gebiß(-sse) *bit*
die Gerte (-n) *crop*
das Geschirr (-e) *harness*
die Kardätsche (-n)
 horse-brush
der Sattel (-) *saddle*
der Steigbügel (-) *stirrup*
der Striegel (-) *curry-comb*
der Zaum (¨e) *bridle*
der Zügel (-) *reins*

die Koppel (-n) *paddock*
der Reitweg (-e) *bridle path*
der Stall (¨e) *stable*

Pferderennen *horseracing*
der Buchmacher (-)
 bookie
das Galopprennen (-)
 flat racing
Gewinner/in *winner*
das Hindernis (-se)
 jump
das Hindernisrennen (-)
 steeplechase
der Jockey (-s) *jockey*
der Parcours (-) *show-jumping course*
die Pferderennbahn (-en)
 racecourse
der Sattelplatz (¨e)
 paddock (racecourse)
das Springreiten *show-jumping*
das Trabrennen (-)
 trotting race
die Wette (-n) *bet*

9 Hobbys und Sport *Hobbies and Sports*

absitzen	*to dismount*
aufsitzen	*to mount*
ausreiten	*to go for a ride*
galoppieren	*to gallop*

herunterfallen	*to fall off*
Schritt gehen	*to walk*
springen	*to jump*
traben	*to trot*

SPORT *SPORTS*

Allgemein *General*

die Anzeigetafel (-n)	*scoreboard*
Olympiasieger/in	*Olympic champion*
die Olympischen Spiele	*Olympic games*
die Tribüne (-n)	*stand*
der Zuschauer (-)	*spectator*

Badminton	***badminton***
das Federball (-spiel)	*badminton for novices!*
der Federball (¨e)	*shuttlecock*
das Netz (-e)	*net*
der Schläger (-)	*racquet*

Basketball	***basketball***
der Korb (¨e)	*basket*

Bergsteigen	***climbing, mountaineering***
Bergwandern	*hill / mountain walking*
Klettern	*rock climbing*
das Seil (-e)	*rope*
das Steigeisen (-)	*crampon*

Billard	***billiards***
Snooker	*snooker*
das Poolbillard	*pool*
die Billardkugel (-n)	*ball*
der Billardtisch (-e)	*table*
der Queue (-s)	*cue*

Bowling, Baccia, Boule	***bowls***
Kegeln	*skittles*
Bowling	*tenpin bowling*

das Boxen	***boxing***
das Ringen	*wrestling*
der Boxhandschuh (-e)	*boxing glove*
der Boxkampf (¨e)	*boxing match*
der Boxring (-e)	*boxing ring*
das K.o. (-s)	*knockout*

das Gewichtheben	*Weightlifting*
Weltmeister im ...	*world ...champion*
Fliegen-	*fly-*
Bantam-	*bantam-*
Feder-	*feather-*
Leicht-	*light-*
Welter-	*welter-*
Mittel-	*middle-*
Schwer-	*heavy-*
Superschwer-gewicht	*super heavyweight*

Darts, Wurfpfeilspiel	***darts***
die Dartscheibe (-n)	*dart board*
der Wurfpfeil (-e)	*dart*

Fechten	***Fencing***
die Fechtmaske (-n)	*fencing mask*
der Degen (-)	*épée*
das Florett (-s)	*foil*
die Klinge (-n)	*blade*
die Parade (-n)	*parry*

9 Hobbys und Sport *Hobbies and Sports*

der Säbel (-)   *sabre*

Fitneßtraining,
Konditionstraining
     fitness training
aerobes Training *aerobic training*
Aerobic   *aerobics*
anaerobes Training
     anaerobic training
das Circuittraining
     circuit training
Gehen   *walking*
die Gewichte   *weights*
der Heimtrainer (-)
     exercise bike
das Joggen, das Laufen
     jogging
das Krafttraining *weight training*
das Stretching, Dehnen
     stretching

Fallschirmspringen
     parachuting
der Fallschirm (-e) *parachute*
Segelflug   ***gliding***
Thermiksegeln *thermal soaring*
Paragliding *paragliding*
Drachenfliegen *hang-gliding*
Ballonfahren *ballooning*

Handball   *handball*

Hockey   ***hockey***
der Schienbeinschoner (-)
     shin pad
Hockeyschläger (-)
     stick

Kampfkunst   ***Martial arts***
Judo   *judo*
das Karate   *karate*
das Taekwondo *taekwondo*

Korbball   *netball*

Rollschuhlaufen *roller skating*
die Rollschuhe   *roller skates*

Rugby   ***rugby***
das Gedränge   *scrum*

Schießen   ***shooting***
das Gewehr (-e) *rifle*
das Luftgewehr (-e)
     air-rifle
der Schießstand ("e)
     rifle range
das Tontaubenschießen
     clay pigeon shooting

Bogenschießen *archery*
der Bogen (")   *bow*
der Pfeil (-e)   *arrow*
die Scheibe (-n) *target*

Skateboardfahren *skate boarding*

Squash   ***squash***
der Squashcourt (-s)
     court

Tischtennis   *table tennis*

(Geräte) Turnen
     gymnastics
die Bank ("e)   *bench*
der Barren (-) *parallel bars*
der Boden   *floor*
die Niedersprungmatte (-n)
     landing mat
das (Seit)Pferd (-e)
     horse
das Reck (-s)   *horizontal bar*
die Ringe   *rings*
die Sprossenwand ("e)
     wall bars
das Sprungbrett (-er)
     springboard
der Stufenbarren (-)
     asymmetric bars

9 Hobbys und Sport *Hobbies and Sports*

das Trampolin (-e)
trampoline

Volleyball   *volleyball*

Das Radsport *Cycling*

das Mountain Biking
mountain-biking
das Rennrad   racing bike
die Bremsen   *brakes*
der Ersatzschlauch (¨e)
spare inner tube
die Kette (-n)   *chain*
der Lenker (-)   *handlebars*

die Luftpumpe (-n)
pump
die Pedale (-n)   *pedal*
der Plattfuß (¨e) *puncture*
das Rad (¨er)   *wheel*
der Rahmen (-)   *frame*
der Reifen (-)   *tyre*
der Rennbügel (-) *toe-clip*
der Sattel (-)   *saddle*
die Schaltung (-en)
gears
die Speiche (-n) *spoke*
der Sturzhelm (-e) *helmet*
das Trikot (-s)   *shirt, jersey*

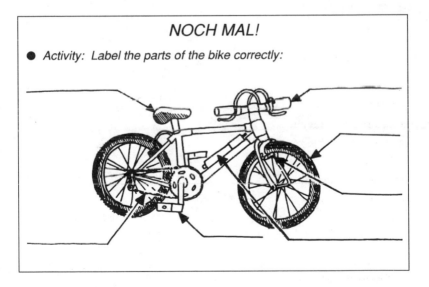

NOCH MAL!

● *Activity: Label the parts of the bike correctly:*

9 Hobbys und Sport *Hobbies and Sports*

Motorsport *Motorsports*

die Formel 1   *Formula One*
der Rennwagen (-)
       racing car
das Motorradrennen (-)
       motorcycle racing
der Seitenwagen (-)
       sidecar

Fußball *Football*

der Club (-s)   *club*
der Fußballplatz ("e)
       football ground
der Kapitän (-e) *captain*
Schiedsrichter/in *referee*
das Spiel (-e)   *match*
Spieler/in   *player*
das Team (-s),
   die Mannschaft (-en)
       team
der Manager (-) *team manager*
Trainer/in   *coach*

die Liga   **league**
die Meisterschaft (-en)
       championship
der Pokal (-e) *cup*
das Turnier (-e) *competition*

das Spiel   **the game**
der Elfmeter (-) *penalty*
das Foul (-s)   *foul*
die gelbe/rote
   Karte (-n)   *yellow / red card*
der Mannschaftskapitän
       captain
der Stürmer (-) *striker*
das Tor (-e)   *goal*
der Torhüter (-) *goalkeeper*

absteigen   *to be relegated*
aufsteigen   *to be promoted*

gewinnen   *to win*
ein Tor schießen *to score*
trainieren   *to train*
üben   *to practise*
unentschieden
   spielen   *to draw*
verlieren   *to lose*

Tennis *Tennis*

der (Tennis-) Ball ("e)
       ball
der Tennisplatz ("e)
       tennis court
der Tennisschläger (-)
       racket
das Tennisspiel (-e)
       match

das Doppel (-)   *doubles*
das Einzel (-)   *singles*
das gemischte Doppel
       mixed doubles
die Linie (-n)   *line*
das Netz (-e)   *net*

Satz und Sieg   **game, set and**
              match
der Aufschlag ("e) *service*
Einstand   *deuce*
null   *love*
der Satz ("e)   *set*
Vorteil . . .   *advantage . . .*

Golf *Golf*

der Golfball ("e) *golf ball*
der Golfclub (-s) *golf club*
der Golfwagen (-) *trolley*

das Tee (-s)   *tee*
der Bunker (-)   *bunker*
der Caddie (-s)   *caddie*
die Flagge (-n)   *flag*

9 Hobbys und Sport *Hobbies and Sports*

das Grün (-s)   *green*
das Loch ("er)   *hole*

Leichtathletik *Athletics*

die Bahn (-en)   *track*
Offizielle/r   *official*
Punktrichter/in *judge*
die Runde (-n)   *lap*
Teilnehmer/in   *competitor*
der Zeitnehmer (-)
     timekeeper

Lauf- und Feldwettbewerb
     field and track events
das Biathlon   *biathlon*
das Querfeldeinrennen
     cross country running
das Diskuswerfen *throwing the discus*
der Dreisprung *triple jump*
das Gehen   *walking*
der Hammerwurf ("e)
     throwing the hammer
der Hochsprung ("e)
     high jump
der Hürdenlauf ("e)
     hurdles
das Kugelstoßen *putting the shot*
das Laufen   *running*
der Marathon (-s) *marathon*
das Speerwerfen *throwing the javelin*
der Sprung ("e) *jump*
der Stabhochsprung
     pole-vault
der Staffellauf ("e)
     relay race
der Weitsprung ("e)
     long jump
der Zehnkampf ("e)
     decathlon

WASSERSPORT
WATER SPORTS

Schwimmen *Swimming*

die Schwimmflossen
     flippers
die Schwimmflügel (-)
     water wings
das Schwimmkissen (-)
     float
die Taucherbrille (-n)
     goggles
das Brustschwimmen
     breast stroke
das Delphinschwimmen
     butterfly
der Freistil   *freestyle*
das Kraulen   *crawl*
das Rückenschwimmen
     back stroke
der Kopfsprung ("e)
     dive
das Sprungbrett (-er)
     diving board

Tauchen   ***underwater diving***
die Sauerstofflasche (-n)
     oxygen cylinder
der Schnorchel (-) *snorkel*
der Taucheranzug ("e)
     wetsuit

rudern   ***rowing***
Floß fahren   *rafting*
das Kajak (-s) *kayak*
Kanufahren   *canoeing*
das Paddel (-) *paddle*
das Ruder (-),
  der Riemen (-) *oar*

das Ruderboot (-e)
    rowing boat
die Schwimmweste (-n)
    lifejacket

segeln   **sailing**
die Regatta (Regatten)
    regatta
das Schlauchboot (-e)
    dinghy
das Segelboot (-e) *sailing boat, yacht*

das Achterschiff *stern*
Backbord   *port*
der Bug (¨e)   *bow*
das Großsegel (-) *mainsail*
das Ruder (-)   *rudder*
das Segel (-)   *sail*
das Segeltuch (¨er)
    canvas
das Seil (-e)   *rope*
Steuerbord   *starboard*

kentern   *to capsize*
vor dem Wind segeln
    to sail downwind
ankern   *to anchor*
einen Segeltörn machen
    to cruise

Wasserski   **water-skiing**
der Außenbordmotor (-en)
    outboard motor
der Monoski (-er) *monoski*
das Motorboot (-e) *motor boat*
der Wasserski (-er)
    water-ski

surfen   **surfing**
das Surfbrett (-er) *surfboard*

WINTERSPORT
WINTER SPORTS
Skifahren *skiing*

die Abfahrt (-en) *downhill*
die Buckelpiste (-n)
    moguls
die Piste (-n)   *piste, run*
der Riesenslalom (-s)
    giant slalom
der Slalom (-s) *slalom*
das Tor (-e)   *gate*
Trickski fahren *freestyle skiing*

die Bindung (-en) *binding*
der Ski (-er)   *ski*
der Skianzug (¨e) *ski suit*
die Skibrille (-n) *goggles*
die Skihose (-n) *ski pants*
der Skistiefel (-) *ski boot*
der Skistock (¨e) *ski pole*
die Sonnenbrille (-n)
    ski glasses

Skilift   **ski lift**
der Schlepplift (-e)
    T-bar lift
die Seilbahn (-en) *cable car*
der Sessellift (-e) *chairlift*
der Skipaß (¨e) *ski pass*

Langlauf   **cross-country skiing**
der Langlaufschuh (-e)
    cross-country boot
die Loipe (-n)   *cross-country course*

Skikurs   **skiing course**
Skilehrer/in   *ski instructor*
der Skiort (-e) *ski resort*
die Skischule (-n) *ski school*

Snowboarden *snowboarding*
das Snowboard (-s)
    board

9 Hobbys und Sport *Hobbies and Sports*

die Halfpipe   *half-pipe*

Skispringen   *ski-jumping*
die Schanze (-n) *ski-jump*

Rodeln *Tobogganing*

der Bob (-s)   *bob (sleigh)*
die Rodelbahn (-en)
              toboggan run
der Schlitten (-) *toboggan*
Schlitten fahren *to go tobogganing*

Eislaufen *Ice-skating*

der Eiskunstlauf *figure-skating*
der Eisschnellauf *speed-skating*
der Eistanz   *ice dance*
das Eisstadion (-stadien)
                 skating rink
der Schlittschuh (-e)
                 skate

Eishockey *Ice hockey*

der Bulli (-s)   *bully-off*
der Kopfschutz *helmet*
der Puck (-s)   *puck*

NOCH MAL!

● *Activity: Name the hobbies and sports. Say which you like and don't like doing.*

10 Der Körper *The body*

DIE KÖRPERTEILE
PARTS OF THE BODY

der Kopf (¨e) *head*
das Gesicht (-er) *face*
das Haar (-e) *hair*
die Stirn (-en) *forehead*
das Ohr (-en) *ear*
die Wange (-n) *cheek*
das Kinn (-e) *chin*
die Nase (-n) *nose*

das Auge (-n) *eye*
die Augenbraue (-n)
    eyebrow
die Augenwimper (-n)
    eyelash
die Netzhaut (¨e) *retina*
die Pupille (-n) *pupil*
die Träne (-n) *tear*

der Mund (¨er) *mouth*
die Lippe (-n) *lip*
der Zahn (¨e) *tooth*
das Zahnfleisch *gums*
die Zunge (-n) *tongue*

der Hals (¨e) *neck*
die Kehle (-n) *throat*
der Nacken (-), das Genick (-e)
    nape of the neck

der Rumpf (¨e) *trunk*
die Schulter (-n) *shoulder*
der Rücken (-) *back*
das Kreuz (-e) *small of the back*
der Brustkorb (¨e) *chest*
die Brust (¨e) *breast*
der Busen (-) *bosom, bust*
der Magen (¨), der Bauch (¨e)
    stomach, belly
die Taille (-n) *waist*
die Hüfte (-n) *hip*

das Gesäß (-e), der Po (-s)
    buttocks, bottom

die Glieder *limbs*
der Arm (-e) *arm*
der Ellbogen (-) *elbow*
das Handgelenk (-e)
    wrist

die Hand (¨e) *hand*
die Faust (¨e) *fist*

der Finger (-) *finger*
der Daumen (-) *thumb*

das Bein (-e) *leg*
das Knie (-e) *knee*
der Knöchel (-),
   das Fußgelenk (-e)
    ankle
der Oberschenkel (-)
    thigh
das Schienbein (-e)
    shin
die Wade (-n) *calf*

der Fuß (¨e) *foot*
die Zehe (-n) *toe*

die Haut (¨e) *skin*

das Skelett (-s) *skeleton*
das Gelenk (-e) *joint*
der Kiefer (-) *jaw*
die Kniescheibe (-n)
    kneecap
der Knochen (-) *bone*
die Rippe (-n) *rib*
der Schädel (-) *skull*
die Wirbelsäule (-n),
   das Rückgrat (-e)
    spine

der Muskel (-n) *muscle*
das Band (¨er) *ligament*

10 Der Körper *The body*

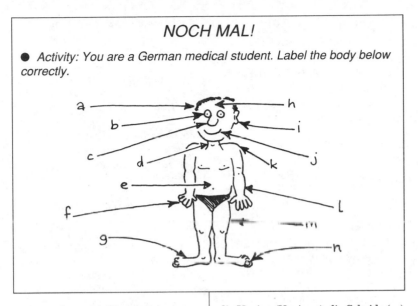

Innere Organe
Internal organs

die Blase (-n)   *bladder*
der Blinddarm (¨e)
                 appendix
der Darm (¨e)   *intestines*
die Gebärmutter (¨)
                 womb
das Gehirn (-e)   *brain*
das Geschlechtsorgan (-e)
                 sexual organ
das Herz (-en)   *heart*
die Herzklappe (-n)
                 valve
die Leber (-n)   *liver*
die Luftröhre (-n)   *windpipe*
die Lunge (-n)   *lung*
die Niere (-n)   *kidney*
der Penis (Penisse/Penes),
   das Glied (-er) *penis*

die Vagina (Vaginen), die Scheide (-n)
                 vagina
die Vorsteherdrüse (-n)
                 prostate gland

das Blut   *blood*
die Ader (-n)   *artery*
die Vene (-n)   *vein*
das Blutgefäß (-e) *blood vessel*
der Kreislauf (¨e) *circulation*
der Puls (-e)   *pulse*
der Herzschlag (¨e)
                 heartbeat

eine Grimasse machen/das Gesicht
   verziehen *to grimace / make a face*
grinsen   *to grin*
lachen   *to laugh*
lächeln   *to smile*
die Stirn runzeln *to frown*

atmen   *to breathe*
keuchen   *to pant*
schwitzen *to perspire, sweat*

10 Krankheit *Illness*

Gute Besserung!
Get well soon!

SCHWERE KRANKHEITEN UND UNWOHLSEIN
SERIOUS ILLNESSES AND INDISPOSITION

Aids; HIV-positiv/negativ
    AIDS; HIV positive / negative
die Anorexie   *anorexia*
die Arthritis   *arthritis*
das Asthma   *asthma*
die Blutung (-en),
  die Hämorrhagie   *haemorrage*
die Blutvergiftung (-en)
    blood poisoning
das Ekzem (-e)   *eczema*
der epileptische Anfall (¨e)
    epileptic fit
die Geschlechtskrankheit (-en)
    VD (venereal disease)
der graue Star   *cataract*
die Hämorrhoiden
    haemorrhoids
die Hepatitis   *hepatitis*
der Herzinfarkt (-e)
    fatal heart attack
der Krebs (-e)   *cancer*

die Leukämie, der Blutkrebs
    leukaemia
die Lungenentzündung (-en)
    pneumonia
das (Magen-) Geschwür (-e)
    (stomach) ulcer
der Nervenzusammenbruch (¨e)
    nervous breakdown
das(der) Rheuma (tismus)
    rheumatism
der Schlaganfall (¨e),
  der Gehirnschlag
    stroke
einen Schlaganfall erleiden
    to have a stroke
die Schüttellähmung (-en)
    Parkinson's disease
die Tb/Tbc   *TB (tuberculosis)*
die Tollwut   *rabies*
der Tumor (-e)   *tumour*
die Verbrennung (-en)
    burn
die Vergiftung (-en)
    poisoning
die Verkrampfung (-en),
  die Zuckung (-en)
    spasm
die Zuckerkrankheit, die Diabetes
    diabetes

Er ist an Krebs gestorben.   *He died of cancer.*
Er ist zuckerkrank.   *He's got diabetes.*

10 Krankheit *Illness*

LEICHTE KRANKHEITEN
MINOR ILLNESSES

die Allergie (-n) *allergy*
die Blase (-n)   *blister*
der hohe/niedrige Blutdruck
    high / low blood
    pressure
die Bronchitis   *bronchitis*
der Durchfall   *diarrhoea*
der blaue Fleck (-en), der Bluterguß
  (-güsse)   *bruise*
die Entzündung (-en)
    inflammation
der Hautausschlag (¨e)
    rash
der Heuschnupfen
    hay fever
die Infektion (-en),
  Entzündung (-en)
    infection
das Jucken, der Juckreiz (-e)
    itching
die Kreislaufstörung (-en)
    circulatory trouble

die Magenverstimmung (-en)
    indigestion
die Masern   *measles*
die Migräne   *migraine*
der Mücken-/Wespenstich (-e)
    mosquito bite / wasp
    sting
die Mumps   *mumps*
das Nasenbluten *nosebleed*
der Pickel (-n)   *spot*

die Reisekrankheit
    travel sickness
die Röteln   *German meales*
der Scharlach   *scarlet fever*
die Schnittwunde (-n)
    cut
der Schorf (-e)   *scab*
der Sonnenbrand (¨e)
    sunburn
die Verdauungsstörung (-en)
    indigestion

die Windpocken *chicken pox*

Sie hat das Bein in Gips.   *She has her leg in plaster.*

---

sich erbrechen *to be sick, vomit*
eine Krankheit bekommen
  to catch a disease,
      an illness
leiden   *to suffer*

ohnmächtig werden, in Ohnmacht
  fallen
    to faint
stöhnen, ächzen *to moan*

10 Der Körper *The body*

BEIM ARZT
AT THE DOCTOR'S

(For First Aid terms see *6: Jobs and Work Safety at work*, page 93.)

der Arzt (¨e)	*doctor, GP*
der Hausarzt (¨e)	*family doctor*
die Praxis (Praxen)	*surgery*
das Rezept (-e)	*prescription*
die Sprechstunde (-n)	*consultation hours*
das Stethoskop (-e)	*stethoscope*

Schmerzen	***aches and pains***
ansteckend	*contagious*
entzündet	*infected*
das Fieber	*fever*
fit/gesund	*fit / healthy*
geschwollen	*swollen*
die Gesundheit	*health*
die Infektionskrankheit (-en)	*disease*
krank	*ill*
die Krankheit (-en)	*illness, sickness*
niesen	*to sneeze*
der Schmerz (-en)	*pain, ache*

Ich hätte gern einen Termin.	*I'd like to make an appointment.*
Ich bin allergisch gegen . . .	*I'm allergic to . . .*
Meine Nase ist verstopft.	*I've got a stuffed-up nose.*
Mir tut alles weh.	*I'm aching all over.*
Ich fühle mich nicht wohl.	*I feel ill.*

Ich habe . . .	*I've got (a) . . .*
Bauchschmerzen	*stomach ache*
eine Erkältung (-en), einen Schnupfen	*a cold*
Fieber	*temperature*
Grippe	*flu*

Halsschmerzen	*sore throat*
Husten	*cough*
Kopfschmerzen	*a headache*
Nasenbluten	*a nosebleed*
Ohrenschmerzen	*earache*

Ich habe mich verbrannt.	*I've burnt myself.*
Können Sie mir bitte etwas verschreiben?	*Can you give me a prescription, please?*
Ich gebe Ihnen eine Spritze.	*I'll give you an injection.*
Ich glaube, ich habe mir . . .	*I think I've . . .*
das Handgelenk verstaucht/geprellt	*sprained my wrist*
den Arm gebrochen	*broken my arm*
Ich bin gestochen worden.	*I've been bitten.*

10 Der Körper *The body*

BEIM ZAHNARZT
AT THE DENTIST'S

die Zahnarztpraxis (-praxen)
    dental surgery
Zahnarzt/Zahnärztin
    dentist
Zahnarzthelferin (-nen)
    dental nurse

der Zahn ("e) *tooth*

der Abszeß (-e) *an abscess*
die dritten Zähne, das Gebiß
    (Gebisse) *false teeth, dentures*
die Füllung (-en), die Plombe (-n)
    filling
der Milchzahn ("e)
    milk tooth
der Weisheitszahn ("e)
    wisdom tooth

Ich habe Zahnschmerzen.   *I've got toothache.*
Ich habe einen Zahn verloren.   *I've lost a tooth.*

bohren   *to drill*
einen Zahn ziehen
    to pull out,
      extract a tooth
plombieren, füllen
    to fill

Beim Optiker
At the optician's

die Brille (-n) *glasses*
die Kontaktlinse (-n)
    contact lens

Ich trage eine Brille/Kontaktlinsen.   *I wear glasses / contact lenses.*
Ich bin kurzsichtig/weitsichtig.   *I'm short-sighted / long-sighted.*

Beim Frauenarzt
At the gynaecologist's

der Abstrich (-e) *smear test*
die Abtreibung (-en)
    abortion
die Menstruation, die Monatsblutung,
   die Periode *menstruation*
die Menstruationbeschwerden
    period pains
die Regel (-n) *period*
schwanger *pregnant*

der Schwangerschaftstest (-s)
    pregnancy test
die Wechseljahre (pl.)
    menopause

Empfängnisverhütung
contraception

die Anti-Baby-Pille (-n)
    contraceptive pill
das Pessar (-e) *pessary*
die Spirale (-n) *coil*
das Verhütungsmittel (-)
    contraceptive

Die Frauenärztin hat einen Abstrich
    gemacht.   *The doctor took a smear.*
Ich habe/bekomme meine Regel.   *I'm having/getting my period.*
Ich bin im fünften Monat schwanger. *I'm five months pregnant.*

Blutspenden   *giving blood*   der Blutspenderpaß (¨e)
Blutspender/in *blood donor*   *blood donor card*
die Blutgruppe (-n)
               blood group

NOCH MAL!

● *Activity: What's the matter? Diagnose these patients' complaints.*

10 Der Körper *The body*

BEHANDLUNG UND HEILMITTEL
TREATMENT AND REMEDIES

der Verbandkasten (¨) *first aid kit*
die Erste Hilfe *first aid*

das Heftpflaster (-) *sticking plaster*
das Pflaster (-) *plaster*
die Schere (-n) *scissors*

die Sicherheitsnadel (-n) *safety pin*
der Verband (¨e),
   die Mullbinde (-n) *bandage, dressing*

die künstliche Beatmung *artificial respiration*
die Wunde (-n) *wound*

Medikamente *Medicines*

das Abführmittel (-) *laxative*
das Antibiotikum (Antibiotika) *antibiotic*
die Antihistaminsalbe (-n) *anti-histamine cream*
die Brandsalbe (-n) *burn cream*
das Desinfektionsmittel (-) *antiseptic*
der Hustensaft (¨e) *cough medicine*
die Hormonbehandlung (-en) *HRT (Hormone Replacement Therapy)*
das Inhaliergerät (-e) *inhaler*
die Pastillen *lozenges*
das Thermometer (-) *thermometer*

das Zäpfchen (-) *suppository*

Tabletten *pills*
das Beruhigungsmittel (-) *tranquillisers*
die Kopfschmerztablette (-n)/
   die Aspirin *headache tablet / aspirin*
das Penizillin *penicillin*
die Schlaftabletten *sleeping pills*
das Schmerzmittel (-) *analgesic*

einreiben *to rub in*
nur äußerlich anwenden *for external use only*
schlucken *to swallow*

Heilmitteln *Other remedies*

die Akupressur (-en) *acupressure*
die Akupunktur (-en) *acupuncture*
ein altes Hausmittel (-) *an old-fashioned remedy*
die Aromatherapie (-n) *aromatherapy*
die Homöopathie *homeopathy*
die natürlichen Heilmittel *natural remedies*
Naturheilkundige (r) *herbalist*
die Therapie (-n) *therapy*

Diät *diet*
der Ballaststoff (-e) *dietary fibre*
Ernährungswissenschaftler/in *dietician*

abnehmen *to lose weight*
sich bewegen *to exercise*
zunehmen *to gain weight*

10 Der Körper *The body*

DAS KRANKENHAUS
HOSPITAL

die Klinik (-en) *clinic*
die Ambulanz *outpatients department*
der Krankenwagen (-) *ambulance*
Patient/in *patient*

Krankenhauspersonal *medical staff*
Arzt/ˉin *doctor*
Chefarzt/ˉin *senior consultant*
Oberarzt/ˉin *senior physician*
Facharzt/ˉin *consultant*
Krankenschwester (-n)/
Krankenpfleger (-) *nurse / male nurse*
Lernschwester (-n) *student nurse*
Oberschwester (-n) *matron*

Station ***ward (department)***
die (Trag)bahre (-n) *stretcher*
die Intensivstation (-en) *intensive care*
der Krankensaal (-säle) *open ward*
das Krankenzimmer (-) *private room*

Chirurgie *surgery*
Anästhesist/in *anaesthetist*
Chirurg/in *surgeon*
die Narkose (-n) *anaesthetic*
die Operation (-en) *operation*
der Sauerstoff *oxygen*

Notfälle *Emergencies*

die Notaufnahme (-n) *casualty (ward)*
der Schock (-e/-s) *shock*
der/die Verletzte (-n) *injured person*
der/die Verunglückte (-n) *casualty (a person)*
bewußtlos/ohnmächtig sein *to be unconscious*
bei Bewußtsein sein *to be conscious*
eingipsen *to plaster*
geröntgt werden *to have an X-ray*
impfen gegen *to vaccinate, inoculate against*
operieren *to operate*
sterilisieren *to sterilise*
heilen *to heal*
sich verbessern *to improve*
sich erholen *to recover*
die Genesung (-en) *convalescence, recuperation*

Sie unterzog sich einer Krebsoperation. *She was operated on for cancer.*
Sein Zustand hat sich verbessert. *His condition has improved.*

10 Der Körper *The body*

ALKOHOL, RAUCHEN UND DROGEN
ALCOHOL, SMOKING AND DRUGS

Alkoholiker/in *alcoholic*
die Alkoholvergiftung (-en)
    alcoholic poisoning
Abstinenzler/in *teetotaller*
betrunken sein *to be drunk*

Raucher/Nichtraucher
    smoker/non-smoker
die Zigarette (-n) *cigarette*
die Kippe (-n) (umg.)
    ciggy (sl.)

der Aschenbecher (-)
    ashtray
das Feuerzeug (-e) *lighter*
das Nikotin *nicotine*
die Pfeife (-n) *pipe*
die Streichhölzer *matches*
der Tabak   *tobacco*
die Zigarre (-n) *cigar*
der (Lungen)Krebs (lung) *cancer*
anzünden *to light a cigarette*
paffen *to puff*
rauchen *to smoke*
mit dem Rauchen aufhören, das
  Rauchen aufgeben
    to give up smoking

Er /Sie trinkt zu viel. *He / She drinks too much.*
Er/Sie hat zuviel getrunken. *He / She is over the limit.*
Er ist ein starker Raucher *He's a heavy smoker.*
Haben Sie Feuer? *Have you got a light?*

Rauschgift ***drugs***
das Cannabis *cannabis*
das Crack *crack*
Dealer/in, Rauschgifthändler/in
    dealer
der/die Drogenabhängige/r
    drug addict
harte/weiche Drogen
    hard / soft drugs
das Haschisch *hashish*
das Heroin *heroin*
das Kokain *cocaine*
das Marihuana *marijuana*
Pusher/in *pusher*

die Spritze (-n) *syringe*
Süchtige/r *addict*

Drogen nehmen *to be on drugs*
eine Entziehungskur machen
    to dry out
Entzugserscheinungen (pl.)
    withdrawal symptoms
kiffen *to smoke dope*
high sein *to be high*
sofortiger Totalentzug
    cold turkey cure
spritzen *to inject*

BANKEN UND FINANZEN *BANKING AND FINANCE*

Deutsche Bank

SPARKASSE

COMMERZBANK

Bank (-en)	*bank*
die Sparkasse (-n)	*savings bank*
Zweigstelle (-n), Filiale	*branch*
die Wechselstube (-n)	*bureau de change*
der Geldwechsel (-)	*foreign exchange*
die Transaktion (-en)	*transaction*
die Kasse (-n)	*cash desk*
Kassierer/in	*cashier, teller*
die Öffnungszeiten	*opening hours*
der Schalter (-)	*counter*
die Auslandsanweisung (-en)	*international money order*
das Bargeld (-er)	*change*
der Betrag (¨e)	*sum*
die Bezahlung (-en), Zahlung (-en)	*payment*
das Geld (-er)	*money*
der Geldautomat (-en)	*cash machine*
die Münze (-n)	*coins*
das Pfund	*pound*
der Schein (-e)	*note*
die Währung (-en), Devisen (-)	*foreign currency*
der Wechselkurs (-e)	*exchange rates*
die Zinsen (pl.)	*interest*
zinsfrei	*interest-free*
der Zinssatz (¨e)	*interest rate*

das Darlehen (-)	*loan*
die Hypothek (-en)	*mortgage*
der Überziehungskredit (-e)	*overdraft facility*
die Bankgebühr (-en)	*bank charge*
das Konto (-s)	*bank account*
der Kontoauszug (¨e)	*statement*
der Kontostand (¨e)	*balance*
das laufendes Konto	*current account*
die Kreditkarte (-n)	*credit card*
die PIN Nummer (-n),	
die Geheimnummer (-n)	*PIN number*
Soll und Haben	*debit and credit*
das Sparbuch (¨er)	*savings book*
das Sparkonto (-s)	*deposit, savings account*
die Überweisung (-en)	*transfer*
die Unterschrift (-en)	*signature*

der Scheck (-s) *cheque*
der Reisescheck (-s)
    traveller's cheque
das Scheckheft (-e) *cheque book*
die Scheckkarte (-n)
    cheque card
der Verrechnungscheck (-s)
    crossed cheque

belasten	*to debit*
einzahlen	*to deposit, to pay in*
fälschen	*to forge*
Geld auf dem Konto haben	
	to be in credit
gutschreiben	*to credit*

in den roten Zahlen sein	
	in the red
leihen	*to borrow*
einen Scheck einlösen	
	to cash a cheque
schulden	*to owe*
sich ausweisen	*to identify oneself*
sparen	*to save*
überweisen	*to transfer*
überziehen	*to overdraw*
wechseln	*to change*
(ver)leihen	*to lend*
ein Darlehen	
zurückzahlen	*to pay off a loan*

Können Sie mir bitte meinen Kontostand geben?	*How much have I got in my account?*
Ich möchte . . . abheben	*I'd like to withdraw . . .*

Geldwechsel *Changing money*

Ich möchte einen Euroscheck/ Reisescheck einlösen.	*I would like to cash a eurocheque / traveller's cheque.*

11 **Institutionen** *Institutions*

Ich möchte Geld wechseln.	*I would like to change some money.*
Ich möchte . . . Pfund in DM wechseln.	*I'd like to change . . . pounds into marks.*
Wie ist heute der Wechselkurs?	*What is today's exchange rate?*
Wieviel Mark bekomme ich für . . . ?	*How many marks do I get for . . . ?*
Darf ich Ihren Paß/Ausweis sehen?	*May I see your passport / identity card?*

Deutscher Aktienindex auf Rekordniveau

die Börse (-n) *Stock exchange*

Aktionär/in	*shareholder*
Börsenmakler/in	*stockbroker*
Kapitalanleger/in	*investor*
die Aktie (-n),	*share*
der Aktienindex (-e)	*share index*
der DAX	*German share index*
der Gewinn (-e)	*profit*
die Inflation (-en)	*inflation*
die Investition (-en)	*investment*
das Kapital	*capital*
der Prozentsatz (¨e)	*percentage*
der Vermögenswert (-e)	*asset*
der Wert (-e)	*value*
die Wertpapiere	*stocks and shares, securities*

die Steuer (-n) *tax*

die Einkommensteuer (-n)	*income tax*
die Mehrwertsteuer (-n), Mwst., die Umsatzsteuer (-n)	*VAT*
Steuerberater/in	*tax consultant*
Steuererklärung (-en)	*tax return*
steuerfrei	*tax free*
Steuerhinterziehung	*tax evasion*
die Steuerkarte (-n)	*tax payment record*
die Steuerrückvergütung (-en)	*tax rebate*
ausgeben	*to spend*
bezahlen	*to pay*
gewinnen	*to gain*
im Wert steigen	*to increase in worth, value*

11 **Institutionen** *Institutions*

investieren, anlegen
    to invest
kosten   *to cost*
spekulieren   *to speculate*
Steuern zahlen *to pay tax*
verkaufen   *to sell*
verlieren   *to lose*
Es ist ... wert. *It's worth ...*

die Währung (-en)
    currency
der australische Dollar
    Australian dollar
die dänische Krone
    Danish krone
die Deutsche Mark
    German mark
die Drachme *drachma*
der Escudo *Portuguese escudo*
die Finnmark *Finnmark, markka*

der französische/belgischer Franc
    French / Belgian franc
der holländische Gulden
    Netherlands guilder
die italienische Lira
    Italian lira
die norwegische Krone
    Norwegian krone
die Peseta *Spanish peseta*
das Pfund Sterling *pound sterling*
der Rubel *rouble*
die Schilling (Österreich)
    schilling (Austria)
die schwedische Krone
    Swedish krona
die schweizer Franken
    Swiss franc
der US-Dollar *US dollar*
der Yen *yen*
der Zloty (Polen) *zloty*

KIRCHE UND RELIGION
CHURCH AND RELIGION

Ich bin ... *I am a / an ...*
Agnostiker/in *agnostic*
Ich gehöre zur Christlichen
  Wissenschaft *Christian Scientist*
Atheist/in *atheist*
Baptist/in *Baptist*
Buddhist/in *Buddhist*
Christ/in *Christian*
Hindu/istin *Hindu*
Jude/Jüdin *Jew*
Katholik/in *Roman Catholic*
Mormone/
  Mormonin *Mormon*
Moslem/Moslime *Muslim*
Protestant/in ⎫
Evangelische/r ⎰ *Protestant*

Quäker/in *Quaker*
Zeuge/Zeugin Jehovas
    Jehovah's witness

der Apostel (-) *apostle*
Christus *Christ*
Gott *God*
Heilige/r *saint*
Heiliger Geist *Holy Ghost*
Herr *Lord*
Jesus *Jesus*
Jünger/in, Anhänger/in
    disciple
Jungfrau Maria *Virgin Mary*

der Bischof (¨e) *bishop*
der Erzbischof (¨e)
    archbishop
der Papst (¨e) *pope*

11 Institutionen *Institutions*

die Gemeinde (-n) *parish*
das Gemeindemitglied (-er)
    parishioner
die Pfarrkirche (-n)
    parish church
der Kaplan, (¨e) *curate, chaplain*
der Meßdiener/in *server, acolyte*
der Pastor (in) *vicar*
der Pfarrer/in *parish priest*
der Priester (-) *priest*
die Seelsorge *spiritual welfare*

der Gottesdienst (-e)
    service
die Beichte (-n) *confession*
die Bibel (-n) *bible*
der Chor (¨e) *choir*
die Firmung (-en)
    confirmation (Catholic)
die Konfirmation (-en)
    confirmation (Protestant)
das Gebet (-e) *prayer*
das Gesangbuch (¨er)
    hymn book
Heilige
    Dreieinigkeit *Holy Trinity*
das Kirchenlied (-er)
    hymn
die Kommunion, das Abendmahl
    Communion
die Messe (-n) *Mass*
die Predigt (-en) *sermon*
der Segen (-) *blessing*
das Vaterunser *The Lord's Prayer*

die Kirche (-n) *Church*
die Kapelle (-n) *chapel*
die Kathedrale (-n),
    der Dom (-e) *cathedral*
das Münster (-) *minster*
die Moschee (-n) *mosque*
die Synagoge (-n) *synagogue*
der Tempel (-) *temple*

der Altar (-e) *altar*
die Glasmalerei (-n)
    stained glass
die Glocke (-n) *bell*
die Kerze (-n) *candle*
die Kirchenbank (¨e)
    pew
der Kirchturm (¨e) *steeple*
das Kreuz (-e) *cross*
die Krypta (Krypten)
    crypt
der Mittelgang (¨e)
    aisle
die Säule (-n) *pillar*

das Kloster(¨) *monastery*
der Abt (¨e) *Abbot*
ehrwürdiger Vater
    Reverend Father
das Nonnenkloster (¨)
    convent
der Kreuzgang (¨e)
    cloister
Mönch (-e) *monk*
Mutter Oberin *Mother Superior*
ehrwürdige Mutter
    Reverend Mother
Nonne (-n) *nun*

der Engel (-) *angel*
der Glaube *faith, belief*
das Gute/das Böse
    good / evil
heilig *holy*
der Himmel (-) /die Hölle
    heaven / hell
ökumenisch *ecumenical*
die Seele (-n) *soul*
der Teufel (-) *devil*
die Sekte (-n) *sect*

anbeten *to worship*
beichten *to confess*

11 **Institutionen** *Institutions*

beten	*to pray*	segnen	*to bless*
glauben/nicht glauben		singen	*to sing, to chant*
	to believe / not believe	sündigen	*to sin*
predigen	*to preach*	verzeihen	*to forgive*

Lasset uns beten
im Namen des Vaters, des Sohnes
  und des Heiligen Geistes.
Lobet den Herrn

*Let us pray
in the name of the Father, the Son
  and the Holy Ghost.
Praise the Lord!*

AUSBILDUNG
EDUCATION

(For punctuation vocabulary see *Arts
and Media – Writing and
punctuation*, page 113.)

die Schule (-n) *School*

die Gesamtschule (-n)
  comprehensive school
die Grundschule (-n)
  primary school
das Gymnasium (Gymnasien)
  grammar school
das Internat (-e) *boarding school*
der Kindergarten (-),
  die Vorschule (-n)
  nursery school

die Orientierungsstufe (-n)
  middle school
die weiterführende Schule (-n)
  secondary school
die Privatschule (-n)
  *private school,
    public school*
die private
  Vorbereitungsschule (-n)
  prep school
die staatliche Schule (-n)
  state school

Erstkläßler/in *new first-year pupil*
Hausmeister/in *caretaker*
Klassenlehrer/in *form teacher*
Klassensprecher/in
  class representative
Lehrer/in *teacher*
Schüler/in *pupil*
Schulleiter/in *headmaster / mistress*
stellvertretende(r) Schulleiter/in
  deputy head
Schulsekretärin (-nen)
  school secretary
Student/in *student*

die Aula (Aulen) *assembly hall*
das Labor (-e) *laboratory*
das Lehrerzimmer (-)
  staff room

147

11 Institutionen *Institutions*

die Pause (-n)   *break*
der Schulhof (¨e) *schoolyard, playground*
das Sekretariat (-e) *office*
die Turnhalle (-e) *gymnasium*

Hitzefrei *holiday because of hot weather*
die Klasse (-n)   *class, year*
die Oberstufe(-n) *upper school*
die Schulferien *school holidays*
das Schuljahr (-e) *school year*

die Schultüte (-n) *big cardboard cone filled with sweets for a child's first day at school.*
das Semester (-) *term*
die Stunde (-n)   *lesson*
der Stundenplan (¨e) *timetable*
die Uniform (-) *uniform*
die Unterstufe (-n) *lower school*
die Versammlung der Schüler/innen *assembly*

Ich bin in der 10. Klasse.   *I'm in year 10.*

---

der Klassenraum (¨e) *classroom*
die Aktentasche (-n) *briefcase*
das Buch (¨er) *book*
die Entschuldigung (-en) *(excuse) note*
das Federmäppchen (-) *pencil case*
der Füller (-) *fountain pen*
das Heft (-e) *exercise book*
das Klassenbuch (¨er) *register*
die Kreide (-n) *chalk*
der Kuli (-s) *biro*
das Lineal (-e) *ruler*
der Overheadprojektor (-en) *overhead projector*
die Schultasche (-n) *school bag*
die Tafel (-n) *blackboard*

das Fach (¨er) *subject*
das Pflichtfach (¨er) *compulsory subject*

das Wahlfach (¨er) *optional subject*
Biologie *Biology*
Chemie *Chemistry*
Deutsch *German*
Englisch *English*
Erdkunde *Geography*
Französisch *French*
Gemeinschaftskunde *General Studies*
Geschichte *History*
Informatik *Computer Studies*
Informationstechnik *Information technology*
Kunst *Art*
Latein *Latin*
Mathematik *Maths*
Musik *Music*
Naturwissenschaft *Science*
Physik *Physics*
Religion *R.E.*
Spanisch *Spanish*
Sport *Games*

11 **Institutionen** *Institutions*

Theater spielen *Drama*
Umweltkunde *Environmental studies*

die Aufgabe (-n) *task*
der Aufsatz (¨e) *essay*
das Diktat (-e) *dictation*
die Hausaufgabe (-n) *homework*
das Projekt (-e) *project*
das Lesen *reading*
die Rechtschreibung *spelling*
die Übersetzung (-en) *translation*
die Übung (-en) *exercise*
das Schreiben *writing*

die Prüfung (-en) *examination*
die Allgemeine Hochschulreife, das Abitur
(roughly equivalent to A-level)
die Mittlere Reife *(roughly equivalent to GCSE higher level, 'O'level)*
der Hauptschulabschluß *(roughly equivalent to GCSE basic level, CSE)*

die Abschlußprüfung (-en) *final exams*
die Antwort (-en) *answer*
der Prüfling (-e) *candidate*
die Frage (-n) *question*
die Klassenarbeit (-en) *test*
die mündliche Prüfung (-en) *oral examination*
die schriftliche Prüfung (-en) *written examination*

der Spickzettel (-) *crib*
das Zeugnis (-se) *report, certificate*

die Note (-n) *mark, grade*
sehr gut *excellent*
gut *good*
befriedigend *satisfactory*
ausreichend *adequate*
mangelhaft *poor (fail)*
ungenügend *unsatisfactory (fail)*

abhaken *to tick*
besuchen *to attend*
fehlen *to be absent*
gut/schlecht sein in . . . *to be good / bad at . . .*
lernen *to learn*
mogeln, schummeln *to cheat*
schwenzen, abklemmen (umg.) *to play truant*
sitzenbleiben *to stay down (a year)*
spicken (umg.) *to copy, to crib (inf.)*
wiederholen *to revise, to repeat a year*

eine Prüfung ablegen *to sit an exam*

eine Prüfung bestehen *to pass an exam*
eine Prüfung nicht bestehen, durchfallen *to fail an exam*
nachschreiben *to re-sit an exam*

die Universität (-en)
University

die Fachhochschule (-n) *college*
das Institut (-e) *institute*

11 Institutionen *Institutions*

die Musikhochschule (-n)
    school of music
die Pädagogische Hochschule (-n)
    teacher training
    college

das Seminar (-e) *department, seminar*
die technische Fachhochschule (-n)
    technical college

Ich besuche die ... Schule.
Ich bin gut in Mathe.
Ich habe am Queen's College in
    Oxford studiert.

I attend ... school.
I'm good at maths.

I studied at Queen's College in Oxford.

der Bakkalaureus (-rei) der
    Geisteswissenschaften
    BA
der Bakkalaureus (-rei) der
    Naturwissenschaften
    BSc
die Doktorwürde (-n),
    der Doktortitel (-)
    doctorate
der erste akademische Grad (-e)
    first degree
der höhere akademische Grad (-e)
    higher degree
der Magister (-) *MA*

der Erstsemestler *fresher*
Student/in   *undergraduate*
Student/in mit Hochschulabschluß
    graduate
Professor/in   *professor*

BaföG   *grant*
Dozent/in   *lecturer*
die Forschung (-en)
    research
der Lehrstuhl (¨e) *chair*
das Studium (Studien)
    studies
die Vorlesung (-en)
    lecture

Sie ist Dozentin für ...

She is a ... lecturer.

Studienfächer *university subjects*
Altphilologie *classics*
Anglistik und Amerikanistik
    English and American studies
Archäologie *archeology*
Betriebswirtschaft *MBA* (Masters
    in Business Administration)
Elektronik *electronics*

Elektrotechnik *electrical engineering*
Geisteswissenschaft (-en)
    humanities
Informatik *computer science*
Jura *law*
Maschinenbau *mechanical*
    engineering
Medizin *medicine*

11 Institutionen *Institutions*

Naturwissenschaft (-en) *sciences*
Neuphilologie *modern languages*
Philosophie *philosophy*
Psychiatrie *psychiatry*
Psychologie *psychology*
Romanistik *Romance languages*
Soziologie *sociology*
Technik *engineering*
Volkswirtschaft *economics*

Forschungsarbeiten durchführen
to carry out research

promovieren *to do a doctorate*
sich spezialisieren auf
to specialize in
studieren *to study, to go to university*
unterrichten *to teach*
eine Vorlesung halten
to give a lecture
. . . als Hauptfach studieren
to major in . . .

Sie hat an der Uni in . . . promoviert. *She did her doctorate at . . . University.*

GESETZ UND ORDNUNG
LAW AND ORDER

Kriminalität und die Polizei
Crime and the police

Kriminelle/r, Verbrecher/in
criminal
Agent/in *agent*
die Bande (-n) *gang*
Dieb/in *thief*
Gauner/in *crook*
die Geisel (-n) *hostage*
Komplize/Komplizin, Mittäter/in
accomplice
Mörder/in *murderer*
der Rowdy (-s), der Krawallmacher (-)
hooligan, yob
Spion/in *spy*
Spitzel (umg.) *informer, nark*
Straftäter/in *offender*
Taschendieb/in *pickpocket*
Terrorist/in *terrorist*
der V-Mann (¨er) *contact*

Wilderer/Wilderin
poacher

das Verbrechen (-), die Straftat (-en)
crime
der Betrug *fraud*
die Brandstiftung (-en)
arson
der Einbruch (¨e) *break-in*
die Entführung (-en)/die Geiselnahme (-n)
kidnapping
die Erpressung (-en)
blackmail
die Fälschung (-en)
forgery
die Flugzeugentführung (-en)
(plane) hi-jacking
die grobe Körperverletzung
grievous bodily harm
der Kampf (¨e),
die Auseinandersetzung (-en)
fight
die Körperverletzung (-en)
assault and battery

11 Institutionen *Institutions*

der Krawall (-e)/der Aufstand (¨e)
    riot
der Ladendiebstahl (¨e)
    shop-lifting
der (versuchte) Mord (-e)
    (attempted) murder
der Raubüberfall (¨e)
    robbery
der sexuelle Mißbrauch (¨e)
    sexual abuse
die Steuerhinterziehung (-en)
    tax evasion
der Straßenraub/der Raubüberfall (¨e)
    mugging
der Totschlag   *manslaughter*
der Überfall (¨e) *hold-up*
der Vandalismus *vandalism*
die Vergewaltigung (-en)/die Notzucht
    rape
das Bestechungsgeld (-er)
    bribe
die Blüte (-n) (umg.)
    forged note
die Gewalt   *violence*
das Gift (-e)   *poison*
das Lösegeld (-er) *ransom*
die Waffe (-n)   *weapon*

angreifen   *to attack*
drohen   *to threaten*
einbrechen   *to burgle*
entführen, kidnappen
    to kidnap
ermorden   *to murder*
erpressen   *to blackmail*
erschießen   *to shoot*
niederstechen   *to stab*
rauben   *to rob*
spionieren   *to spy*
stehlen   *to steal*
eine Straftat begehen
    to commit an offence

töten, umbringen *to kill*
überfallen   *to hold up*
vergewaltigen   *to rape*

Polizist/in   ***policeman/woman***
die Bereitschaftspolizei
    riot police
das Betrugsdezernat (¨e)
    fraud squad
der Bulle (umg.), die Bullen (umg.)
    cop, the fuzz
die Handschelle (-n)
    handcuff
die Kriminalpolizei,
  die Kripo (umg.)
    CID
Polizeibeamte/beamtin
    police officer
der Polizeiwagen (-)/der Streifenwagen (-)
    police, patrol car
der Privatdetektiv (-e)
    private investigator
die Razzia (Razzien)
    (police) raid
der Sicherheitsdienst (-e)
    Special Branch
die Sittenpolizei, die Sitte (umg.)
    vice squad
Streifenpolizist/in
    officer on the beat
die Trachtengruppe (umg.)
    boys in blue (coll.)
Verdächtige/r   *suspect*
die Verkehrspolizei
    traffic police
die Wache (-n) *police station*
die Zivilpolizei *plain-clothes police*

durchsuchen   *to search*
verhaften   *to arrest*
verhören   *to question, interrogate*

11 Institutionen *Institutions*

Im Gerichtssaal *In court*

Angeklagte/r	*defendant*
Gefangene/r	*prisoner*
das Schöffengericht (-e)	
	jury
Rechtsanwalt, Rechtsanwältin	
	lawyer, solicitor,
	barrister
Richter/in	*judge*
Zeuge, Zeugin	*witness*

die Anklage (-n) *charge*
die Berufung (-en) *appeal*
die Beschwerde (-n)
    complaint
das Beweismaterial
    evidence
die Bürgschaft (-en), die Kaution (-en)
    bail
das Geständnis (-se)
    confession
der Fall (¨e), der Rechtsstreit (-e)
    case
die Freisprechung (-en)
    acquittal
das Gefängnis (-se),
   die Strafvollzugsanstalt (-en)
    prison
der Gerichtssaal (-säle)
    law court

der Prozeß (-sse),
   das Gerichtsverfahren (-)
    trial
der Schadensersatz
    damages
die Schuld   *guilt*
das Urteil (-e) *verdict*
die Verteidigung (-en)
    defence
die Zelle (-n) *cell*

das Zivilrecht *civil law*
Friedensrichter/in
    Justice of the Peace,
    magistrate
vorläufiges/endgültiges
   Scheidungsurteil
    decree nisi / absolute
der Unterhalt *maintenance*

anklagen	*to charge*
bezeugen	*to testify*
entlassen	*to release*

ins Gefängnis gehen
    to go to jail
ein Geständnis ablegen
    to make a confession
leugnen   *to deny*
sich schuldig/nicht schuldig bekennen
    to plead guilty / not
    guilty
unschuldig sein *to be innocent*
verklagen *to sue*
zugeben   *to confess*

---

jdn. verurteilen
Seine Strafe wurde zur Bewährung
   ausgesetzt.
Der Richter verurteilte ihn zu
   3 Jahren Haft.

to sentence

He was given a suspended sentence.
The judge sentenced him to
   3 years' imprisonment.

11 Institutionen *Institutions*

Er wurde zu lebenslänglichem
  Freiheitsentzug verurteilt.
Er wurde für schuldig befunden.
Er wurde zu einer Geldstrafe von
  DM 300,- verurteilt.
Er ist Geschworener.

He was sentenced to life imprisonment.
He was found guilty.

He was fined DM 300.
He is sitting on the jury.

DAS MILITÄR
THE MILITARY

die Streitkräfte **armed forces**
Freiwillige/r   *volunteer*
der Kriegsdienstverweigerer (-)
            conscientious objector
Militärgericht (-e) *court martial*
der Wehrdienst *military service*

der Krieg (-e) *War*

der Angriff (-e) *attack*
der Befehl (-e) *order, command*
die Blockade (-n) *blockade*
der Coup (-s)   *coup*
die Feuerpause (-n)
            ceasefire
der Flüchtling (-e) *refugee*
die Gefahr (-en) *threat*
der Guerilla (-s) *guerrilla*
die Invasion (-en) *invasion*
die Kapitulation (-en)
            surrender
Kriegsgefangene/r
            prisoner of war
Mannschaftstransportwagen
  /-transportflugzeug
            personnel carrier
militärisch   *military (adj.)*
das Opfer (-)   *victim*
der Rückzug (¨e) *withdrawal, retreat*

der Luftschutzkeller (-)
            air raid shelter
die Schlacht (-en) *battle*
die Sondereinheit (-en),
  die Spezialeinheit (-en)
            taskforce
die Überwachung (-en)
            surveillance

den Krieg erklären (gegen)
            to declare war (on)
den Krieg gewinnen/verlieren
            to win / lose the war

die Armee (-n) *Army*

der Feldmarschall (¨e)
            field marshall
der General (¨e) *general*
der Hauptmann (¨er)
            captain
die Kompanie (-n)
            company

154

11 **Institutionen** *Institutions*

die Mannschaft (-en)
    enlisted men
der Oberst   *colonel*
der Offizier (-e) *officer*
der Rekrut (-en) *recruit*
der Soldat (-en) *soldier*
die Truppe (-n) *troop*
der Unteroffizier (-e) *NCO*
    (non-commissioned officer)
die Wache (-n) *sentry*
der Zeitsoldat (-en)
    regular soldier

die Artillerie   *artillery*
das Biwak (e),
  das Lager (-) *camp*
das Exerzieren *drill*
das Hauptquartier (-e)
    HQ
die Infantrie   *infantry*
die Kaserne (-n) *barracks*
die Patrouille (-n) *patrol*
der Verwundete (-n)
    casualty

die Marine *Navy*

der Admiral (¨e) *admiral*
der Kapitän (-e) *captain*
der Matrose (-n) *sailor*
der Navigationsoffizier (-e)
    navigator
der Schiffsingenieur (-e)
    chief engineer

die Besatzung (-en)
    crew
die Flotte (-n) *fleet*
der Flugzeugträger (-)
    aircraft carrier
die Fregatte (-n) *frigate*
das Geschwader (-)
    squadron

der Kreuzer (-) *cruiser*
das Kriegsschiff (-e)
    battleship
das U-Boot (-e) *submarine*
die Wache (-n) *watch*

die Luftwaffe *Air force*

der Brigadegeneral (¨e)
    Air Commodore
der General (¨e) *Air Chief Marshal*
der Jagdflieger (-) *fighter pilot*
der Kapitän(-e) *captain*
Luftwaffenpilot/in
    air force pilot

der Bomber (-s) *bomber*
der Düsenjäger (-) *jet fighter*
der Hubschrauber (-)
    helicopter
das Jagdflugzeug (e)
    fighter plane

der Flugplatz (¨e) *air field*
die Luftbrücke (-n)
    air lift
der Luftwaffenstützpunkt (-e)
    air base
der Navigator (-en)
    navigator
das Radar (-s) *radar*
die Staffel (-n) *squadron*
die Wartung (-en) *maintenance*

die Waffen *Weapons*

die Atomwaffe(-n) *nuclear weapon*
die Bombe (-n) *bomb*
das ferngelenkte Geschoß
  (Geschosse) /die Lenkwaffe (-n)
    guided missile

11 **Institutionen** *Institutions*

die Feuerwaffe (-n)
gun
das Gewehr (-e) *rifle*
die Granate (-n) *shell*
die Handgranate (-n)
hand grenade
die Kugel (-n) *bullet*
das Maschinengewehr (-e)
machine gun
die (Land)Mine (-n)
(land) mine
die Munition *ammunition*
der Panzer (-) *tank*
die Rakete (-n) *rocket*
der Revolver (-) *revolver*
der Torpedo(-s) *torpedo*
das Ziel (-e) *target*
(er)schießen *to shoot*
besetzen *to occupy*
besiegen *to defeat*
Bomben abwerfen
to bomb
desertieren *to desert*
eine Stadt einnehmen
to take a town
einmarschieren *to invade*
explodieren *to explode*
fliegen *to fly*
kämpfen *to fight*
kapitulieren, sich ergeben
to surrender
das Kommando führen
to be in command
stürmen *to storm*
überleben *to survive*
verteidigen *to defend*
zurückziehen *to retreat,*
to withdraw

auf Wache sein *to be on sentry duty*
Wehrdienst ableisten
to do military service

der Frieden *Peace*

die (atomare) Abrüstung (-en)
(nuclear)
disarmament
Alliierte, Verbündete
allies
das Abkommen (-)
agreement
die Friedensverhandlungen
peace talks
einen Friedensvertrag unterzeichnen
to sign a peace treaty
das Gipfeltreffen (-)
summit meeting
neutral *neutral*
der Pakt (-e) *pact*
die Sanktion (-en) *sanctions*
UN Soldaten, Blauhelme
United Nations forces

POLITIK UND REGIERUNG
*POLITICS AND
GOVERNMENT*

die Wahl (-en) *Election*

Anhänger/in *supporter*
Kandidat/in *candidate*
die Koalition (-en) *coalition*
die Nominierung (-en), die Ernennung (-en)
nomination
die Parlamentswahl (-en),
die Bundestagswahl (-en)
general election
der Wahlkampf (¨e)
election campaign
der Wahlkreis (-e) *constituency*
der Wähler (-) *voter, electorate*

11 **Institutionen** *Institutions*

die (politische)
    Partei (-n) *(political) party*
die Fraktion (-en) *parliamentary party*
linker/rechter Flügel (-)
    left / right wing

Bündnis 90/Die Grünen
    Green party
Christlich Demokratische
  Union (CDU) *Conservative party*
Christlich Soziale Union in
  Bayern (CSU)
    Conservative party
    in Bavaria
Freie Demokratische Partei (FDP)
    Liberal party
Republikaner, REP
    Republicans
Sozialdemokratische Partei, SPD
    Social Democratic
    party

die Christdemokraten
    Christian Democrats
die Grünen   *Greens*
die Konservativen *Conservatives*
die Liberalen   *Liberals*
die Sozialdemokraten
    Social Democrats

Kapitalist/in   *capitalist*
Kommunist/in   *communist*
Nationalist/in   *nationalist*
Sozialist/in   *socialist*

die Bundesregierung
Federal Government

das Parlament (-e)
    parliament
die Regierung (-en)
    government

die Bundesregierung (-en)
    National / federal
    government
die Landesregierung (-en)
    State government
die Bezirksregierung (-en)
    regional
    administration
der Bundestag *government, lower*
    house
der Bundesrat *upper house*
das Oberhaus *House of Lords*
    (in Britain)
das Unterhaus *House of Commons*
    (in Britain)

Abgeordnete/r *member of parliament*
der Bundeskanzler
    (Federal) Chancellor
das Kabinett (-e) *cabinet*
die Opposition (-en)
    opposition
Parteivorsitzende/r
    party leader
Politiker/in   *politician*
Premierminister/in
    prime minister

die Politik, politische Linie
    politics, policy
die Debatte (-n) *debate*
die Demokratie *democracy*
das Gesetz (-e) *law, Act*
    of Parliament
das Grundgesetz (-e)
    (German) constitution
der Haushalt (-e) *budget*
der Parteitag (-e) *party conference*
die Staatsangelegenheiten (pl.)
    affairs of state

11 **Institutionen** *Institutions*

einen Minister vereidigen
to swear in a minister

... Minister | *Secretary of State for ..., Minister of State for ...*
Arbeits- | *Employment*
Außen- | *Foreign affairs*
Bau- | *Building*
Familien- | *Health and Social Security*
Finanz- | *Chancellor of the Exchequer*
Forschungs- | *Research and development*
Gesundheits- | *Social Services*
Innen- | *Home Department*
Justiz- | *Justice*
Kultus- | *Education and Science*
Landwirtschafts- | *Agriculture, (Fisheries and Food)*
Post- | *Postmaster General*
Umwelt- | *Environment*
Verkehrs- | *Transport*
Verteidigungs- | *Defence*
Wirtschafts- | *Industry*

das Ministerium (Ministerien)
ministry
das Auswärtiges Amt , AA
Foreign Office
der Bundesgerichtshof
Federal Supreme Court
das Bundeskriminalamt/BKA
Federal Criminal Police Office

der Bundesnachrichtendienst
Federal Intelligence Service
der Bundesrechnungshof
Federal Audit office

(Bundes-)Präsident/in
(Federal) President
die Botschaft (-en)
embassy
Botschafter/in | *ambassador*
Diplomat/in | *diplomat*
Konsul/in | *consul*
das Staatsoberhaupt ("er)
head of state

abstimmen | *to take a vote*
einen Antrag einbringen
to propose a motion
debattieren | *to debate*
regieren | *to govern*
eine Rede halten | *to give a speech*
tagen | *to sit*
einen Vorschlag machen
to make a proposal
Wahlwerbung machen
to canvass
wählen | *to vote, elect*
zurücktreten | *to resign*

die Stadtverwaltung (-en)
Local government

Abgeordnete/r | *elected representative*
Bürgermeister/in | *mayor, mayoress*

11 Institutionen *Institutions*

Finanzbeamter/-beamtin
 financial officer
die Gemeinde (-n), Kommune (-n)
 community
die Gemeindesteuern,
 die Kommunalsteuern *rates*
das Rathaus (¨er) *town hall*
der Stadtrat (¨e) *town council*

Städtische Dienststellen,
 Ortsverwaltung
  local government offices
das Amt für öffentliche
 Ordnung/die Polizeibehörde
  law and order

das Amt für Sozialversicherung
 social security
das Amtsgericht (-e)
 county court
das Arbeitsamt (¨er)
 employment office
das Finanzamt (¨er)
 tax office
das Notariat (-e) *notary's office*
das Schulamt (¨er)
 education department

12 die Stadt und Einkaufen *Town and shopping*

die Stadt (¨e) *town*
das Dorf (¨er) *village*
die Stadt, die Großstadt (¨e)
    city
die Industriestadt (¨e)
    industrial town
die Hafenstadt (¨e)
    port, harbour town
die Hauptstadt (¨e)
    capital city
die historische Stadt (¨e)
    historical town
die Kleinstadt (¨e) *small town*
das Kuhdorf (¨e), Kuhkaff (¨er) (umg.)
    backwater, one-horse town

die Trabantenstadt (¨e)
    satellite town
die Universitätsstadt (¨e)
    university town
Frank wohnt j.w.d.
    Frank lives at the
    back of beyond.
der Stadtkern (-e)
    town centre
der Stadtteil (-e),
  das Stadtviertel (-)
    district
der Vorort (-e) *suburb*

DAS STADTZENTRUM, DIE STADTMITTE
THE TOWN CENTRE

der Bahnhof (¨e) *station*
die Bank (-en) *bank*
die Bar (-s) *bar*
die Bibliothek (-en), die Bücherei (-en)
    library
der botanischer Garten (¨)
    botanical gardens
das Büro (-s) *office*
der Busbahnhof (¨e)
    bus station
der Dom (-e) *cathedral*
die Einkaufspassage (-n)
    shopping arcade
die Feuerwehr (-en), Feuerwache (-n)
    fire station
der Friedhof (¨e) *cemetery*
der Friseur (-e) *hairdresser's*
das Fußballstadion (-stadien)
    football stadium
die Galerie (-n) *art gallery*
das Hotel (-s) *hotel*

die Imbißbude (-n)
    snack stand
die Imbißstube (-n)
    snack bar
das Kino (-s) *cinema*
die Kläranlage (-n)
    sewage works
der Markt (¨e) *market*
die Markthalle (-n)
    market hall
der Marktplatz (¨e)
    market place
das Münster (-) *minster*
das Museum (Museen)
    museum
der Park (-s) *park*
das Parkhaus (¨er) *multi-storey car park*
der Parkplatz (¨e) *car park*
das Planetarium (-)
    planetarium
die Polizeiwache (-n)
    police station
die Post *post office*
das Rathaus (¨er) *town hall*
das Restaurant (-s)
    restaurant

12 die Stadt und Einkaufen *Town and shopping*

das Rotlichtviertel (-), der Kiez (-e)
  red-light district
das Schloß (Schlösser)
  castle
die Schule (-n) *school*
das Schwimmbad ("er)
  swimming pool
der Sportplatz ("e) *sports ground*
die Stadthalle (-n) *concert hall*
die Stadtverwaltung (-en)
  council offices
die Stadtwerke *Gas and Electricity
  Board*
das Sportzentrum (-zentren)
  leisure centre

das Stehcafe (-s) *self-service café
  (standing only)*
der Tante Emma
  Laden (") *corner shop*
das Theater (-) *theatre*
der U-Bahnhof ("e)
  *underground railway
  station*
das Verkehrsamt ("er),
  Tourist Information
  tourist office
der Zoo (-s) *zoo*

(For motoring see 13 *Travel and
Tourism*, page 185.)

die Allee (-n) *avenue*
die Einbahnstraße (-n)
  one-way street
die Gasse (-n) *lane, alley*
die Sackgasse (-n) *dead end*
die Straße (-n) *street, road*
der Weg (-e) *path, way*

die Ampel (-n) *traffic lights*
der Bordstein (-e) *kerb*
der Bürgersteig (-e)
  pavement
die Bushaltestelle (-n)
  bus stop
der Fahrradweg (-e)
  cycle path

der Fußgängerüberweg (-e)
  pedestrian crossing
die Fußgängerzone (-n)
  pedestrian area
das absolute Halteverbot (-e)
  double yellow lines
der Kreisel (-),
  der Kreisverkehr (-e)
  roundabout
die Laterne (-n) *lamp post*
mitten auf der Straße
  *in the middle of the
  road*
die Parkuhr (-en) *parking meter*
die Straßenbahnhaltestelle (-n)
  tram stop

12 die Stadt und Einkaufen *Town and shopping*

das Straßenschild (-er)
    street sign
der Taxistand (¨e) *taxi stand, rank*

die Unterführung (-en)
    subway
der Wegweiser (-) *signpost*
die Zufahrt (-en) *access*

Er steht im (absoluten) Haltevorbot. *He's parked on a (double)
    yellow line.*

GESCHÄFTE UND EINKÄUFE
SHOPS AND SHOPPING

(For buying clothes see *Clothes and
fashion*, page 63.)

der Laden (¨),
das Geschäft (-e) *shop*
das Antiquitätengeschäft
    antique shop
das Antiquariat (-e)
    *second-hand book
    shop*
die Apotheke (-n) *dispensing chemist*
die Bäckerei (-en) *bakery*
der Blumenladen (¨)
    flower shop
die Boutique (-n) *boutique*
die Buchhandlung (-en)
    bookshop
die Drogerie (-n) *non-dispensing
    chemist*
die Eisen- und
    Haushaltswarenhandlung (-en)
    *ironmonger's and
    household goods*
das Elektrogeschäft (-e)
    electrical goods
das Fischgeschäft (-e)
    fishmongers
das Fotogeschäft (-e)
    photographer's

der Friseursalon (-s)
    hairdresser's
der Gebrauchtwarenladen (¨),
    Second-Hand-Laden
    second-hand shop
der Gemüseladen (¨)
    greengrocers
das Geschenkartikelgeschäft (-e)
    gift shop
der Juwelier (-e) *jeweller's*
das Kaufhaus (¨er)
    department store
der Kiosk (-e) *small newsagent's*
das Bekleidungsgeschäft (-e)
    clothes shop
die Konditorei (-en)
    cake shop
der Kosmetiksalon (-s)
    beautician's
das Lebensmittelgeschäft (-e)
    grocers
das Lederwarengeschäft (-e)
    leather goods shop
die Metzgerei (-en), der Schlachter (-)
    butcher's
der Naturkostladen (¨), der Bioladen (¨)
    wholefood shop
das Reformhaus (¨er)
    health food shop
die (chemische) Reinigung (-en)
    dry cleaner's
das Reisebüro (-s) *travel agent's*

12 die Stadt und Einkaufen *Town and shopping*

der Schreibwarenladen (¨)
    stationer's
das Schuhgeschäft (-e)
    shoe shop
das Sportgeschäft (-e)
    sports shop
das Süßwarengeschäft (-e)
    sweet shop
der Tabak(waren) laden (¨)
    tobacconist
der Waschsalon (-s)
    launderette
der Zooladen (¨) *pet shop*

Einkaufen *Shopping*

Haben Sie . . .? *Have you got . . .?*
Ich möchte . . . *I would like a . . .*

einen Beutel   *sachet of . . .*
ein Glas . . .   *jar of . . .*
eine Schachtel . . . *box of . . .*
eine Dose . . .   *can, tin of . . .*
eine Flasche . . . *bottle of . . .*

eine Kiste . . . *case of, crate of . . .*
eine Kiste
    Bier   *crate of beer*
eine Packung . . . *packet of . . .*
eine Tube . . . *tube of . . .*

frisch/ Dosen-   *fresh / tinned*
Dosentomaten   *tinned tomatoes*
roh/gekocht   *raw / cooked*

Wieviel?   *How much? / How
          many?*
ein Kilo   *1 kilo*
ein halbes Kilo/fünfhundert
    Gramm/ein Pfund
          *½ kilo / 500g /
          1 pound*

ein Liter   *1 litre*
ein halber Liter *½ litre*
ein Dutzend   *a dozen*
ein(e) Sechserpack (ung)
          a packet, or box of six
eine Scheibe   *a slice*
ein Stück   *a piece*

Beim Einkaufen *Making purchases*

Werden Sie schon bedient?   *Are you being served?*
Das ist alles/Das war's, danke. *That's all, thanks.*
Es tut mir leid. Ich habe kein
    Kleingeld.   *I'm sorry I haven't got any change.*
Tut mir leid, kleiner habe ich   *Sorry, I haven't got anything*
    es nicht.   *smaller.*
Das ist zu viel.   *It's too much.*

teuer   *expensive* | beschädigt   *damaged*
billig   *cheap* |

12 die Stadt und Einkaufen *Town and shopping*

Haben Sie ein/eine/einen . . .?	*Have you got a / some . . .?*
Wo kann man . . . kaufen?	*Where can I find . . .?*
Woher kommt es/kommen die?	*Where is it / are they from?*
Woraus ist es/sind die gemacht?	*What is it / are they made of?*
Welche Marke ist das?	*What make is it?*
Kann ich einen/eine/ein bestellen?	*Can I order one?*
Wann kann ich . . . abholen?	*When can I collect . . .?*
Wieviel kostet das?	*How much does it cost?*
Wo kann ich bezahlen?	*Where can I pay?*
Nehmen Sie Euroschecks?	*Do you take Eurocheques?*

IM KAUFHAUS
IN THE DEPARTMENT STORE

Untergeschoß	Erdgeschoß	1. Obergeschoß
Cafe	Foto	Herrenbekleidung
Delikatessen	Stoffe	Damenbekleidung
Haushaltswaren	Kurzwaren	Abendbekleidung
Hobby-Heimwerker	Kosmetik	Anzüge
Heimtierbedarf	Lederwaren	Damenwäsche
	Musik und Radio	Miederwaren
	Parfümerie	Bademoden
	Reisebüro	
	Schreibwaren	

Basement	*Ground floor*	*First Floor*
Cafe	*Photography*	*Menswear*
Delicatessen	*Fabrics*	*Ladies Wear*
Kitchenware	*Haberdashery*	*Evening wear*
DIY and hobbies	*Cosmetics*	*Suits*
Pet's corner	*Leather goods*	*Lingerie*
	Music and Radio	*Corsetry*
	Perfumery	*Swimwear*
	Travel agency	
	Stationery	

2. Obergeschoß	3. Obergeschoß	4. Obergeschoß
Haus- und Heimtextilen	Computer	Restaurant
Weißwaren	Elektrogeräte	Kundendienstbüro
Kinderbekleidung und	Fernsehen und Video	WC
Spielwaren	Möbel	
Porzellan und Glaswaren	Teppiche	
Sportartikel		
Geschenkartikel		
Geschenk-Hochzeits-		
Service		

Second Floor	*Third Floor*	*Fourth Floor*
Home Furnishings	*Computers*	*Restaurant*
Linen	*Electrical goods*	*Customer services*
Childrenswear and	*Television and videos*	*Toilets*
* toys*	*Furniture*	
China and glassware	*Carpeting*	
Sports and sportswear		
Gifts and fancy foods		
Wedding list		

Orientierung im Laden
      Directions in a store
Wo ist . . .?   *Where is the . . .?*
der Ausgang (¨e) *exit*
der Fahrstuhl (¨e) *lift*

die Kasse (-n) *cash desk*
das Regal (-e) *shelf*
die Reihe (-n) *row*
die Rolltreppe (-n)
      escalator

BEIM FRISEUR
AT THE HAIRDRESSERS

(For more on hair styles and colours,
see *Personal appearance,* page 43.)

das Haar (-e) *Hair*

der Knoten (-), der Dutt (-s) (umg.)
      bun
die Perücke (-n) *wig*
der Pferdeschwanz (¨e)
      ponytail

der Pony (-s) *fringe*
das Toupet (-s) *toupee, hairpiece*
der Zopf (¨e) *plait, bunch*
der Meckyputz *crop*
der Bubikopf *bob*

die Dauerwelle (-n)
      perm

die Strähne (-n) *streak*
das Haarfärbemittel (-)
      dye

12 die Stadt und Einkaufen *Town and shopping*

die Schere (-n) *scissors*		bleichen	*to bleach*
das Shampoo (-s) *shampoo*		färben	*to colour*
die Spülung (-en) *conditioner*		fönen	*to blow dry*
das Tönungsmittel (-)		in Locken legen	*to curl*
tint		legen	*to set*
		schneiden	*to cut*
der Fön (-e) *hairdryer*		tönen	*to tint*
die Trockenhaube (n)		toupieren	*to backcomb*
hairdryer (at the salon)		waschen	*to wash*

Ich muß zum Friseur.	*I need a haircut.*
Ich möchte die Haare schneiden lassen.	*I'd like my hair cut.*
Etwas kürzer . . .	*A bit shorter . . .*
Nicht zu kurz . . .	*Not too short . . .*
Nur die Spitzen . . .	*Only the ends . . .*
Ich hätte den Scheitel gern rechts/links.	*I'd like the parting on the right / left.*
Ich trage einen Pferdeschwanz.	*I have a pony tail.*
Es ist gut so, danke.	*That's fine, thanks.*

NOCH MAL!

● *Activity: How do you want your hair?*

12 die Stadt und Einkaufen *Town and shopping*

In der Drogerie *At the non-dispensing chemist's*

(For medicines see 10 *The Body*, page 132.)

Toilettenartikel
Toiletries

die Après Sun Creme (-s), Lotion (-en)
after-sun cream

das Deodorant (-s), Deo
deodorant

die Feuchtigkeitscreme (-s)
moisturiser

die Handcreme (-s)
hand-cream

der Kulturbeutel (-)
sponge-bag

der Schwamm (¨e) *sponge*

die Seife (-n)   *soap*

die Sonnencreme (-s)
sun cream

die wasserfeste Sonnenmilch (-s)
water-resistant sun milk

das Talkumpuder (-)
talcum powder

der Waschlappen (-)
face-cloth, flannel

die Watte (-n)   *cotton wool*

Nägel   nails
die Nagelfeile (-n) *nail file*

die Papiernagelfeile (-n)
emery board

die Nagelschere (-n)
nail scissors

der Nagellack (-e) *nail varnish*

der Nagellackentferner (-)
nail varnish remover

das Tempo (-s)®,
   das Papiertaschentuch (¨er)
paper handkerchief

Intimpflege   *female hygiene*
die Damenbinde (-n)
sanitary towel

der Tampon (-s) *tampon*

Haarpflege   *hair care*
die Haarbürste (-n)
hairbrush

die Haarklammer (-n)
hairgrip

die Haarspange (-n)
slide

das Haarspray (-s)
hairspray

der Kamm (¨e)   *comb*

der Lockenstab (¨e)
curling tongs

der Schaumfestiger (-)
styling mousse

Das Rasierzeug *shaving gear*
das After-shave (-s),
   das Rasierwasser (-)
after shave

der Rasierapparat (-),
   der Rasierer (-)
razor, electric razor

die Rasierklinge (-n)
razor blade

das Rasiermesser (-)
cut-throat razor

der Rasierpinsel (-)
shaving brush

der Rasierschaum (¨e)
shaving foam

der Wegwerfrasierer (-)
disposable razor

Verhütungsmittel
contraceptives

das Kondom (-e), das Präservativ (-e)
condom

12 die Stadt und Einkaufen *Town and shopping*

Mundpflege   *oral hygiene*
das Mundwasser (-)
          mouthwash
die Zahnbürste (-n)
          toothbrush
die Zahnpasta (-pasten)
          toothpaste
die Zahnseide (-n) *dental floss*
der Zahnstocher (-)
          toothpick

Kosmetik und Parfum
Cosmetics and perfume

der Augenbrauenstift (-e)
          eyebrow pencil
der Eyeliner (-) *eyeliner*
die Gesichtspackung (-)
          face pack
das Gesichtspuder (-)
          face powder
die Grundierungscreme (-s)
          foundation cream
die Kosmetiktasche (-n)
          make-up bag
der Lidschatten (-)
          eyeshadow
der Lippenstift (-e)
          lipstick
das Make-up (-s)
          make-up
der Make-up Entferner (-)
          make-up remover
die Wimperntusche (-n)
          mascara
die Nachtcreme (-s)
          night cream

der Pinsel (-)   *make-up brush*
die Pinzette (-n) *tweezers*
das Rouge (-)   *blusher*
das Schminkset (-s)
          make-up kit
der Spiegel (-)   *mirror*
die Tagescreme (-s)
          day cream
das Wachs (-e)   *leg wax*

Parfüm   *perfume*
blumig   *flowery*
der Duft (¨e)   *fragrance*
das Kölnisch Wasser (-)
          toilet water
das Lavendel(öl)*lavender*
das Moschus(öl) *musk*
das Parfümfläschchen (-)
          perfume, scent bottle
der Zerstäuber (-)
          spray

auftragen   *to put on (cream)*
benutzen   *to use*
die Fingernägel lackieren
          to varnish one's nails
Nagellack entfernen
          to remove varnish
die Haare waschen/fönen
          to wash / dry your hair
bürsten   *to brush*
die Zähne putzen *to clean one's teeth*
schminken/abschminken
          *to put on / take off
          make-up*
sich waschen   *to wash*

12 die Stadt und Einkaufen *Town and shopping*

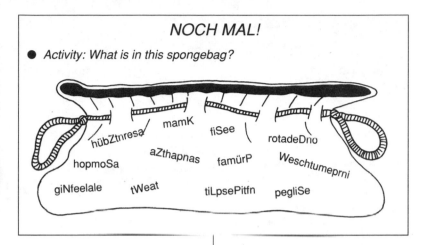

NOCH MAL!

● *Activity: What is in this spongebag?*

mamK
fiSee
hübZtnresa
rotadeDno
hopmoSa
aZthapnas
famürP
Weschtumeprni
giNfeelale
tWeat
tiLpsePitfn
pegliSe

AUF DER POST
AT THE POST OFFICE

(For bank see 11 *Banking and Finance*, page 142.
For Telephone see 7 *The Company*, page 106.)

der Absender (-) *sender*
der Brief (-e)   *letter*
der Briefkasten (¨)
            post box
die Briefmarke (-n)
            stamp
der Briefmarkenautomat (-en)
            stamp machine
Briefträger/in   *postman*
der Briefumschlag (¨e)
            envelope
die Drucksache (-n)
            printed matter
per Einschreiben *recorded delivery*

das Gewicht   *weight*
per Luftpost   *by air mail*
das Maß (-e)   *size*
per Nachnahme *cash on delivery*
das Päckchen (-) *small parcel*
das Paket (-e)   *parcel*
das Porto   *postage*
die Postanweisung (-en)
            postal / money order
die Postkarte (-n) *postcard*
das Postfach (¨er) *PO Box*
postlagernd   *poste restante*
die Postsparkasse (-n)
            post office savings bank
der Poststempel (-)
            postmark
der Schalter (-) *counter*
das Telegramm (-e)
            telegram

12 die Stadt und Einkaufen *Town and shopping*

Ich möchte eine Briefmarke für einen Brief/eine Postkarte nach ...
Vier Briefmarken zu ... Pfennig/ Mark, bitte.
Was kostet ein Brief/eine Postkarte

I'd like a stamp for a letter / post card to ...
Four ... pence stamps, please.

---

das Lotto *lottery*
die Lottozahlen *lottery numbers*
der Lottoschein *lottery ticket*

der Lottogewinn *lottery prize*
die Rubbelkarte *scratchcard*

---

auf der Polizei revier
at the police station
der Diebstahl (¨e) *theft*
stehlen *to steal*

verlieren *to lose*
aufbrechen, einbrechen
to break into

Ich möchte einen Diebstahl/ Verlust melden.
Ich habe meine Kreditkarte/mein Scheckheft/mein Geld verloren.
Was soll ich tun?
Mein Fotoapparat ist gestohlen worden.
Mein Auto ist aufgebrochen worden.

I'd like to report a theft / loss.
I have lost my credit card / cheque book / money.
What should I do?
My camera has been stolen.
My car has been broken into.

---

auf dem Verkehrsbüro
at the tourist office
die Broschüre (-n) *brochure*
der englischsprechenden Fremdenführer (-)
English-speaking guide

das Hotelverzeichnis (-se)
list of hotels
der Stadtplan (¨e) *town plan*
die Stadtrundfahrt (-en)
sightseeing tour
der Veranstaltungskalender (-)
calendar of events

Wo ist das Verkehrsbüro?
Gibt es Führungen in englischer Sprache?

Where is the tourist office?
Are there guided tours in English?

12 die Stadt und Einkaufen *Town and shopping*

RICHTUNGSANGABEN
DIRECTIONS

Wie komme ich bitte zur Messe?	*How do I get to the fair?*
Wie weit ist das?	*How far is it?*
Ist es in der Nähe?	*Is it near here?*
Kann man dahin zu Fuß gehen?	*Can I get there on foot?*
Biegen Sie nach . . . ab	*Turn . . .*
links	*left*
rechts	*right*
Gehen Sie immer geradeaus	*Go straight ahead*
Nehmen Sie die erste/zweite Straße	*You take the first / second road*
rechts/links.	*on the right / left.*
Gehen Sie/Fahren Sie . . .	*Go . . .*
bis zur Ampel	*to the crossing*
bis zum Bahnübergang.	*to the level crossing.*
um die Ecke	*around the corner*
den Fluß entlang	*along the river bank*
rechts/links am Museum vorbei	*to the left / right of the museum*
Gehen Sie über die Straße/den	
Marktplatz.	*Cross the road / market place.*
Gehen Sie durch die Unterführung.	*Take the underpass.*
Am/An der . . . gehen/fahren Sie nach . . .	
	When you come to the . . ., you turn . . .
Es ist weit/nicht weit.	*It's far / not far.*
Es ist fünf Minuten von hier.	*It's five minutes from here.*
Es ist gleich hier vorn!	*It's right here!*
dort oben/unten	*up / down there*

irgendwo	*somewhere*	Ich weiß nicht, wo es ist!	
		I don't know where it is!	

Wo ist der Bahnhof/die Post/	**Where is the station/**
das Rathaus?	**post office/town hall?**
Er/Sie/Es ist . . .	*It's . . .*
auf der linken/rechten Seite	*on the left / right*
dort drüben	*over there*
in der . . . Straße.	*in . . . Road / Street*
in der ersten/nächsten Straße	*in the first / next street*

12 die Stadt und Einkaufen *Town and shopping*

nach der Ampel	*after the lights*
auf der anderen Straßenseite	*on the other side of the road*
auf dem Marktplatz	*in the market place*
am Fuß der Treppe	*at the bottom of the steps*
auf dem Weg zur Burg	*on the way to the castle*

nehmen	*to take*	folgen	*to follow*
gehen	*to walk*	überqueren	*to cross*
fahren	*to drive*	an/am . . . vorbei gehen/fahren	
abbiegen	*to turn*		*to go past . . .*

Learning tip
· · · · · · · · · · · · · · · · · ·

Remember: **gehen** means to *go on foot* or *walk* and **fahren** is *to go by car* or *drive*.

NOCH MAL!

● *Activity: How do I get to . . . ?*

Give directions to all the buildings from Ihr Standort.

Ihr Standort
= You are here

13 Reisen und Tourismus *Travel and tourism*

REISEN *TRAVEL*

die Abfahrt (-en) *departure*
die Ankunft ("e) *arrival*
der Ausflug ("e) *excursion*
der Fahrplan ("e)
    timetable
der Fahrpreis (-e) *fare*
das öffentliche Verkehrsmittel (-)
    public transport

der Paß ("e) *passport*
die Paßkontrolle (-n)
    passport control
die Reise (-n) *journey*
die Rundreise (-n), Rundgang ("e)
    tour
die Schlange (-n) *queue*

Er machte einen Rundgang durch
   das Schloß.　　　*He went on a tour of the castle.*

Mit dem Zug fahren
Travel by train

Deutsche Bahn **DB**

der Bahnhof ("e) *station*
der Ausgang ("e) *exit*
die Auskunft *information*
der Bahnsteig, das Gleis
    platform
der Eingang ("e) *entrance*
der Entwerter *machine for*
    stamping tickets
der Fahrgast ("e) *passenger*
die Gepäckaufbewahrung
    left-luggage
der Kofferkuli (-s) *trolley*
der Warteraum ("e)
    waiting room
der Schalter (-) *ticket office*
die Platzreservierung (-en)
    seat reservation
die Verspätung (-en)
    delay

die Fahrkarte (-n) *ticket*
die Bahncard (-s)
    railcard
die Einzelfahrkarte (-n)
    single ticket
die Rückfahrkarte (-n)
    return ticket
der Fahrkartenautomat (-en)
    ticket machine

halber/voller Fahrpreis
    half/full fare
die Ermäßigung (-en)
    reduction
der Erwachsene *adult*
das Kind (er) *child*
erster/zweiter Klasse
    first/second class
der Zuschlag ("e)
    supplement

Züge *trains*
der Autoreisezug (ARZ)
    motorail
der Schnellzug (D)
    fast train
der EuroCity (EC)
    EC

13 **Reisen und Tourismus** *Travel and tourism*

der InterCity (IC)
Inter-city
der InterCityExpress (ICE)
ICE
der InterRegio (IR)
regional
die S-Bahn (S) *suburban train*
der StadtExpress (SE)
city express
der Bummelzug (¨e)
slow train
der Güterzug (¨e)
freight train

die Lokomotive (-n)
engine
der Wagen (-) *railway carriage*
die Notbremse (-n)
communication cord
Raucher/NichtRaucher
Smoking / non-smoking
der Schlafwagen (-)
sleeping-car
Zugbegleiter/in, Schaffner/in
guard, conductor
das Zugrestaurant (-s)
restaurant car

Wann fährt der (nächste) Zug? *What time does the (next) train leave?*
Auf welchem Gleis? *Which platform?*
Muß ich umsteigen? *Do I have to change?*
Fährt dieser Zug nach . . .? *Is this the train for . . .?*
Zweimal nach . . . hin und
zurück, bitte. *Two return tickets to . . ., please.*
Gibt es von Köln einen Anschluß nach . . . ?
Is there a connection from Cologne to . . .?
Der Zug nach . . . hat eine Stunde *The train to . . . is running*
Verspätung. *one hour late.*

---

aussteigen *to get off*
den Zug bekommen
to catch a train
eine Fahrkarte entwerten
to validate
a ticket

einen Sitzplatz reservieren
to reserve a seat
schwarzfahren *to travel without*
a ticket
umsteigen *to change*
zusteigen *to board*

174

NOCH MAL!

● *Activity: Ask where you can find the following:*

Fliegen *Travel by plane*

das Düsenflugzeug (-e)
   jet
die Fluggesellschaft (-en)
   airline
das Flugzeug (-e)
   plane
der Flughafen (¨)
   airport

die Abfertigung (-en)
   check-in
der Abflug (¨e)   *departures*
die Ankunft (¨e) *arrivals*
der Flugplan (¨e)
   plane timetable
der Flugschein (-e)
   air ticket

der Ausgang (¨e) *gate*
die Gepäckausgabe
   luggage claim
der Schalter (-) *desk*
der Terminal (-s)
   terminal

der Flug (¨e)   *flight*

der Charterflug (¨e)
   charter flight
der Linienflug (¨e)
   scheduled flight

die Club-Klasse *club class*
die Touristenklasse
   economy class

die Landung (-en)   *landing*
der Transfer   *transfer*
die Zwischenlandung (-en)
   stop-over

die Bordkarte (-n)
   boarding card
das Handgepäck (-e)
   hand luggage
der Kofferkuli(-s)*luggage trolley*
der Sitz am Gang/Fenster
   aisle/window seat

Pilot/in   *pilot*
Steward, Stewardess
   steward, stewardess
die Notlandung (-en)
   emergency landing
landen   *to land*
starten   *to take off*

Die Passagiere nach Rom, Flug Nummer ... werden gebeten, sich zum Ausgang ... zu begeben.	*Will passengers for Rome, flight number ... please go to gate number ...*
Bitte das Rauchen einstellen und anschnallen.	*Please extinguish all cigarettes and fasten your seat belts.*
An wen kann ich mich wenden?	*Whom can I speak to?*

Mit dem Boot fahren
Travel by boat

(For sailing, rowing and fishing, see 9 *Hobbies – fishing* and *water sports*, pages 123 and 129.)

die Kreuzfahrt (-en)
    cruise
die Überfahrt (-en)
    crossing

der Hafen (¨) *dock, harbour, port*
der Kai (-e) *quay*
der Pier (-e) *pier*

das Schiff (-e) *ship*
das Containerschiff (-e)
    roll-on-roll-off, container ship
der Dampfer (-) *steamer*
die Fähre (-n) *ferry*
der Frachtkahn (¨e)
    freight barge
das Hausboot (-e) *barge, houseboat*
die Jacht (-en) *yacht*
das Motorboot (-e)
    motor boat
das Passagierschiff (-e)
    cruise liner

das Segelboot (-e)
    sailing ship
der Tanker (-) *tanker*

die Crew (-s), Besatzung (-en)
    crew
der Kapitän (-e) *captain*
der Offizier (-e) *officer*
der Seemann (-leute)
    sailor
der Steward (-s) *steward*
der Zahlmeister (-)
    purser

der Anker (-) *anchor*
auf Deck *on deck*
die Kabine (-n) *cabin*
das Rettungsboot (-e)
    lifeboat
die Bugklappe (-n)
    vehicle loading doors

(mit dem Schiff) fahren
    to sail
an Bord/von Bord gehen
    to embark / disembark
anlegen *to dock*
seekrank sein *to be seasick*
sinken *to sink*

Wann legen wir in . . . an?
Wie lange dauert die Überfahrt?
Die See ist rauh/ruhig.

When do we dock in . . .?
How long does the crossing take?
The sea is rough/calm.

die Zollkontrolle (-n)
      At customs
das Visum (Visa)
    visa

Zollbeamter, -beamtin
    customs officer
zollfrei   *duty-free*

Haben Sie etwas zu verzollen?
Ihren Paß, bitte.
Sie müßen für die Zigaretten Zoll
   bezahlen.
Haben Sie einen Impfschein?

Have you anything to declare?
May I see your passport, please?
You will have to pay duty on
   these cigarettes.
Have you got a certificate
   of vaccination?

Mit dem Bus fahren
Travel by bus

der Busbahnhof ("e)
    bus station
Busfahrer/in   *driver*
die Bushaltestelle (-n)
    bus stop
der Fahrkartenautomat (-en)
    ticket machine
die Linie (-n)   *number, route*
der Reisebus (-se)
    coach

die Straßenbahn (-en)
    tram
die U-Bahn(-en)
    underground, tube

13 Reisen und Tourismus *Travel and tourism*

Kann ich dort mit öffentlichen Verkehrsmitteln/dem Bus/dem Auto hinkommen?

Can I get there by public transport / bus / car?

Welche Linie fährt nach . . .? *Which number goes to . . .?*

Wie oft fährt der Bus/die Straßenbahn? *How often does the bus / tram run?*

Alle zehn Minuten. *Every ten minutes.*

Sie können eine Tageskarte/24 Stunden Karte kaufen.

You can buy a day / 24 hour ticket.

Mit dem Taxi fahren *Travel by taxi*

der Fahrpreis (-e)	*fare*
Taxifahrer/in	*taxi driver*
Zum Bahnhof, bitte.	*To the station, please.*
Wieviel kostet es nach/zum/zur . . .?	*How much is it to . . .?*
Das ist für Sie.	*That's for you.*

Mit dem Rad fahren
Travel by bike

(For bicycle see 9 *Hobbies and sports*, page 127.)

das Mofa (-s)   *small moped*

das Moped (-s)   *moped*

das Motorrad (¨er)
   motor bike

der Motorroller (-)
   scooter

der Sturzhelm (-e)
   crash helmet

13 **Reisen und Tourismus** *Travel and tourism*

NOCH MAL!

● *Activity: How do you prefer to travel?*

TOURISMUS   *TOURISM*

Sehenswerte Orte und Gegenden   **Places and areas to visit**
Overleaf are a few of the places and sights worth taking in when you visit
a German-speaking country.

ÖSTERREICH

DIE SCHWIEZ

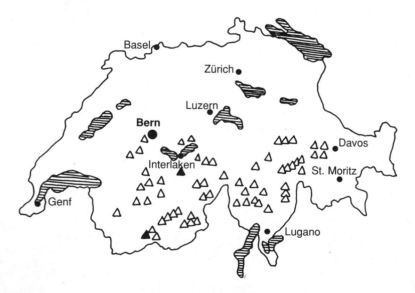

DEUTSCHLAND

13 Reisen und Tourismus *Travel and tourism*

Ich möchte die Sehenswürdigkeiten
   besichtigen!   *I want to see the sights!*

It will help you to remember the words in this list if you look at a map and
find out where these well-known sights are located.

der Berg (-e)	*mountain*
die Zugspitze in Bayern; Eiger und	
Jungfrauenjoch in der Schweiz	
die Wart**burg** bei Eisenach in	
Thüringen	*fortress*
der Kölner **Dom**	*cathedral*
der Bamberger Dom in Bamberg	
historisches Denkmal	*ancient monument*
der Römer und die Bremer	
Stadtmusikanten in Bremen	
der Fastnachts**brunnen** in Basel	*fountain*
Denkmal (¨er), **Monument**	*monument*
der Herkules in Kassel	
Gedenkstätte (-n)	*memorial*
die Walhalla bei Regensburg	
historisches Gebäude (-n)	*historic building*
das Knochenhaueramtshaus in	
Hildesheim	
die Bing**höhle** bei Streitberg in Bayern	*cave*
die Frauen**kirche** in Dresden;	*church*
die Gedächtnis**kirche** in Berlin	
Kloster Eberbach	*abbey*
Freiburger **Münster**	*minster*
Museum Ludwig in Köln;	*museum*
Sprengel **Museum** in Hannover	
Palast	*palace, stately home*
Sanssouci Potsdam	
Schloß	*castle*
Neuschwanstein in Bayern	
Schlucht	*gorge*
die Höllentalklamm bei Garmisch-Partenkirchen	
der Starnberger **See** bei München;	*lake*
Wörther **See** in Österreich	
der Schwarz**wald**	*forest*
der Thüringer **Wald**	

13 Reisen und Tourismus *Travel and tourism*

Im Reisebüro
At the travel agent's

die Broschüre (-n)
    brochure
Reisebürokaufmann/-frau
    travel agent
die Reiseversicherung (-en)
    holiday insurance
das Reservierungs formular (-e)
    booking form

der Urlaub (-e) *holiday*
Tourist/in   *The tourist*
Besucher/in   *visitor*
Reisende/r   *traveller*
Urlauber/in   *holidaymaker*

der Freizeitpark (-s)
    theme park
der Nationalpark (-s)
    national park
der Urlaubsort (-e)
    holiday resort
die Pauschalreise (-n)
    package tour
der Aktivurlaub (-e)
    activity holiday

der Tagesausflug (¨e)
    day trip
die Kreuzfahrt (-en)
    cruise
mit dem Rucksack unterwegs
    backpacking
der Wanderurlaub (-e)
    walking holiday
die Kurzreise (-n) *weekend break*
der Abenteuerurlaub (-e)
    adventure
    holiday
die Städtereise (-n)
    city holiday
besuchen, besichtigen
    to visit
bleiben   *to stay*
fotografieren *to photograph*
ins Ausland reisen
    to go abroad
reisen   *to travel*
reservieren, buchen
    to book
übernachten *to stay overnight*
verbringen *to spend (time)*

URLAUBSUNTERKUNFT *HOLIDAY ACCOMMODATION*

Wir übernachten . . .
  in einem Feriendorf
  in einem Ferienhaus
  in einer Ferienwohnung
  in einem Gasthaus
  in einer Pension

We are going to stay . . .
  in a holiday camp
  in a holiday house
  in a holiday flat
  at an inn, at a bed and breakfast
  at a guesthouse

13 **Reisen und Tourismus** *Travel and tourism*

Im Hotel *At the hotel*

der Gesellschaftsraum (¨e)
    lounge
der Portier   *porter*
das Restaurant (-s)/
   der Speisesaal (-säle)
    *restaurant / dining
    room*

die Rezeption, der Empfang
    reception
das Schwimmbad (¨er)
    pool
der Umkleideraum (¨e)
    changing room
das Zimmer (-) *room*
der Zimmerservice
    room service

Ich möchte ein . . . reservieren.   *I'd like to book a . . .*

Doppelzimmer	*double room*
Dreibettzimmer	*room with three beds*
Einzelzimmer	*single room*
Zimmer mit Bad/Dusche	*room with a bath / shower*
für zwei Erwachsene und ein Kind	*for two adults and one child*
mit Balkon	*with a balcony*
mit Blick aufs Meer	*wih a sea view*
mit Fernseher	*with TV*
mit Telefon	*with phone*
Voll-/Halbpension	*full / half board*
mit Frühstück	*with breakfast*

Ich habe reserviert.	*I've made a reservation.*
Füllen Sie bitte das Anmeldeformular aus.	*Would you complete this registration form, please?*
Ich hätte gern meinen Schlüssel.	*Could I have my key, please.*
Gibt es eine Nachricht für mich?	*Are there any messages for me?*
Wir sind voll ausgebucht.	*We're fully booked.*
Wo kann ich den Wagen abstellen?	*Where can I park my car?*
Wecken Sie mich bitte morgen früh um . . . Uhr.	*I'd like a morning call at . . . .*

abfahren	*to depart*	Kaution bezahlen	*to pay a deposit*
ankommen	*to arrive*	übernachten	*to stay overnight*
sich anmelden	*to register*		

Auf dem Campingplatz
On the camp-site

das Wohnmobil (-e)	*camper van*
der Wohnwagen (-)	*caravan*
das Zelt (-e)	*tent*

Campinganlagen
camping facilities

Abfallbehälter	*rubbish bin*
Bügelplatz	*ironing place*
Duschen	*showers*
Gasverkauf	*gas on sale*
Geschirrspülbecken	*sinks for washing-up*
Hundeverbot	*no dogs*
Kinderspielplatz	*children's playground*

Kochgelegenheit	*cooking range*
Lebensmittelverkauf	*food shop*
Minigolfanlage	*minigolf*
mit Stromanschluß	*with electricity*
Sanitäreinrichtung für Körperbehinderte	*facilities for the disabled*
Steckdosen	*electric points*
überwiegend schattig	*predominantly shaded*
Waschbecken	*sinks, washbasins*
Waschmaschine	*washing machine*
Waschräume	*washing facilities*
Wasserzapfstellen	*water taps*

NOCH MAL!

● *Activity: What do these signs mean?*

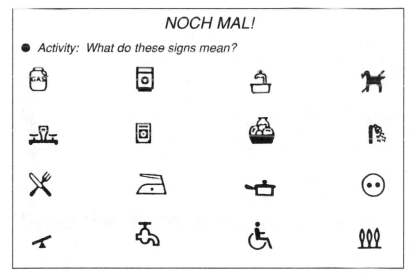

13 Reisen und Tourismus *Travel and tourism*

die Ausrüstung (-en)
Equipment

die Hängematte (-n)
    hammock
der Hering (-e) *peg*
die Lampe (-n) *lamp*
die Luftmatratze (-n)
    air bed
der Schlafsack (¨e)
    sleeping-bag
die Taschenlampe (-n)
    torch
der Zeltboden (¨) *groundsheet*
die Zeltstange (-n)
    tent pole

zelten   *to camp*

In der Jugendherberge
In the youth hostel

die Mitgliedskarte (-n)
    membership card
der Schlafsaal (¨e)
    dormitory
der Aufenthaltsraum (¨e)
    recreation room
die Hausordnung (-en)
    regulations
Herbergsvater/mutter
    warden

NOCH MAL!

● *Activity: Complete this registration form*

Name _____

Wohnort _____

Geburtsort _____

Geburtsdatum _____

Ausweisnummer _____

Autokennzeichen _____

Ankunft _____

Nationalität _____

Abfahrt _____

13 Reisen und Tourismus *Travel and tourism*

AM MEER
AT THE SEASIDE

For diving and swimming see 9
Hobbies and Sports, page 129.
For sportswear see 3 *Clothes and
Fashion*, page 64.

die Bucht (-en) *bay*
der Fels (-en) *rocks*
die Insel (-n) *island*
der Kanal (¨e) *channel*
die Klippe (-n) *cliff*
der Leuchtturm (-e)
    lighthouse

das Meer (-e), die See
    sea
die Ebbe *low tide*
die Flut *high tide*

AUTO UND AUTOFAHREN
CARS AND MOTORING

Fahrzeuge *vehicles*
das Auto (-s), der Wagen (-),
  der PKW (-s), *car*
der Kleintransporter (-)
    commercial van
der Lieferwagen (-)
    delivery van
der LKW (-s), Lastwagen (-)
    *HGV heavy
      goods vehicle*
der Tankwagen (-)
    tanker

die Automatik *automatic*
das Hecktürmodell (-e)
    hatchback
der Hinter-/Vorderradantrieb (-e)
    *rear / front-
      wheel drive*
der Kleinwagen (-)
    small car

die Welle (-n) *wave*

der Strand (¨e) *beach*
FKK-Strand (¨e) (Freikörperkultur)
    nudist beach
der Liegestuhl (¨e)
    deck chair
die Möwe (-n) *seagull*
der Sand *sand*
die Sonnenbrille (-n)
    sun glasses
der Strandkorb (¨e)
    *wicker beach seat
      with a hood*
der Windschutz (-e)
    wind break

sich entspannen *to relax*
in der Sonne liegen
    to sunbathe

der Kombi (-s) *estate car*
die Limousine (-n)
    saloon car
der Sportwagen (-)
    sports car

Die Autoteile *parts of the car*
der Dachgepäckträger (-)
    roof rack
das Kennzeichen (-)
    registration
die Antenne (-n)
    aerial
der Auspuff (-e) *exhaust*
der Benzintank (-s)
    petrol tank
die Haube (-n) *bonnet*
der Katalysator (en)
    catalytic converter
der Kofferraum (¨e)
    boot
das Nummernschild (-er)
    number plate

13 Reisen und Tourismus *Travel and tourism*

das Standlicht (¨er)
    side lights
der Reifen (-)   *tyre*
der Scheibenwischer (-)
    windscreen wipers
der Scheinwerfer (-)
    headlights
das Schiebedach (¨er)
    sun roof
die Stoßstange (-n)
    bumper
das Warnblinklicht (-er)
    hazard warning light
die Windschutzscheibe (-n)
    windscreen

das ABS   *ABS braking*
der Airbag (-s) *airbag*
der Blinker (-) *indicators*
die Bremse(-n) *brake*
das Armaturenbrett (-er)
    dashboard
die Tankanzeige (-n)
    petrol gauge
der Gang (¨e)   *gear*

das Gas(pedal (-e)
    accelerator (pedal)
der Gurt (-e)   *seat belt*
die Handbremse (-n)
    hand-brake
die Klimaanlage (-n)
    air-conditioning
das Lenkrad (¨er) *steering wheel*
die Kupplung (-en)
    clutch
das Pedal (-e)   *pedal*
der Rückspiegel (-)
    rear-view mirror
der Sitz (-e)   *seat*
die Zündung (-en) *ignition*

bremsen   *to brake*
fahren   *to drive*
parken   *to park*
schalten   *to change gear*
steuern   *to steer*
überholen   *to overtake*
zurücksetzen   *to reverse*
den Motor
  abwürgen   *to stall the engine*

Ich fahre immer rückwärts in die Garage.	*I always reverse into the garage.*

Unter der
Haube und   *Under the bonnet*
Reparaturen *and repairs*
die Batterie (-n) *battery*
der Keilriemen (-)
    fan belt

abgenutzt   *worn*
defekt   *defective*

der Kühler (-) *radiator*
der Luft-/Ölfilter (-)
    air / oil filter
der Motor (-en) *engine*

überhitzt   *overheated*
undicht   *leaking*

13 Reisen und Tourismus *Travel and tourism*

die Leistung (-en)
     performance
die PS   *horsepower*
Liter pro hundert
   Kilometer   *litres per 100 km*
der Verbrauch   *consumption*

Fahrschule (-n) *driving school*
Fahrschüler/in   *learner driver*
die Fahrstunde (-n)
     driving lesson
die Fahrprüfung (-en)
     practical driving test
die Theorieprüfung (-en)
     theory test

der Führerschein (-e)
     driving licence
die Fahrzeugpapiere
     car papers
der Fahrzeugbrief (-e)
     registration
     document, log book
die Grüne Karte (-n)
     green card
der TÜV   *MOT*
die vorläufige   *provisional*
   Fahrerlaubnis   *licence (only in GB)*
die Versicherung (-en)
     insurance

die Panne (-n)   *breakdown*
der Abschleppdienst (-e)
     breakdown service
der ADAC   *German Automobile*
     Association
die Pannenhilfe (-n)
     breakdown assistance
die Karambolage (-n)
     crash, collision

der Stau (-s)   *(traffic) jam*

abschleppen   *to tow away*

eine Panne haben
     to break down
zusammenstoßen
     to collide
(zu) schnell fahren
     to speed

13 Reisen und Tourismus *Travel and tourism*

Können Sie mir beim Reifenwechsel helfen?

Can you help me change the tyre?

Rufen Sie schnell die Polizei/einen Krankenwagen.

Call the police / an ambulance.

Ist jemand (schwer) verletzt? *Is anyone (seriously) hurt?*

Wo ist die nächste Notrufsäule? *Where is the nearest emergency phone?*

NOCH MAL!

● Activity: Name the parts of the car:

Straßen und Verkehrsschilder
Roads and road signs

die Autobahn (-en)

motorway

die Spur (-en) *lane*

die Hauptstraße (-n)

main road

die Landstraße (-n)

country road

die Ringstraße (-n)

ring road

die Seitenstraße (-n)

side road

die Schnellstraße (-n), zweispurige Straße (-n)

dual carriageway

die Umgehungsstraße (-n)

bypass

das Verkehrsschild (-er)
    road sign
Baustelle   *road works*
Doppelkurve   *double bend*
Eingang freihalten
    Keep entrance clear
Gegenverkehr   *two-way traffic*
Geschwindigkeitsbeschränkung
    speed restriction
Kreuzung   *intersection*
Schleudergefahr *aquaplaning*

(Trecker)dürfen überholt werden
    overtaking of (tractors) allowed
Überholverbot   *no overtaking*
Umleitung   *diversion*
unbefestigter Fahrbahnrand/
  Seitenstreifen
    soft verge
Vorfahrt gewähren in 100m
  Entfernung   *Give way in 100m*
Vorfahrtstraße   *Right of way on*
    this road
Stop!   *Stop*

NOCH MAL!

● *Activity 2: What do these signs mean?*

An der Tankstelle
    at the petrol
    station
das Benzin   *petrol*
die Zapfsäule (-n)
    petrol pump
Diesel   *diesel*
Normal   *2-star*
Super   *4-star*
Super Plus   *super plus*

bleifrei   *unleaded*
verbleit   *leaded*

die Autowäsche (-n)
    car wash
das Ersatzteil (-e)
    spare part
der Luftdruck (¨e)
    tyre pressure

13 Reisen und Tourismus *Travel and tourism*

das Öl (-e)   *oil*
die Straßenkarte (-n)
                road map

der Verbandskasten (¨)
                first-aid kit
das Warndreieck (-e)
                warning triangle

Volltanken, bitte.   *Fill it up, please.*
Ich möchte . . . Liter Super, bitte.   *I'd like . . . litres of 4-star, please.*

An der Raststätte
        at the services
Telefax   *Telefax*
Service für Behinderte
                Service for the
                disabled
Geldautomat vorhanden
                cash machine
                available
Baby-Wickelraum
                baby changing room

Kinderspielplatz
                playground
Hunde-Bar   *'dog bar' (water*
                bowl)
AutobahnKapelle
                motorway church
Autobahnübergang
                bridge
Tankstelle   *petrol station*
Raststätte   *services*
Motel   *motel*

14 Die Natur *The Natural World*

DAS LAND
THE COUNTRYSIDE

(For flowers and plants see 5 *House and Home – Garden*, page 88.)

die Landschaft (-en)
landscape
der Bach (¨e)   stream
der Felsbrocken (-)
     rock, boulder
der Fluß (Flüsse)
     river
die Heide (-n)   *heath*
das Hochmoor (-e)
     moor
die Hohle (-n),
   die Grotte (-n) *cave*
die Marsch(e)   *marsh*
der See (-n)   *lake*
das Tal (¨er)   *valley*
das Ufer (-)   *(river) bank*
der Wasserfall (¨e)
     waterfall

der Berg (-e)   **mountain**
das Gebirge (-) *mountain range*
der Gipfel (-)   *summit*
der Hügel (-)   *hill*

der Fußweg (-e) *footpath*
der Wald (¨er)   *wood, forest*

der Weg (-e)   *path*
die Wiese (-n)   *field*

der Baum (¨e) *tree*
der Ast (¨e)   *branch*
das Blatt (¨er)   *leaf*
die Rinde (-n)   *bark*
der Stamm (¨e)   *trunk*
die Wurzel (-n)   *root*
der Zweig (-e)   *twig*

der Laubbaum (¨e)
     deciduous tree
der Bergahorn (-e)
     sycamore
die Buche (-n)   *beech*
die Eiche (-n)   *oak*
die Kastanie (-n)
     chestnut
die Kiefer (-n)   *pine*
die Weide (-n)   *willow*
die Weißbirke (-n)
     silver birch

der Nadelbaum (¨e)
     conifer
die Eibe (-n)   *yew*
die Kiefer (-n)   *pine*
die Lärche (-n)   *larch*
die Tanne (-n)   *fir*
der Tannenzapfen (-)
     pine cone
die Zeder (-n)   *cedar*

NOCH MAL!

● *Activity: What do the symbols mean?*

AUF DEM BAUERNHOF
ON THE FARM

(For horses see *Hobbies and sports – Riding*, page 124.)

der Ackerbau *farming (crops)*
die Landwirtschaft
    agriculture
urbar, anbaufähig
    arable

die Viehzucht *farming (cattle breeding)*
das Milchvieh *dairy cattle*
die Schlachtrinder
    beef cattle
das Weidevieh *grazing cattle*

der Hof (¨e) *farmyard*
Bauer/Bäuerin, Landwirt/in
    farmer,
      farmer's wife
das Bauernhaus (¨er)
    farmhouse
der Gutshof (¨e) *large farm*
die Hecke (-n) *hedge*
der Land arbeiter/in
    farmhand
der Mist, der Dünger
    manure
der Rinderstall (¨e)
    cowshed
die Scheune (-n) *barn*
der Schweinestall (¨e)
    pigsty
der Stall (¨e) *stall, byre*
der Zaun (¨e) *fence*

der Mähdrescher (-)
    combine harvester
der Pflug (¨e) *plough*
der Traktor (-en), der Schlepper (-)
    tractor

Nutztiere auf dem Bauernhof
Farm animals

die Herde (-n) *herd, flock*

die Kuh (¨e) *cow*
der Bulle (-n) *bull*
das Kalb (¨er) *calf*
der Ochse (-n) *ox*

das Mutterschaf (-e)
    ewe
das Schaf (-e) *sheep*
der Schafbock (¨e), Widder (-)
    ram
das Lamm (¨er) *lamb*

das Schwein (-e) *pig*
die Sau (-en) *sow*
das Ferkel (-) *piglet*

das Pferd (-e) *horse*
der Esel (-) *donkey*

die Ente (-n) *duck*
der Erpel (-) *drake*
das Entenküken (-)
    duckling

die Gans (¨e) *goose*
der Ganter (-) *gander*
das Gänschen (-)
    gosling

das Huhn (¨er) *chicken, hen*
die Henne (-n) *hen (fem)*
das Küken *chick*
der Hahn (¨e) *cockerel*

der Truthahn (¨e)
    turkey (cock)
die Truthenne (-n)
    turkey (hen)

die Ziege (-n)/die Geiß (-e)
    goat / nanny goat
der Ziegenbock (¨e)
    billy goat

das Zicklein (-s), das Kitz (-e)
 kid

die Feldfrüchte *arable crops*
das Getreide *grain, corn*
der Mais *maize, sweetcorn*

der Hafer *oats*
das Heu *hay*
das Stroh *straw*

anbauen *to cultivate*
ausbrüten *to hatch*
bewässern *to irrigate*
Eierlegen *to lay eggs*
ernten, einfahren
 to harvest
melken *to milk*
nisten *to nest*
pflanzen *to plant*
pflücken *to pick, gather*
pflügen *to plough*
säen *to sow*
Tiere füttern *to feed animals*

TIERE *ANIMALS*

die Amphibie (-n)
 amphibian
das Reptil (-ien) *reptile*
das Säugetier (-e)
 mammal

die Waldtiere *woodland creatures*
der Dachs (-e) *badger*
das Eichhörnchen (-)
 squirrel
die Fledermaus ("e)
 bat
der Fuchs ("e), die Füchsin (-nen)
 fox, vixen
der Hase (-n), die Häsin (-nen)
 hare, doe
der Hirsch (-e), das Reh (-e)
 stag, roe deer

der Igel (-) *hedgehog*
der Maulwurf ("e)
 mole
die Maus ("e) *mouse*
die Nacktschnecke (-n)
 slug
die Ratte (-n) *rat*
die Schnecke (-n)
 snail
der Regenwurm ("er)
 earthworm

Am Teich **at the pond**
der (Fisch) otter (-)
 otter
der Biber (-) *beaver*
der Frosch ("e) *frog*
die Kröte (-n) *toad*

Großwild und andere Tiere
Big game and other animals

auf Safari *on safari*
die Jagd/das Jagen
 hunt / hunting

der Bär (-en) *brown bear*
der Büffel (-) *buffalo*
der Elefant (-en)*elephant*
das Fluß-/Nilpferd (-e)
 hippopotamus
die Giraffe (-n) *giraffe*
das Kamel (-e) *camel*
das Känguruh (-s)
 kangaroo
der Koala (-s) *koala*
das Krokodil (-e) *crocodile*
das Nashorn ("er)
 rhinoceros
die Schlange (-n) *snake*
das Zebra (-s) *zebra*

der Affe (-n) *monkey*
der Gorilla (-s) *gorilla*

14 Die Natur *The Natural World*

der Orang-Utan (-s)
    orangutang
der Gepard (-e) *cheetah*
der Leopard (-en)
    leopard
der Löwe (-n), die Löwin (-nen)
    lion, lioness
der Panther (-) *panther*
der Tiger (-) *tiger*
der Wolf (¨e) *wolf*

der Delphin (-e) *dolphin*
der Seehund (-e) *seal*
der Wal (-e) *whale*
das Walroß (-rosse)
    walrus

die Antilope (-n) *antelope*
das Rentier (-e) *reindeer*

das Fell (-e) *coat*
die Flosse (-n) *fin, flipper*
der Stoßzahn (¨e)
    elephant tusk
das Horn (¨er) *horn*
die Kralle (-n) *claw*
das Maul (¨er) *mouth*
der Pelz (-e) *fur*
die Pfote (-n) *paw*
der Rüssel (-) *trunk*
die Schale (-n), das Gehäuse (-)
    shell
der Schwanz (¨e), der Schweif (-e)
    tail

die Vögel *Birds*

Vogelbeobachtung
    bird-watching

die Greifvögel *birds of prey*
der Adler (-) *eagle*
die Eule (-n) *owl*

der Geier (-) *vulture*
der Habicht (-e) *hawk*
der Uhu (-s) *eagle-owl*

die Singvögel **songbirds**
die Amsel *blackbird*
die Drossel *thrush*
die Blaumeise (-n)
    blue-tit
der Eisvogel (¨) *kingfisher*
die Elster (-n) *magpie*
die Krähe (-n) *crow*
der Kuckuck (-e)*cuckoo*
die Nachtigall (-en)
    nightingale
das Rotkehlchen (-)
    robin
die Schwalbe (-n)
    swallow
der Spatz (-en) *sparrow*
der Zaunkönig (-e)
    wren

die Möwe (-n) *seagull*
der Pelikan (-e) *pelican*
der Pfau (-en) *peacock*
der Specht (-e) *woodpecker*
der Schwan (¨e) *swan*
die Taube (-n) *dove, pigeon*
der Storch (¨e) *stork*

Wild vögel **game birds**
der Fasan (-e) *pheasant*
das Rebhuhn (¨er)
    partridge
die Schnepfe (-n)
    snipe
das Waldhuhn (¨er)
    grouse

der Schnabel (¨) *beak, bill*
die Feder (-n) *feather*
das Nest (-er) *nest*
der Flügel (-) *wing*

14 **Die** Natur *The Natural World*

Insekten *Insects*

die Biene (-n)   *bee*
die Hummel (-n) *bumble bee*

die Ameise (-n) *ant*
die Fliege (-n)   *fly*
der Floh (¨e)   *flea*
der Grashüpfer (-)
                       grasshopper
die Grille (-n)   *cricket*
der Käfer (-)   *beetle*

der Marienkäfer (-)
                       ladybird
die Mücke (-n) *midge*
die Raupe (-n) *caterpillar*
der Schmetterling (-e)
                       butterfly
die Spinne (-n) *spider*
die Stechmücke (-n)
                       mosquito
die Wespe (-n) *wasp*

UMWELTTHEMEN
ENVIRONMENTAL ISSUES

Halten Sie die
Anlage bitte sauber

die Umwelt *Environment*

die Verschmutzung (-en)
                       pollution
die grüne/alternative Bewegung
                       green movement
die Ökologie   *ecology*
das Ökosystem (-e)
                       ecosystem
der Schadstoff (-e)
                       pollutant
die Umweltwerschmutzung (-en)
                       environmental
                       pollution
umweltfreundlich
                       environmentally
                       friendly

umweltverträglich
                       ecologically
                       harmless
umweltschädlich *ecologically harmful*
das Umweltministerium (-ministerien)
                       Department of
                       the Environment
der Umweltschutz
                       environmental
                       protection
Umweltschützer/in
                       environmentalist

der Abfall (¨e), der Müll
                       waste
die Altkleidersammlung (-en)
                       collection of old clothes
die Beseitigung (-en)
                       disposal
der Giftmüll   *toxic waste*
der Kunststoff (-e)
                       plastic
die Müllkippe (-n), die Mülldeponie (-n)
                       waste dump
die Mülltonne (-n)
                       dustbin

der Sondermüll *hazardous waste (oil, paint)*
die Verpackung (-en) *packaging*

**das Recycling, die Wieder-
verwertung (-en)
recycling**
der Altglascontainer (-) *bottle bank*
der blaue Umweltengel (-) *eco-friendly product symbol*
die Mehrwegflasche (-n) *returnable bottle*
der Recyclinghof (¨e) *recycling plant*
das Umweltpapier (-e) *recycled paper*
die Wiederaufbereitungsanlage (-n) *reprocessing plant*

**die Wasserverschmutzung (-en)
water pollution**
das Abwasser (-)*sewage*
die Alge (-n) *algae*
das Grundwasser *ground water*
die Kläranlage (-n) *sewage plant*
das Trinkwasser *drinking water*

**die Luftverschmutzung (-en)
air pollution**
die Abgase *fumes*
die Autoabgase *exhaust fumes*
die Atmosphäre (-n) *atmosphere*
das Kraftwerk (-e) *power station*
der Regenwald (¨er) *rainforest*
der saure Regen *acid rain*
der Schadstoffausstoß (¨e) *harmful emission*

der Smog *smog*
das Waldsterben *dying forests*
die Zerstörung, die Vernichtung *destruction*

bleifrei *unleaded*
die Energieeinsparung (-en) *energy efficiency*
die Erhaltung *conservation*
der Kat(alysator), (-s) (-en) *catalytic converter*

die Ozonschicht *ozone layer*

ausgestorben *extinct*

Ozonloch im Süden so groß wie noch nie

die Bodenerosion (-en) *soil erosion*
die Eiskappen der Pole *polar ice caps*
das FCKW (-s) *CFC (Chloro-Fluoro-Carbon)*
die globale/weltweite Erwärmung *global warming*
das Kohlendioxid (-e) *carbon dioxide*
die Landrückgewinnung (-en) *land reclamation*
der Meeresspiegel *sea level*
der Ozonalarm *ozone warning*
das Ozonloch (¨er) *hole in the ozone layer*
die Spraydose (-n) *aerosol*
der Treibhauseffekt *greenhouse effect*

14 **Die** **Natur** *The Natural World*

das Überleben *survival*
die UV-Strahlung (-en)
        ultraviolet radiation
die Wüste (-n) *desert*

die alternativen Energiequellen
alternative sources of energy
der fossile Brennstoff (-e)
        fossil fuels
die Solarenergie *solar power*
durch Wasserkraft erzeugte Energie
        hydroelectric power
die Vorräte, Ressourcen
        resources

die Nuklearenergie
        nuclear power
der Atommull, die radioaktiven
  Abfälle *radioactive waste*

die Strahlung (-en)
        radiation
die Langzeitwirkungen
        long-term effects
mißgebildet *deformed*

austrocknen *to dry up*
betreffen, erfassen
        to affect
reduzieren, verringern
        to reduce
schaden *to damage*
schmelzen *to melt*
überschwemmen *to flood*
verschmutzen *to pollute*
verschwenden *to waste*
verseuchen *to contaminate*
verursachen *to cause*
wiederverwerten *to recycle*

Wir müssen Energie sparen und
  weniger Abfall produzieren.
Die Autoabgase verschmutzen die
  Atmosphäre.
Der Treibhauseffekt führt zur
  Zerstörung der Ozonschicht.

*We must save energy and
  produce less waste.*
*Car exhaust fumes pollute
  the atmosphere.*
*The greenhouse effect leads to the
  destruction of the ozone layer.*

WETTER UND KLIMA
WEATHER AND CLIMATE

die (Wetter)Vorhersage (-n)
        (weather)forecast
die Atmosphäre (-n)
        atmosphere
das Barometer (-) *barometer*
der Grad (-e) *degree*
der Himmel (-) *sky*
das Klima (-s) *climate*

die Luft *air*
der Luftdruck (¨e)
        atmospheric pressure
die Luftfeuchtigkeit
        humidity
der Meteorologe (-n)
        weatherman
die Sichtweite (-n)
        visibility
die Temperatur (-en)
        temperature

das Thermometer (-)
thermometer
der Wetterbericht (-e)
weather report
die Wetterkarte (-n)
weather map

gutes Wetter **good weather**
die Aufheiterung (-en)
bright interval
die Brise (-n) *breeze*
die Hitze *heat*
die Hitzewelle (-n)
heat wave
der Hochdruck, das
Hochdruckgebiet (-e)
high pressure
der Regenbogen (¨)
rainbow
die Sonne *sun*
die Warmfront (-en)
warm front

Es ist . . . *It is . . .*
beständig *settled*
heiß *hot*
heiter *brightening up*
mild *mild*
schön *fine*
schwül, drückend
humid
sonnig *sunny*
trocken *dry*
warm *warm*
wolkenlos *clear*

das schlechte Wetter
bad weather
der Tiefdruck, das
Tiefdruckgebiet (-e)
low pressure
die Kaltfront (-en)
cold front

der Regen **rain**
der Dunst *mist*
der Nebel *fog*
der Niederschlag (¨e)
rainfall
der Nieselregen *drizzle*
die Pfütze (-n) *puddle*
der Regenguß (-güsse)
downpour
der Regentropfen (-)
raindrop
das Schauer (-) *shower*
der Schneeregen *sleet*
die Überschwemmung (-en)
flood

der Schnee **snow**
der Eiszapfen (-) *icicle*
der Frost (¨e) *frost*
das Glatteis *black ice*
der Graupel *sleet*
der Schneesturm (¨e)
snowstorm
das Tauwetter *thaw*

Wind **wind**
schwacher . . . *light . . .*
mäßiger . . . *moderate . . .*
kräftiger . . . *strong . . .*
. . . aus dem *. . . from the*
Norden/Osten/ *north / east /*
Süden/Westen *south / west*
die Brise (-en) *breeze*

der Sturm (¨e), das Gewitter (-)
storm
die Bö (-en) *gust*
Donner und Blitz
thunder and
lightning
der Hagel *hail*
der Orkan (-e) *hurricane*
die Wolke (-n) *cloud*

14 Die Natur *The Natural World*

Es ist . . .	*It is . . .*	hageln	*to hail*
bedeckt	*overcast*	nieseln	*to drizzle*
dunkel	*dark*	regnen	*to rain*
frostig	*frosty*	scheinen	*to shine*
kalt	*cold*	schmelzen	*to melt*
kühl	*cool, chilly*	schneien	*to snow*
naß	*rainy, wet*	sich aufheitern	*to clear up*
naßkalt	*chilly and damp*	tauen	*to thaw*
nebelig	*foggy*	verbessern	*to improve*
stürmisch	*stormy*	wehen	*to blow*
unangenehm	*nasty*		
wechselhaft	*changeable*	Das Wetter ist . . .	
windig	*windy*		*The weather is . . .*
wolkig	*cloudy*	Es ist . . .	*It's . . .*
		Es war . . .	*It was . . .*
ändern	*to change*	Der Himmel ist . . .	
frieren	*to freeze*		*The sky is . . .*
gießen	*to pour*	Es wird . . .	*There will be . . .*

Es ist sonnig.	*It's sunny.*
Es regnet in Strömen.	*It's pouring.*
Ein schwacher Wind weht aus Osten.	*There is a light easterly wind blowing from the west.*
Das Haus wurde vom Blitz getroffen.	*The house was struck by lightning.*

NOCH MAL!

● *Activity: What's the weather like?*

DEUTSCHLAND

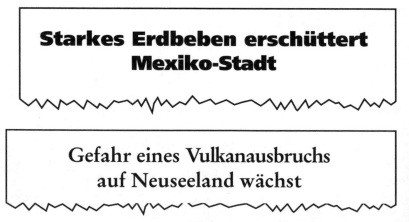

UMWELTKATASTROPHEN
NATURAL DISASTERS

der Brand (¨e)   *fire*
die Dürreperiode (-n)
        drought
die Epidemie (-n)
        epidemic
der Erdrutsch (-e)
        landslide
die Flut (-en), die Überschwemmung (-en),
  das Hochwasser
        flood
die Hungersnot (¨e)
        famine
die Lawine (-n)   *avalanche*
die Seuche (-n)   *plague*

der Taifun (-e)   *typhoon*
der Tornado (-s)   *tornado*
der Vulkanausbruch (¨e)
        volcanic eruption
der Wirbelsturm (¨e)
        hurricane
der Zyklon (-e)   *cyclone*

das Erdbeben (-)
        earthquake
das Erdbebengebiet (-e)
        earthquake zone
der Seismograph (-en)
        seismograph
die Verwerfung (-en)
        fault
der Riß (Risse)   *crack*

15 Die große weite Welt *The Wider World*

DIE WELT
THE WORLD

die Erde	*the Earth*
der Globus	*the Globe*

der Nordpol	*North Pole*
der Südpol	*South Pole*
die Arktis	*Arctic*
der nördlicher Polarkreis	
	Arctic Circle
die Antarktis	*Antarctic*
der südlicher Polarkreis	
	Antarctic Circle

der Äquator	*equator*
der Breitengrad (-e)	
	line of latitude
der Längengrad (-e)	
	line of longitude

die Tropen	*the tropics*
der Wendekreis des Krebses/	
	Tropic of Cancer /
Steinbocks	*Capricorn*
der Kompaß (-sse)	
	compass

Nord	*North*
Süd	*South*
Ost	*East*
West	*West*

der Kontinent (-e)
continent

Afrika	*Africa*
Antarktika	*Antarctica*
Asien	*Asia*
Australien und	*Australia and*
das Ozeanien	*Oceania*
Europa	*Europe*
Nordamerika	*North America*
Südamerika	*Südamerika*

der Ferne Osten	*Far East*
der Nahe Osten	*Middle East*

... Ozean (-e) ... *Ocean*

der Atlantische	*Atlantic*
der Indische	*Indian*
der Stille, der Pazifische	
	Pacific
das Nordpolarmeer	
	Arctic Ocean

DIE EUROPÄISCHEN LÄNDER
THE COUNTRIES OF EUROPE
Großbritannien *Great Britain*

Land	Einwohner	Sprache	*country*	*inhabitant*	*language*
Europa	Europäer	—	*Europe*	*European*	*—*
Großbritannien	Brite	—	*Great Britain*	*British*	*—*
England	Engländer	Englisch	*England*	*Englishman /*	
				woman	*English*
Wales	Waliser	Walisisch	*Wales*	*Welshman /*	*Welsh / (English)*
				woman	
Nordirland	Ire	Gälisch	*Northern Ireland*	*Irishman /*	*English*
				woman	

15 Die große weite Welt *The Wider World*

Schottland	Schotte	Schottisch	*Scotland*	*Scotsman / woman*	*Scottish Gaelic*
Irland	Ire	Gälisch	*Ireland*	*Irishman / woman*	*Irish Gaelic (English)*

Skandinavian *Scandinavian*

Finnland	Finne	Finnisch	*Finland*	*Finn*	*Finnish*
Schweden	Schwede	Schwedisch	*Sweden*	*Swede*	*Swedish*
Norwegen	Norweger	Norwegisch	*Norway*	*Norwegian*	*Norwegian*
Dänemark	Däne	Dänisch	*Denmark*	*Dane*	*Danish*

Westeuropa *Western Europe*

Niederlande	Niederländer	Nieder- ländisch	*The Netherlands*	*Dutch*	*Dutch*
Belgien	Belgier	Flämisch	*Belgium*	*Belgian*	*Flemish*
Luxemburg	Luxemburger	Französisch	*Luxembourg*	*Luxembourger*	*French*
Deutschland	Deutscher	Deutsch	*Germany*	*German*	*German*
Frankreich	Franzose	Französisch	*France*	*Frenchman / woman*	*French*
Italien	Italiener	Italienisch	*Italy*	*Italian*	*Italian*
Portugal	Portugiese	Portugiesisch	*Portugal*	*Portuguese*	*Portuguese*
Spanien	Spanier	Spanisch	*Spain*	*Spaniard*	*Spanish*
Schweiz	Schweizer	Deutsch/ Französisch/ Italienisch	*Switzerland*	*Swiss*	*German / French / Italian*

Mitteleuropa *Central Europe*

Österreich	Österreicher	Deutsch	*Austria*	*Austrian*	*German*
Czechische Republik	Czechen	Czechisch	*Czech Republic*	*Czech*	*Czech*
Polen	Pole	Polnisch	*Poland*	*Pole*	*Polish*
Ungarn	Ungar	Magyarisch	*Hungary*	*Hungarian*	*Hungarian*
Slovakei	Slovake	Slovakisch	*Slovenia*	*Slovak*	*Slovakian*
Kroatien	Kroate	Serbo- Kroatisch	*Croatia*	*Croatian*	*Serbo-Croat*
Bosnien - Herzegowina	Bosnier	Serbo- Kroatisch	*Bosnia- Herzegovina*	*Bosnian*	*Serbo- Croat*
Montenegro	Montenegran	Serbo- Kroatisch	*Montenegro*	*Montenegran*	*Serbo-Croat*
Rumänien	Rumäne	Rumänisch	*Romania*	*Romanian*	*Romanian*

15 Die große weite Welt *The Wider World*

Bulgarien	Bulgare	Bulgarisch	*Bulgaria*	*Bulgarian*	*Bulgarian*
Estland	Estländer, Este	Estländisch	*Estonia*	*Estonian*	*Estonian*
Lettland	Lette	Lettisch	*Latvia*	*Latvian*	*Lettish*
Litauen	Litauer	Litauisch	*Lithuania*	*Lithuanian*	*Lithuanian*
Rußland	Russe	Russisch	*Russia*	*Russian*	*Russian*
Griechenland	Grieche	Griechisch	*Greece*	*Greek*	*Greek*
Türkei	Türke	Türkisch	*Turkey*	*Turk*	*Turkish*

Note: The masculine form for inhabitants is given in the list.
For the feminine form add **-in** and drop the final **e** where necessary, for example: e.g. Schotte– Schot**tin**.

Asien *Asia*

Japan	*Japan*
China	*China*
Indien	*India*
Afghanistan	*Afghanistan*

Der Mittlere Osten
The Middle East

Iran	*Iran*
Irak	*Iraq*
Kuwait	*Kuwait*
Türkei	*Turkey*

Der Nahe Osten
The Near East

Israel	*Israel*

Afrika *Africa*

Ägypten	*Egypt*
Algerien	*Algeria*
Tunesien	*Tunisia*
Kenia	*Kenya*

Australien *Australia*

Neuseeland	*New Zealand*

Nordamerika *North America*

Kanada	*Canada*
Vereinigten Staaten von Amerika, US	*United States, USA*

Südamerika *South America*

Brasilien	*Brazil*
Argentinien	*Argentina*

Europäische Städte
European cities

Braunschweig	*Brunswick*
Hannover	*Hanover*
Köln	*Cologne*
München	*Munich*
Athen	*Athens*
Basel	*Basle*
Brüssel	*Brussels*
Den Haag	*The Hague*
Kopenhagen	*Copenhagen*
Lissabon	*Lisbon*
Mailand	*Milan*
Moskau	*Moscow*
Nizza	*Nice*
Rom	*Rome*
Venedig	*Venice*

15 Die große weite Welt *The Wider World*

Warschau	*Warsaw*	der Bodensee	*Lake Constance*
Wien	*Vienna*	die Ostsee	*Baltic Sea*
		das Mittelmeer	*Mediterranean*

NOCH MAL!

● *Activity: How many of the EU countries can you name in German?*

15 Die große weite Welt *The Wider World*

NATIONALE UND INTERNATIONALE VERBÄNDE UND ORGANISATIONEN
NATIONAL AND INTERNATIONAL AGENCIES

Nationale Organisationen
National organisations

(AA) Anonyme Alkoholiker	*AA Alcoholics Anonymous*
Aids-Hilfe	*Aids Advice*
Berufsberatung	*Careers Advisory Service*
(BUND) Bund für Umwelt und	*Association for the environment*
Naturschutz Deutschland	*and protection of nature*
Caritas	*Catholic welfare organisation*
(DFB) Deutscher Fußball-Bund	*German Football Association*
(DGB) Deutscher Gewerkschaftsbund	*Federation of German Trade Unions*
(DJH) Deutsches	*(YHA) (German Youth Hostel*
Jugendherbergswerk	*Association)*
(DLRG) Deutsche	
Lebensrettungsgesellschaft	*RNLI*
(DRK) Deutsches Rotes Kreuz	*Red Cross*
(IHK) Industrie- und Handelskammer	*Chamber of Commerce*
Pro Familia	*Family planning organisation*
Tierschutzverein	*RSPCA*
die Verbraucherzentrale	*Citizens Advice Bureau*

Internationale Organisationen *International organisations*

Greenpeace	*Greenpeace*
(IGFM) Internationale Gesellschaft	*International Society for*
für Menschenrechte	*Human Rights*
(IOK) Internationales Olympisches	*(IOC) International Olympic*
Komitee	*Committee*
(IRK) Internationales Rotes Kreuz	*(IRK) International Red Cross*
(IWF) Internationaler Währungsfonds	*(IMF) International Monetary Fund*
(NATO) Nordatlantische	*(NATO) North Atlantic*
Verteidigungs-Organisation	*Treaty Organisation*
(UN) Vereinte Nationen	*(UN) United Nations*
(UNICEF) Weltkinderhilfswerk	
der UNO	*(UNICEF)*
(WWF) Welttierschutzorganisation	*World Wildlife Fund*

15 Die große weite Welt *The Wider World*

die EU (Europäische
   Union)   **European Union**
der Europarat *Council of Europe*
das Europa-Parlament
     *European
       Parliament*

die Europäische Kommission
     *European
       Commission*
Europäische Weltraum Organisation
     *European Space
       Agency*

DER WELTRAUM *SPACE*

die Galaxie (-n) *galaxy*
der Globus, die Erdkugel
     globe
der Komet (-en) *comet*
mit Licht-/Schallgeschwindigkeit
     *at the speed of
       light / sound*
das Lichtjahr (-e)
     light year
der Meteor (-e) *meteor*
das schwarzes Loch (¨er)
     black hole
das Sonnensystem (-e)
     solar system
das Universum, Weltall
     universe

der Mond (-e) *moon*
Neumond/Vollmond
     new moon / full moon

die Astronomie
     astronomy
der Himmel *sky, heaven*
der Stern (-e) *star*
das Fernrohr (-e)
     telescope
der UFO (-s) *UFO*

die Milchstraße (-n)
     Milky Way
der Planet (-en) *planet*
der Sterngucker (-)
     star gazer
der Sternkreis (-e)
     zodiac
die Sternschnuppe (-n)
     shooting star

die Raumfahrt
     space travel
Astronaut/in *astronaut*
die Erdanziehung
     gravitation
die Raumfähre (-n)
     shuttle
das Raumlabor (-e)
     space lab
das Raumschiff (-e)
     spaceship
der Satellit (-en) *satellite*
die Umlaufbahn (-en)
     orbit
der Wiedereintritt (-e)
     re-entry

der Krieg der Sterne
     star wars
ankoppeln *to dock*

16 Koda *Coda*

ABKÜRZUNGEN   *ABBREVIATIONS*

Abb.	Abbildung	*illus.*	*illustration*
BLZ	Bankleitzahl	*bank sorting code*	
b.w.	bitte wenden	*PTO*	*please turn over*
bzw.	beziehungsweise	*or that is to say*	
ca.	circa	*approx.*	*approximately*
d.h.	das heißt	*i.e.*	*that is*
C	Celcius	*C*	*Celcius, Centigrade*
ggf	gegebenenfalls	*if necessary, if applicable*	
Hrsg.	Herausgeber	*ed.*	*editor*
i.A.	im Auftrag	*pp*	*per pro*
i.R.	im Ruhestand	*retired*	
IQ	Intelligenzquotient	*IQ*	*Intelligence Quotient*
j.w.d.	weit entfernt (umg.)	*the back of beyond*	
Kfz	Kraftfahrzeug	*motor vehicle*	
Lkw	Lastkraftwagen	*HGV*	*heavy goods vehicle*
m	meter	*m*	*metre*
Mwst.	Mehrwertsteuer	*VAT*	*value added tax*
Nr.	Nummer	*no.*	*number*
p.a.	per annum	*p.a.*	*per annum*
Pkw	Personenkraftwagen	*car*	
PLZ	Postleitzahl	*postcode*	
PS	Postskriptum	*PS*	*postscript*
PS	Pferdestärke	*hp*	*horsepower*
sog.	sogenannt	*as it / he, etc. is called, so-called*	
Str.	Straße	*St.*	*street*
Tel.	Telefon	*Tel.*	*telephone*
u. U.	unter Umständen	*possibly*	
usw.	und so weiter	*etc.*	*et cetera*
WC	Toilette	*WC*	*water closet*
z. B.	zum Beispiel	*e.g.*	*for example*
z.H.	zur Hand	*attn.*	*for the attention of*
z.Z.	zur Zeit	*at the moment*	
AA	Auswärtiges Amt	*FO*	*Foreign Office*
AA	Anonyme Alkoholiker	*AA*	*Alcoholics Anonymous*
ADAC	Allgemeiner Deutscher Automobil-Club	*AA*	*Automobile Association*
AG	Aktiengesellschaft	*PLC*	*Public Limited company*
BAT	Bundesangestelltentarif	*statutory salary scale*	
BGB	Bundesgesetzbuch	*Federal Law Code*	
BRD	Bundesrepublik Deutschland	*Federal Republic of Germany*	

16 Koda *Coda*

DAAD	Deutscher Akademischer Austauschdienst	*German Academic*	*Exchange Service*
DAX	Deutcher Aktienindex	*German share index*	
Dr. med.	Arzt/Ärztin	*MD*	*Doctor of Medicine*
ECU	Europäische Währungseinheit	*ecu*	*European currency unit*
EDV	elektronische Datenverarbeitung	*EDP*	*electronic data processing*
EG	Europäische Gemeinschaft	*EC*	*European Community*
GG	Grundgesetz	*Federal Constitution*	
GmbH	Gesellschaft mit beschränkter Haftung	*Ltd*	*Limited*
MdE	Mitglied des europäischen Parlaments	*MEP*	*Member of the European Parliament*

UMGANGSSPRACHE UND SCHIMPFWÖRTER
COLLOQUIAL PHRASES, SLANG AND SWEAR WORDS

Das ist Spitze!	*Great!*
Laß mich in Ruhe!	*Leave me alone!*
Quatsch!	*Nonsense!*
Halt die Klappe!	*Shut it / shut your trap!*
Renate hat eine große Klappe.	*Renate is a bigmouth.*
Das ist Murks!	*That's a botch-up!*
Ich habe die Nase gestrichen voll / Mir reicht's.	*I'm sick of it / I've had enough.*
Es ist mir schnuppe.	*I don't give a damn.*
Sandra ist völlig **ausgeflippt**.	*Sandra cracked up / freaked out.*
Daniel hat **einen über den Durst getrunken.**	*Daniel had one over the eight.*
Er ist blau.	*He's drunk / pissed.*
Er ist stockbesoffen.	*He's legless.*
Hans hat gestern **blau gemacht**.	*Hans skipped work yesterday.*
Ralf hat immer **die Nase vorn**.	*Ralf is always one step ahead.*
Ich bin blank.	*I'm broke.*
Das **geht in die Hose**.	*It'll be a cock-up / disaster.*
Er hat **die Hose voll Schiß**.	*He's scared shitless.*
Die Party war absolut **tote Hose**.	*The party was a dead loss.*
Die Firma hat **mich über den Tisch gezogen**.	*The company ripped me off.*

16 Koda *Coda*

Er hat **mich übers Ohr gehauen**.	*He conned me.*
Mein Auto hat **den Geist aufgegeben**.	*My car's packed up.*
Er **hat keinen Durchblick** .	*He hasn't got a clue.*
Das **schnalle/checke** ich nicht.	*I don't get it. (understand)*
Er **kriegt es** nicht **auf die Reihe**.	*He can't get his act together.*
Ich **kann ihn nicht ausstehen**.	*I can't stand him.*
Er ist ein **Hasenfuß**/ein **Waschlappen**.	*He's a wimp / chicken.*
Ich **sitze in der Klemme**.	*I'm snookered / in a tight spot.*
Das wäre beinahe **ins Auge gegangen**.	*That was a close shave.*
Jetzt **schlägt's** aber **dreizehn**!	*That takes the biscuit!*
Ich bin **ins Fettnäpfchen getreten**.	*I've put my foot in it.*

die Bude	*pad, place*
Kiste, Karre	*wheels (car)*
(heißer) Ofen	*big bike*
Knete, Kies, Kohle, Eier	*readies, dough (money)*
Geizkragen	*stingy, tight person*
Macker, Typ	*geezer, bloke*
Zoff	*slanging match, row*
sehen, wie der Hase läuft	*to see how the wind blows*
eine brenzlige Situation	*a tricky situation*
absahnen	*to rake in*

You are advised **not** to use the following language yourself as it is likely to give offence, but you may find it useful to be able to understand it! It is especially difficult for a non-native speaker to judge when vulgarisms can be used. Ask yourself how you would react to being sworn at by a foreigner and try to find other ways of responding!

Arschloch!	*Asshole!*
Verzieh dich!/Du kannst mich mal!	*Piss off / Get stuffed!*
Scheiße!	*Shit!*
Verdammt!	*Blast / Damn!*
verdammter Mist!	*Bloody hell*
Verpiß dich!	*F*** off!*
zum Teufel nochmal!	*Oh hell!*
Motz nicht so 'rum!	*Stop whingeing / whining!*
Zieh Leine!/Hau ab!	*Get lost / Piss off!*
Was zum Teufel willst du?	*What the hell do you want?*
Er ist beknackt.	*He's mental.*
Es ist zum kotzen!	*It makes you sick!*
Es ist beknackt.	*It's crap.*

Mir ist kotzübel!	*I'm going to throw up!*	vögeln, ficken	*to screw*
eine Tussi	*tart*	es miteinander treiben, bumsen	
aufgedonnert	*tarted up*		*to have it off*

UNREGELMÄßIGE VERBEN
IRREGULAR VERBS

Infinitive	Imperfect	Past Participle	
beginnen	begann	begonnen	*to begin*
bitten	bat	gebeten	*to ask*
bleiben	blieb	geblieben	*to stay*
bringen	brachte	gebracht	*to bring*
denken	dachte	gedacht	*to think*
dürfen	durfte	gedurft	*to be allowed to, may*
essen	aß	gegessen	*to eat*
fahren	fuhr	gefahren	*to go, to drive*
fallen	fiel	gefallen	*to fall*
finden	fand	gefunden	*to find*
fliegen	flog	geflogen	*to fly*
gehen	ging	gegangen	*to go*
haben	hatte	gehabt	*to have*
helfen	half	geholfen	*to help*
kennen	kannte	gekannt	*to know (a person, a place)*
kommen	kam	gekommen	*to come*
können	konnte	gekonnt	*to be able to, can*
lassen	ließ	gelassen	*to leave*
mögen	mochte	gemocht	*to like*
müssen	mußte	gemußt	*to have to, must*
nehmen	nahm	genommen	*to take*
schlafen	schlief	geschlafen	*to sleep*
schreiben	schrieb	geschrieben	*to write*
schwimmen	schwamm	geschwommen	*to swim*
sehen	sah	gesehen	*to see*
sein	war	gewesen	*to be*
sollen	sollte	gesollt	*to be supposed to, ought to*
sprechen	sprach	gesprochen	*to speak*
stehen	stand	gestanden	*to stand*
tragen	trug	getragen	*to carry / to wear*
treffen	traf	getroffen	*to meet*

16 Koda *Coda*

trinken	trank	getrunken	*to drink*
verlieren	verlor	verloren	*to lose*
waschen	wusch	gewaschen	*to wash*
werden	wurde	geworden	*to become*
wissen	wußte	gewußt	*to know (a fact)*
wollen	wollte	gewollt	*to want*

HILFE! *HELP!*

Sprechen Sie Englisch?
Do you spreak English?

Es tut mir leid. *I'm sorry.*
Wie bitte? *Pardon?*
Entschuldigung. *Pardon? / I'm sorry / Excuse me.*

Ich verstehe das nicht. *I don't understand.*
Ich habe das/Sie/ nicht verstanden. *I didn't understand that / you.*
Würden sie das bitte wiederholen. *Can you repeat that please?*
Würden Sie bitte etwas langsamer sprechen? *Can you say it more slowly?*
Wie heißt das auf Englisch? *What does that mean in English?*
Sprechen Sie ... *Do you speak...*
Wie buchstabiert/schreibt man das? *How do you spell / write it?*
Würden Sie das bitte für mich aufschreiben? *Can you write that down for me please?*

Entschuldigen Sie, bitte. *Excuse me, please.*
Können Sie mir helfen? *Can you help me?*
Verstehen Sie das? *Do you understand?*
Hör zu! *Listen!*

bitte	*please*
Danke/Vielen Dank	*Thank you (very much).*
Danke. Bitte.	*Thank you. You're welcome.*

Gern geschehen, bitte. *It's a pleasure.*
Nichts zu danken. *Don't mention it.*

Bitte has two meanings: *Please* and *You're welcome.*

214

16 Koda *Coda*

Entschuldigung, das habe ich
 falsch verstanden. *I'm sorry, I've misunderstood.*
Ich fürchte, Sie haben mich da
 mißverstanden. *I'm afraid you've misunderstood me.*
Tut mir leid, ich wollte Sie nicht *I'm sorry, I didn't mean to*
 beleidigen/verletzten. *give offence.*
Es war mein Fehler. *It was my fault.*
Es war überhaupt nicht mein Fehler. *It was not MY fault.*
Es war Dein /Ihr Fehler. *It was your fault.*

Achtung! *Danger!* | Sei vorsichtig! *Be careful!*
Paß auf!/Vorsicht!
 Watch out!

Key to the Activities

Greetings   *p. 14* (*a*) Guten Morgen! (*b*) Guten Tag! (*c*) Guten Abend! (*d*) Gute Nacht/Auf Wiedersehen!/Tschüs!   (*p. 15*) (1) (*a*) Herr . . . (*b*) Fräulein . . . (*c*) Frau . . . (*p. 15*) (2) (*a*) Sehr geehrter Frank, . . . Mit freundlichen Grüßen (*b*) Liebe Steffi, . . . Alles Liebe, (*c*) Sehr geehrte Damen und Herren, . . . Mit freundlichen Grüßen,

The calendar   (*p. 20*) (*a*) Am Montag, den zehnten März. (*b*) Am Mittwoch, den sechzehnten Juni. (*c*) Am Freitag, den zweiundzwanzigsten Juli. (*d*) Am Dienstag, den ersten August. (*e*) Am Donnerstag, den fünfzehnten Oktober.

The clock   (*p. 22*) (*a*) Viertel nach eins (*b*) halb drei (*c*) Viertel vor drei/dreiviertel drei (*d*) vier Uhr (*e*) Viertel vor fünf, dreiviertel fünf (*f*) dreizehn Uhr fünf (*g*) vierzehn Uhr fünfundzwanzig (*h*) sechzehn Uhr fünfundfünfzig (*i*) zweiundzwanzig Uhr sechsundvierzig (*j*) dreiundzwanzig Uhr neunundfünfzig

Adverbs   (*p. 27*) (*possible answers:*) (*a*) sehr (*b*) ziemlich (*c*) fast (*d*) mehr (*e*) ungefähr (*f*) Leider, vielleicht

Where?   (*p. 29*) (*a*) Er ist hinter der Mauer. (*b*) Er ist unter dem Tisch. (*c*) Er ist vor dem Kino. (*d*) Er sitzt zwischen zwei großen Leuten.

When?   (*p. 30*) (*possible answers:*) (*a*) Nächstes Jahr (*b*) oft, manchmal (*c*) immer, heute (*d*) Gestern, Am Wochenende (*e*) jetzt, später

Question Words   (*p. 31*) (1) Wie spät ist es? (2) Wieviel kostet das? (3) Wie heißt er? (4) Was für ein Auto hast du?

Articles, pronouns and conjunctions   (*p. 33*) (der → einen/keinen; die → eine/keine; das → ein/kein) (*a*) **der** PC Ich habe **einen/keinen** PC. (*b*) **der** Tisch (*c*) **der** Stuhl (*d*) **die** Lampe. Ich habe **eine/keine** Lampe. (*e*) **das** Telefon. Ich habe **ein/kein** Telefon. (*f*) **der** Briefumschlag (*g*) **der** Taschenrechner (*h*) **der** Füller (*p. 36*) With **der** words: (ii) dieser (iii) mein (iv) ihr (v) dein/euer/Ihr/ihr With **die** (fem. and pl.) words: (ii) diese (iii) meine (iv) ihre (v) deine/eure/Ihre/ihre With **das** (neuter) words: (ii) dieses (iii) mein (iv) ihr (v) dein/euer/Ihr/ihr (*a*) **der** Hund (*b*) **der** Füller (*c*) **das** Auto (*d*) **die** Schuhe (*e*) **das** Haus (*f*) **der** Kamm (*g*) **die** Bücher (*h*) **der** Regenschirm

Verbs   (*p. 40*) Er ist angeln gegangen. Er spielt Golf. Er wird Fahrrad fahren. Sie hat am Computer gearbeitet. Sie macht Hausarbeit. Sie wird weggehen!

1 Zur Person (*p. 45*) Sie ist groß und schlank. Sie hat kurzes, lockiges, blondes Haar und Sommersprossen.   Er hat langes, glattes, dunkles Haar, braune Augen, große Ohren und Quadratlatschen. Er sieht schmuddelig aus.   Er hat eine Glatze, einen Vollbart, einen Bierbauch und eine Boxernase.

2 Geburt, Hochzeit und Tod   (*p. 56*) die Windel; die Rassel; die Nuckelflasche; der Schnuller; das (Hand)tuch; das Lätzchen; das Baby!

3 Kleidung und Mode   (*p. 67*) Der Pullover ist (*a*) zu lang (*b*) zu eng (*c*) zu kurz (*d*) zu weit   (*p. 70*) (*possible answers*) **Jens** trägt **eine** blaue Hose, **ein** rotweiß**es** karier**tes** Hemd, gelbe Socken, weiße Turnschuhe und ein**e** blaue Jacke. **Sylvia** trägt **eine** weiße Bluse, **einen** kurz**en**, schwarz**en** Rock, **einen** roten Schal, goldene Ohrringe, **eine** weiße Strumpfhose und rote hochhackige Schuhe.

Key to the Activities

4 Essen und Trinken (p. 76) (1) Gurke (2) Karotte (3) dicke Bohnen (4) Wirsing (5) Erbsen (6) Spargel (7) Fenchel (8) Lauch (9) Zwiebeln (10) Spinat = RADIESCHEN

(p. 76) Ich möchte . . . (a) zwei Weißwein und einen Rotwein (b) drei Bier (c) eine Tasse Kaffee und zwei Tassen heiße Schokolade

5 Das Zuhause (p. 83) 2 (a) 3-Zimmer Wohnung, 93 Quadratmeter Küche, Badezimmer, Zentralheizung, Balkon. Kaltmiete Eintausendundfünfzig Mark plus hundertfünfzig Mark Nebenkosten plus Kaution. Telefon . . . (b) Einfamilienhaus circa zweihundertzehn Quadratmeter. Baujahr 1993. Zentrumnah, Einbauküche, 2 Bäder, Ölzentralheizung, Wintergarten, Sauna und Garten. Verhandlungsbasis 800,000 Mark. Telefon . . . (p. 85) **der** words: **einen neuen . . .; die** words: **eine neue . . .; das** words: **ein neues . . .** (a) der Sessel (b) der Spiegel (c) die Lampe (d) das Waschbecken (e) der Herd (f) das Bett (g) die Kommode (h) die Waschmaschine

7 Die Firma (p. 106) Datei Bearbeiten Ansicht Einfügen Format Extras Tabelle Fenster ? (p. 109) Tut mir leid . . . (a) ich muß zum Zahnarzt. (b) ich habe den Bus verpaßt. (c) mein Auto wollte nicht anspringen. (d) ich spiele Golf. (e) ich bin beschäftigt. (f) ich habe keine Zeit!

8 Arts and Media (p. 120) Sport – Fußball; Tennis; Nachrichten; Serie; Musik; Krimiserie; Dokumentarfilm; Kulturmagazin; Talkshow; Spielfilm; Quizshow; Report

9 Sport (p. 131) Ich spiele (nicht) gern Hockey; Ich schwimme (nicht) gern. Ich spiele (nicht) gern Fußball; Ich reite (nicht) gern. Ich fahre (nicht) gern Ski; Ich angele (nicht) gern. Ich spiele (nicht) gern Tennis; Ich fahre (nicht) gern Rad. Ich tanze (nicht) gern; Ich spiele (nicht) gern Golf. Ich fechte (nicht) gern.

10 Der Körper (p. 133) (a) der Kopf (b) das Auge (c) die Nase (d) der Hals (e) der Bauch (f) die Hand (g) der Fuß (h) die Stirn (i) das Ohr (j) der Mund (k) die Schulter (l) der Arm (m) das Bein (n) die Zehe (p. 138) Er hat eine Erkältung/einen Schnupfen. Er hat das Bein gebrochen. Sie ist gestochen worden. Sie hat Rückenschmerzen. Er hat Kopfschmerzen. Sie hat Zahnschmerzen.

12 die Stadt und Einkaufen (p. 166) Ich möchte . . . eine Dauerwelle . . . die Haare waschen lassen . . . die Haare schneiden lassen . . . die Haare fönen lassen. (p. 169) Zahnbürste; Kamm; Seife; Deodorant; Shampoo; Zahnpasta; Parfüm; Nagelfeile; Watte; Lippenstift; Wimperntusche; Spiegel

13 Reisen und Tourismus (p. 179) mit dem Bus; mit der Jacht; mit dem Flugzeug; mit der Straßenbahn; mit dem Motorrad; mit dem Hausboot; mit dem Zug; mit dem Passagierschiff (p. 188) (1) die Zapfsäule (2) rauchen verboten (3) das Dach (4) die Windschutzscheibe (5) der Scheibenwischer (6) die Tür (7) der Kofferraum (8) das Nummernschild (9) der Reifen (1) die Haube (11) das Lenkrad (12) der Scheinwerfer (p. 189) What do these road signs mean? Baustelle; Doppelkurve; Schleudergefahr; Kinder; Autobahn; Vorfahrtstraße

Die Natur (p. 191) What do the symbols mean?
Marsch; Laubbaum; Nadelbaum; Berg; Schloß; See; Kirche